Harvest of Blessings

2673 TR 421
Sugarcreek, OH 44681

Carlisle Printing
OF WALNUT CREEK Ltd.

Table of Contents

Abbreviations

cup = c.	ounce = oz.	envelope = env.
pint = pt.	pound = lb.	dozen = doz.
quart = qt.	teaspoon = tsp.	package = pkg.
gallon = gal.	tablespoon = Tbsp.	

Prayer for a Good Day

Dear Lord, as I arise
And bend my knee to pray,
I ask please place your guiding hand
Upon this busy day.

All my yesterdays are said and done,
Tomorrow may never be,
But I give you full reign over this day
To make the best of me.

May each little word I speak
Be filtered through your love.
May all my thoughts be connected
To the heavenly courts above.

And use my feet to take me
To where you want me to be.
Guard my eyes that they would only
See what you want me to see.

Give me a heart that longs to show
Others the way back home,
And with these two hands help me
Fashion glory for your throne.

From the great expanse of eternity
One day is all I can borrow,
So help me, Lord, to take care of today,
And we'll talk again tomorrow.

Introduction

We, the Yoders, would like to introduce you to a special cookbook that uses God's wonderful garden blessings we all love so well. We are using a special harvest symbol for any recipes that use food we so readily harvest such as broccoli, cauliflower, lettuce, radishes, tomatoes, potatoes, beans, peas, pumpkins, etc. and starring among them all is the wonderful zucchini plant. There are many recipes, some new and unusual, and also some tried and true ways, to use up those extra zucchini.

There are many never before published recipes in this special cookbook. Making meals will become a joyful experience as you cook with *Harvest of Blessings Cookbook.*

We wish to thank our many friends and family for sharing their best recipes for this harvest collection. Last but not least, a big thank you to my husband, Freeman, for your support and also to the children, who used their God-given talent in providing artwork for our dividers. May God richly bless you all.

Happy harvest cooking,

Freeman & Mabel Yoder

Charlene, Amy, Lonnie, LuAnn, Jason, Mervin, Jay Lee and Lanae

Unto thee, O God, do we give thanks, unto thee do we give thanks: for that thy name is near thy wondrous works declare.

Psalm 75:1

Life's Garden

Life is like a garden,
Each day a budding flower,
Unfolding at the dawning
To close at sunset hour.

Life is like a garden
With a bit of sun and rain,
Helping it to grow
And strength and beauty gain.

Life is like a garden
Where we may sow the seeds
Of happiness, contentment and faith,
By kind and constant deeds.

Life is like a garden
Rich and fertile as the sod,
Where we may reap our blessings
With the help of God.

And sow the fields, and plant vineyards, which may yield fruits of increase.

Psalm 107:37

It is a good thing to give thanks unto the Lord,
and to sing praises unto thy name, O most High.
Psalm 92:1

Appetizers, Beverages & Dips

Emergency Phone Number List

When in sorrow call...John 14
When men fail you call...Psalm 27
When you have sinned call...Psalm 51
When you worry call...Matthew 6:19-34
When you are in danger call...Psalm 91
When God seems far away call...Psalm 91
When your faith needs stirring call...Hebrews 11
When you are lonely and fearful call...Psalm 23
When you grow bitter and critical call...I Corinthians 13
When you feel down and out call...Romans 8:31
When you want peace and rest call...Matthew 11:25-30
When the world seems bigger than God call...Psalm 90
When you want Christian assurance call...Romans 8:1-30
When you leave home for labor or travel call...Psalm 121
When your prayers grow narrow or selfish call...Psalm 67
When you want courage for a task call...Joshua 1
When you think of investments and returns call...Mark 10
If you are depressed call...Psalm 27
If your pocketbook is empty call...Psalm 37
If you are losing confidence in people call...I Corinthians 13
If people seem unkind call...John 15
If discouraged about your work call...Psalm 126
If self pride/greatness takes hold call...Psalm 19
If you want to be fruitful call...John 15
For understanding of Christianity call...II Corinthians 5:15-19
For a great invention/opportunity call...Isaiah 55
For how to get along with people call...Romans 12
For Paul's secret to happiness call...Colossians 3:12-17

*Emergency numbers may be dialed direct. No operator
assistance is necessary. All lines to heaven are open 24
hours a day! Feed your faith, and doubt will starve to death.*

Alternate Numbers

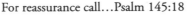

For dealing with fear call...Psalm 34:7
For security call...Psalm 121:3
For assurance call...Mark 8:35
For reassurance call...Psalm 145:18

Vegetable Roll-Ups

...Mrs. David (Barbara) Wagler

4 c. (1 pkg.) broccoli
4 c. (1 head) cauliflower
2 c. (4 peppers) peppers
2 c. carrots
2 lb. cherry tomatoes
1 lb. cheese
20 soft tortillas
2 (16 oz.) sour cream
½ c. or 2 pkg. Ranch dressing

Finely chop all vegetables except tomatoes, and put in a large mixing bowl. Mix Ranch powder with sour cream and add to chopped vegetables, mixing thoroughly. Fold in shredded cheese. Put ½ c. mixture on one tortilla shell; spread out and lay a row of cherry tomatoes across the middle, then roll it up, and wrap in Saran wrap. Refrigerate overnight or until it hangs together. Unwrap from Saran wrap and slice to desired width.

Taco Roll-Ups

...Mrs. Gerald (Rosanna) Schrock

1½ lbs. browned hamburger
1½ c. onions
1 pkg. taco seasoning
4 oz. chives, optional
8 oz. cream cheese
8 oz. sour cream
1 c. shredded cheese
9 – 10" flour tortillas

Fry hamburger with onions, then add rest of ingredients in the order given. Spread a thin layer of meat mixture on tortillas and roll up. Refrigerate for 1 hour before cutting into slices. Serve with taco sauce or salsa. These work great at picnics and finger food meals.

Vegetable Dip

...Mrs. John (Mary) Hochstetler

8 oz. cream cheese
1 c. buttermilk
1 c. sour cream
1 c. mayonnaise
1 pkg. Hidden Valley Ranch
   dressing mix

Soften cream cheese. Add dressing mix. Slowly add buttermilk. Add rest of ingredients. Beat until smooth with wire whip. Yield: 1 qt.

Fruit Dip

...Mrs. Freeman (Mabel) Yoder

1 (14 oz.) can sweetened
   condensed milk
4-6 oz. plain yogurt
8 oz. container Cool Whip

Mix well. Use to dip assorted fruits.

Fruit Dip

...Mrs. David (Emma) Hershberger

2 c. pineapple juice
2 Tbsp. clear jel
8 oz. Cool Whip
1/2 c. sugar
8 oz. cream cheese

Cook pineapple juice, sugar and clear jel until thick. When cool, add cream cheese and Cool Whip. Mix together until creamy. Serve with sliced apples, bananas, oranges and grapes. Apples and bananas may be dipped in lemon juice to keep from turning brown. Delicious.

Crunchy Apple Dip

...Mrs. Freeman (Mabel) Yoder

1 (8 oz.) pkg. cream cheese
1/2 c. creamy peanut butter
1/3 c. brown sugar
1 tsp. vanilla
1/2 c. miniature marshmallows
1 (11 3/4 oz.) jar hot fudge ice
   cream topping
2 Tbsp. chopped peanuts or
   mixed nuts
apple wedges
lemon juice

Beat cream cheese, peanut butter, brown sugar and vanilla. Stir in marshmallows. Spoon half into a small glass bowl; spread with hot fudge sauce. Repeat layers; sprinkle with nuts. Toss apple slices with lemon juice to keep from turning brown.

Apple Brickle Dip

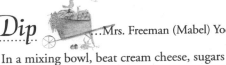

...Mrs. Freeman (Mabel) Yoder

1 (8 oz.) pkg. cream cheese,
   softened
1/2 c. packed brown sugar
1/4 c. sugar
1 tsp. vanilla
1 (7 1/2 oz.) pkg. almond brickle
   chips or 10 oz. English toffee bits
3 med. tart apples, cut into chunks

In a mixing bowl, beat cream cheese, sugars and vanilla. Fold in brickle chips. Serve with apples. Refrigerate any leftovers. Yield: 2 c.

Dorito Chip Dip

...Mrs. Simon (Esta) Miller

8 oz. cream cheese 8 oz. sour cream ¾ c. mayonnaise	Beat until smooth. Spread on a glass plate and refrigerate for 1 hour.
1 lb. hamburger with taco seasoning 1 pt. salsa	Fry hamburger with taco seasoning and salsa. Cook and stir for 5 minutes. Spread on cream cheese layer. Refrigerate.
2 c. shredded cheddar cheese 4 c. chopped lettuce 2 tomatoes, chopped 1 green pepper, chopped 1 small onion, chopped	Before serving spread on cheese, lettuce, tomatoes, green pepper and onion. Dip and serve with Doritos or your favorite dipping chips.

Bacon Tomato Spread

...Mrs. Freeman (Mabel) Yoder

1 (8 oz.) pkg. cream cheese 2 tsp. prepared mustard ½ tsp. celery seed 1 med. tomato (take out seeds and chop fine) ½ c. chopped green pepper ¼ tsp. salt ⅛ tsp. pepper 8 slices bacon, fried and crumbled crackers or raw veggies	In a bowl, combine cream cheese, mustard and celery seed until well blended. Add everything else and refrigerate for 1 hour or so. Serve with crackers or veggies. Yum!

Pizza Bites

...Mrs. Freeman (Mabel) Yoder

10 slices American cheese 40 slices pepperoni 40 round snack crackers (Ritz)	Cut each cheese slice into 4 pieces. Spray a large cookie sheet with nonstick cooking spray. Place crackers on cookie sheet, top with cheese and a slice of pepperoni. Bake at 300° for 10 minutes or until warm. A child pleasing snack!

Cocoa
...Mrs. Freeman (Mabel) Yoder

1¼ c. powdered coffee creamer
1½ c. mini milk chocolate
  chips (a must)
1½ c. powdered sugar
1½ c. chocolate-flavored
  drink mix
1⅔ c. powdered milk
dash salt

Mix all together. To serve, place 2 Tbsp. into a cup and add 1 c. boiling water. Serve with marshmallows. At Christmas time it is nice to add 1.75 oz. bottle Betty Crocker decor sprinkles to the mix in red and green color. These are soft and chewy, not the hard pebbles. Then put this in pint jars and decorate with a recipe card attached for a gift.

Creamy Hot Chocolate
...Mrs. Freeman (Mabel) Yoder

½ c. cocoa
1 (14 oz.) can sweetened
  condensed milk
⅛ tsp. salt
2 tsp. vanilla extract
8 c. water

In a large kettle, combine cocoa, milk and salt. Cook over low heat; gradually add water. Cook until heated through. For a richer drink, use milk instead of water. Stir in vanilla. Serve with marshmallows. Yield: 9 c.

Peppermint Cocoa
...Mrs. Freeman (Mabel) Yoder

1 c. coffee creamer
¾ c. sugar
¾ c. powdered sugar
1 c. chocolate drink mix
1 c. dry milk
½ c. red and white
  peppermint candy

Place candy in a freezer bag and tap with hammer to crush. Combine all ingredients and mix well. Mix 2 Tbsp. mix to a cup of boiling water. Top with whipped topping if desired. Refreshing.

The greatest of all faults is to imagine you have none.

6

Cappuccino

...Mrs. Melvin (Mary) Stutzman
...Mrs. Richard (Verna Kay) Stutzman

4 c. coffee creamer
4 c. dry milk
1 c. instant chocolate milk mix
$^{3}/_{4}$ c. instant coffee
1$^{1}/_{2}$ c. vanilla sugar
$^{1}/_{2}$ c. powdered sugar
$^{1}/_{2}$ tsp. salt

Mix all together. To serve, use 5 tsp. in 8 oz. hot water.
Vanilla sugar—Mix in 2 tsp. vanilla and 1 tsp. maple flavoring with the sugar. Line jelly roll pan with waxed paper. Spread out the sugar and let dry. Or instead of making vanilla sugar use flavored coffee creamer.
Verna Kay uses less creamer, dry milk and coffee.

Russian Tea

...Mrs. John (Mary) Hochstetler

$^{1}/_{2}$ c. instant tea (Nestlé)
2$^{1}/_{2}$ c. white sugar
2 c. Tang
1 tsp. cloves
2 tsp. cinnamon
2 pkg. Kool-Aid lemonade

Mix ingredients together. Store in covered jar. Dissolve 2-3 tsp. in 1 c. hot water and serve.

Springtime Punch

...Mrs. David (Barbara) Wagler

2 c. sugar
2$^{1}/_{2}$ c. water
1 c. fresh lemon juice
  (3-4 lemons)
1 c. fresh orange juice
  (2-3 oranges)
1 (6 oz.) can frozen pineapple
  juice concentrate, thawed
2 qt. ginger ale, chilled

In a saucepan, bring sugar and water to a boil. Boil for 10 minutes; remove from heat. Stir in the lemon, orange and pineapple juices. Refrigerate. Just before serving, combine with ginger ale in a large punch bowl.
Yield: about 3 qt.

Love never asks how much must I do,
but how much can I do.

Punch
...Mrs. Melvin (Mary) Stutzman

1 (6 oz.) pkg. cherry gelatin
³/₄ c. sugar
2 c. boiling water
1 (46 oz.) can pineapple juice
6 c. cold water
2 liters ginger ale, chilled

Dissolve gelatin and sugar in boiling water. Stir in pineapple juice and cold water. Cover and freeze overnight. Remove from freezer 2 hours before serving. Add ginger ale.

Fruity Punch
...Mrs. Freeman (Mabel) Yoder

3 qt. pineapple juice
12 oz. frozen lemonade concentrate
2 (12 oz.) cans frozen orange juice concentrate
2 c. sugar
1 gal. ginger ale
2 qt. water
ice ring—cranberries or strawberries and lime rind

Mix first 6 ingredients together and chill. To make ice ring you need to plan ahead. Place 4 c. water in a ring mold lightly sprayed with nonstick cooking spray. Cut tree shapes or whatever shape you wish with a sharp cookie cutter. Place shapes upside down in top of ring mold. Save lime pulp for another use. Place cranberries or strawberries between lime peel shapes. Rearrange as mold freezes if necessary. Freeze until solid. Unmold and float this in your punch bowl. Very pretty! Another punch tip—freeze strawberries, pit cherries, raspberries or grapes or mint in ice cube trays using some of the punch you are using or water and float these cubes in your punch.

Mennonite Wine
...Mrs. Sam (Mary) Hershberger

1 (12 oz.) can frozen orange juice
1 (12 oz.) can frozen grape juice
1 – 2 liter Sprite or 7-Up
¹/₄ c. ReaLemon
1 c. sugar

Mix this all in gallon container then fill with water. Enjoy!

*Happiness is the art of making a bouquet
of those flowers within reach.*

Our Favorite Grape Punch

...Mrs. Glen (Pollyanna) Hochstetler

2 qt. chilled grape juice
2 pk. Concord grape Kool-Aid
sugar to taste
1 liter Sprite

Mix first three ingredients well. Add Sprite and ice. Pour into crystal clear glasses and serve with a smile!

Iced Tea

...Mrs. Willis (Mary) Bontrager

4 c. water
2 c. tightly packed fresh tea leaves
1 1/2 c. sugar

Boil water and sugar together for 5 minutes. Add tea leaves, cover and let stand 6-7 hours or overnight. Strain. Can be frozen. Use 1 c. concentrate to 2 qt. water or to suit taste. Very refreshing!

Homemade Frappuccino

...daughter, Amy Yoder

6 c. milk
1 c. chocolate syrup
1 1/2 c. cold coffee
1/2 c. sugar
1 c. whipped cream, optional

Mix first four ingredients. Stir until sugar is dissolved. Add whipped cream last. Yield: approx. 2 qt. Serve very cold. Delicious!

Dreamsicle Drink Mix

...Mrs. Freeman (Mabel) Yoder

1/2 c. sugar
2/3 c. powdered coffee creamer
1 c. dry milk
1/2 c. powdered sugar
2/3 c. orange-flavored drink mix
dash salt

Mix all ingredients well. To use, mix 3 Tbsp. mix to 1 c. boiling water; top with marshmallows. To serve cold, place a scoop of vanilla ice cream, 1 c. milk and 1/3 c. dreamsicle mix in a quart jar and shake until well mixed and enjoy.
Variation: 1/3 c. mix, 1 c. milk and ice cubes blended together is another good cooler.

Hints for Breads

- To avoid lumps in bread batter, add a pinch of salt to the flour before it is wet.

- When cool-rise dough "rests", the resting takes the place of the first rising in other methods.

- Over kneading may cause large air holes in the crust.

- A small dish of water in the oven while baking bread will keep it from getting a hard crust.

- When making rolls, add only enough flour to keep dough from sticking to your hands or the board. Keep the dough as soft as possible.

- After rolls have baked, remove from pan immediately to prevent steam from forming and making them heavy.

- Brush rolls with one beaten egg and ¼ c. water before baking. Sprinkle with sesame seed, poppy seed, etc., for that professional look.

- Let nut breads and other quick breads stand for 10 minutes before removing from the pan to allow them to become firmer. Do not cool completely in the pan or they will become soggy.

- For tender muffins, mix liquid and dry ingredients until just moistened. Over mixing causes muffins to be tough, coarse-textured and full of tunnels.

- Use the divider from an ice tray to cut biscuits in a hurry. Shape dough to conform with size of divider and cut. After baking, biscuits will separate at dividing lines.

- Kneading the dough for a half minute after mixing improves the texture of baking powder biscuits.

- Use cooking or salad oil in waffles and hotcakes instead of shortening. No extra pan or bowl to melt the shortening and no waiting.

- A rib of celery in your bread bag will keep the bread fresh for a longer time.

- Freshen dry bread by wrapping in a damp towel and placing it in the refrigerator for 24 hours. Remove towel and heat in oven for a few minutes.

- Put frozen bread loaves in a clean brown paper bag and place in 325° oven for 5 minutes to thaw completely.

- Substitutes that can be used for bread crumbs are dry cereal and potato flakes.

- Cut "figure eight" yeast rolls with a doughnut cutter. Pick up the ring, stretch it, then twist. No ends to tuck under and a pretty roll for the pastry or bread platter.

- To raise bread dough in your oven, preheat the oven at lowest possible setting for 10 minutes. Turn the oven off and then put in mixing bowl of dough, covered.

To shew forth thy lovingkindness in the
morning and thy faithfulness every night.
Psalm 92:2

Breads & Rolls

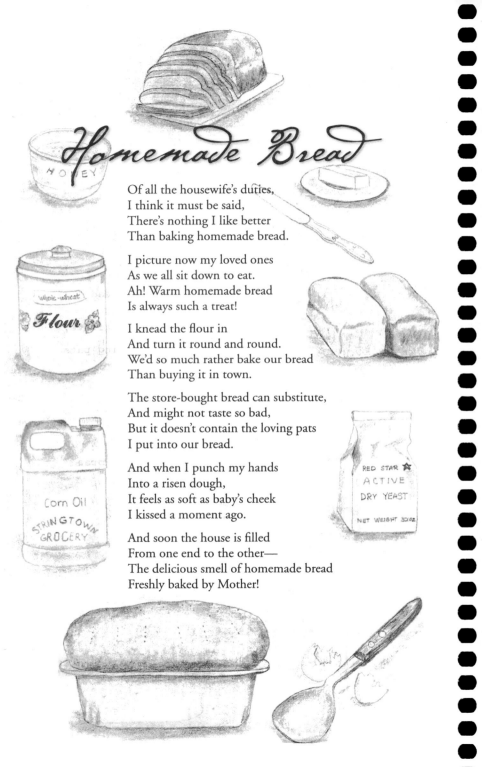

Homemade Bread

Of all the housewife's duties,
I think it must be said,
There's nothing I like better
Than baking homemade bread.

I picture now my loved ones
As we all sit down to eat.
Ah! Warm homemade bread
Is always such a treat!

I knead the flour in
And turn it round and round.
We'd so much rather bake our bread
Than buying it in town.

The store-bought bread can substitute,
And might not taste so bad,
But it doesn't contain the loving pats
I put into our bread.

And when I punch my hands
Into a risen dough,
It feels as soft as baby's cheek
I kissed a moment ago.

And soon the house is filled
From one end to the other—
The delicious smell of homemade bread
Freshly baked by Mother!

Pizza Crust
...Mrs. Lonnie (Norma) Bontrager

2 Tbsp. yeast
2 c. warm water
2 tsp. salt
$^{1}/_{2}$ c. oil
2 tsp. sugar
1 c. wheat flour
4 c. white flour

Mix yeast and water until yeast is dissolved. Then add remaining ingredients. Bake at 350° for 15 minutes or until golden brown. Yield: 2 large crusts.

Biscuit Mix
...Mrs. Jonathan (Naomi) Wagler

8 c. flour
8 tsp. sugar
$^{1}/_{3}$ c. baking powder
2 tsp. cream of tartar
2 tsp. salt
1$^{3}/_{4}$ c. shortening

Sift together dry ingredients and cut in shortening. Pack loosely in airtight container. When ready to use, mix 1 c. mix to $^{1}/_{3}$ c. milk, blend lightly with fork only until flour is moistened and dough pulls away from sides of bowl. Place on lightly greased pan. Bake at 450° for 10-12 minutes.

Never-Fail Biscuits
...Mrs. Freeman (Mabel) Yoder

2 c. flour
$^{1}/_{2}$ tsp. salt
1 Tbsp. baking powder
$^{1}/_{2}$ tsp. cream of tartar
1$^{1}/_{2}$ Tbsp. sugar
1 egg, slightly beaten
$^{1}/_{2}$ c. margarine
$^{2}/_{3}$ c. milk

Mix dry ingredients. Then cut in shortening; add egg and milk. Mix just until it hangs together. Drop onto a baking sheet and bake at 375° for 20 minutes or until golden.

Jesus is our pattern,
The Bible is our guide,
The life He leads is perfect,
In Him we shall abide.

Pepperoni Biscuits
...Mrs. Freeman (Mabel) Yoder

2 c. flour
$1/2$ tsp. salt
4 tsp. baking powder
$1/2$ tsp. cream of tartar
2 tsp. sugar
$1/2$ c. shortening or margarine
$2/3$ c. milk
$1/2$ tsp. garlic powder
$1/2$ tsp. Italian seasoning
1 ($3^1/2$ oz.) pkg. pepperoni
   slices, finely chopped
$2/3$ c. shredded cheddar cheese

Mix dry ingredients. Cut in shortening. Gradually add milk and stir in pepperoni and cheese just until combined. Drop by tablespoons on ungreased cookie sheets. Bake at 400° until golden brown, approximately 15-20 minutes. Serve warm. This is good with a spaghetti dish or sausage gravy.

Bacon Cheese Biscuits
...Mrs. Freeman (Mabel) Yoder

2 c. flour
1 Tbsp. sugar
$1/2$ tsp. baking soda
$1/2$ c. softened butter,
   margarine or shortening
1 c. buttermilk or sour milk*
1 lb. bacon cooked, crumbled
   and drained
1 c. shredded cheese
1 Tbsp. baking powder
1 tsp. salt

In a large bowl, combine dry ingredients. Cut in shortening. Stir in milk just until combined. Fold in cheese and bacon. Turn onto a floured surface. Knead 4 or 5 times. Roll out to $1/2$" thick and cut with a biscuit cutter. Place on greased baking sheet. Bake at 375°-400° until golden. These can be dropped. Serve with sausage gravy or your favorite soup.
*To make sour milk place 1 Tbsp. vinegar in a measuring cup and fill up with milk.

Build a little fence of trust today;
Fill the space with loving deeds and therein stay;
Look not through the sheltering bars upon tomorrow;
God will help bear what comes of joy and sorrow.

14

Italian Bread Twists
...daughter, Amy Yoder

2-3 c. flour
1 Tbsp. yeast
¹/2 tsp. salt
³/4 c. warm water
6 Tbsp. vegetable oil, divided
2 tsp. honey
2 Tbsp. butter, melted
5 tsp. Parmesan cheese
1 Tbsp. parsley flakes
1 tsp. garlic salt

In a large bowl place warm water, yeast, 3 Tbsp. oil and honey. Add flour gradually and salt. Knead until smooth and elastic. Cover and let rise for 15 minutes. Punch down and roll out into an approximately 9" x 14" rectangle. Cut into strips, twist each strip and place on greased cookie sheet. Combine butter and remaining oil. Brush liberally over bread twists. Sprinkle with Parmesan cheese, garlic salt and parsley. Bake at 350° for 15-20 minutes or until light brown. Serve with warmed pizza sauce. Yield: 10 breadsticks.

Sesame Onion Twists
...Mrs. Jonathan (Wilma) Hochstetler

2 Tbsp. butter
1¹/2 c. finely chopped onions
¹/4 tsp. paprika
1 (16 oz.) loaf frozen bread
   dough, thawed
1 egg, beaten
1 Tbsp. sesame seeds

Melt butter in medium skillet. Add chopped onion and paprika; cook until onion is tender, stirring occasionally. Remove from heat. Grease work surface and roll dough into a 14" x 12" rectangle. Spread onion mixture on one side of dough. Fold dough over onion mixture to make a 14" x 6" rectangle. Pinch 14" edge of dough to seal over onion mixture. Cut dough into 14 lengthwise dough strips. Gently twist strips 2 times and place on greased baking sheet. Press down both ends of strips to prevent curling. Let twists rise in warm place until double in size. Brush with beaten egg; sprinkle with sesame seeds. Bake at 375° for 15-18 minutes or until golden. Serve immediately with salsa or cheese dip.

Sour Cream Twists
...Mrs. Steve (Linda) Kauffman

³/₄ c. sour cream
¹/₈ tsp. soda
1 tsp. salt
3 Tbsp. sugar
2 Tbsp. butter
1 egg, beaten
1 Tbsp. yeast in
   ¹/₄ c. warm water
2¹/₂-3 c. flour

Bring sour cream to a boil and add soda. Add remaining ingredients. Knead and let set for 5 minutes in a warm place. Then roll out and make twist and let set until doubled. Bake at 350° for 10-15 minutes. Frost with maple icing. If baked in an airbake, should be in oven more like 18 minutes.

Herb Rolls
...Mrs. Sam (Viola) Miller

2 pkg. dry yeast
2³/₄ c. warm water
1 egg
1/3 c. vegeteble oil
1/4 c. honey or molasses
1 Tbsp. salt
2 tsp. thyme
2 tsp. basil
1 tsp. onion powder
2 tsp. dill weed
4 c. whole wheat flour
4-4¹/₂ c. white flour

Dissolve yeast in ¹/₂ c. warm water. Add next nine ingredients and remaining water. Beat until smooth and gradually add rest of flour. Grease 48 muffin cups. Let rise until double. Punch down; form 1" balls. Put 3 in each cup. Let rise until double. Bake at 375° for 12-15 minutes.

Refrigerator Potato Rolls
...Mrs. Melvin (Mary) Stutzman

2 c. warm water
1 (1 Tbsp.) pkg. yeast
²/₃ c. sugar
1¹/₂ tsp. salt
²/₃ c. vegetable oil
2 eggs
1 c. mashed potatoes, cooled
6¹/₄-6³/₄ c. flour

Soak yeast in part of the water. Mix the remaining ingredients (except the flour) and beat well. Add yeast and flour, 2 c. at a time, beating well after each addition. Cover and let rise. Punch down. Roll out on floured surface and cut with a biscuit cutter. Cover and let rise. Bake at 350°. Dough can be stored in refrigerator. Rolls can be baked and frozen, then warmed up. These rolls are light and fluffy. Have plenty of butter, jam and apple butter on hand to serve with them.

Melt-in-Your-Mouth Dinner Rolls
...Mrs. Allen (Elsie) Bontrager

1 pkg. dry yeast ¹/₂ c. warm water	Dissolve together.
1 Tbsp. sugar 1 tsp. baking powder	Add and let stand for 20 minutes.
¹/₃ c. butter, melted 1 c. milk, scalded ¹/₃ c. sugar dash of salt	Meanwhile, mix together and cool.
2 eggs, beaten 4¹/₂ c. flour yeast mixture	Add. Stir with spoon, as it is very sticky. Cover and refrigerate overnight. Shape into balls and place in greased muffin tins or you can put them in a 9" x 13" pan. Let rise 2 hours. Bake at 425° until golden.

Dinner Rolls
...Mrs. Owen (Treva) Yoder

2 c. warm water 2 Tbsp. yeast ¹/₂ c. sugar 2 tsp. salt ¹/₄ c. oil 2 eggs, beaten 1 c. mashed potatoes approx. 6 c. flour	Soften yeast in water. Add rest of ingredients, adding only half of the flour. Let set a few minutes then add more flour to make a soft dough. Shape into dinner rolls or roll out ³/₄" thick and cut out for soft homemade hamburger buns. Let rise until light. Bake at 350° for about 20 minutes.

Easy Rolls
...Mom, Elsie Yoder

1 c. shortening or butter 2 c. hot water 1 Tbsp. salt ¹/₂ c. sugar 2 beaten eggs 2 Tbsp. yeast approx. 5 c. flour	Use hot water to melt shortening. Cool to lukewarm. Add salt, sugar, beaten eggs and yeast. Add enough flour for a soft dough. Roll them out right away. Spread with butter, brown sugar and cinnamon and set in a warm place to rise about 1-1¹/₂ hours. Bake at 350°. We bake 10 minutes on bottom rack and 5 minutes on top. Frost with your favorite frosting.

Best Burger Buns
...Mrs. David (Fannie) Miller

³/₄ c. whole wheat flour
1 Tbsp. instant yeast
1 tsp. salt
3 Tbsp. sugar
1 c. warm water
2 Tbsp. butter, melted
1 egg, beaten
2-2¹/₂ c. flour

Dissolve yeast in warm water. Add salt, sugar, beaten egg and melted butter with wire whip a little at a time. Then knead on floured surface, adding only enough flour to keep dough from sticking. A soft dough makes lighter buns. Cover and let rise in greased bowl 1 hour or until doubled. Divide into 12 pieces and form into smooth balls, greasing hands if necessary. Place on greased sheet and flatten with your hand. Cover and let rise 30-40 minutes. Bake at 375° for 10-12 minutes until golden.

Double-Quick Dinner Buns
...Mrs. Steve (Linda) Kauffman

³/₄ c. warm water (not hot)
1 pkg. active dry yeast or 1 Tbsp.
¹/₄ c. sugar
1 tsp. salt
2¹/₄ c. sifted flour
1 egg
¹/₄ c. soft shortening or butter

Dissolve yeast in water in mixing bowl. Add sugar, salt and about half the flour. Beat thoroughly for 2 minutes. Add egg and shortening. Then beat in gradually the remaining flour until smooth. Let rise in bowl for 40-50 minutes in a warm place. Stir down the batter and drop into greased muffin cups. Let rise another 30 minutes or until double in bulk. Heat oven to 425°. Bake for 10 minutes. Yield: 1 dozen.

But without faith it is impossible to please him; for he that cometh to God must believe that he is, and that he is a rewarder of them that diligently seek him.
—Hebrews 11:6

Cinnamon Yeast Rolls
...Mrs. Owen (Treva) Yoder

1 Tbsp. yeast
1 c. lukewarm milk
¼ c. sugar
3 c. bread flour
1 tsp. salt
2 eggs, beaten
¼ c. vegetable oil

Soften yeast in milk. Add sugar and 1½ c. flour and mix. Let set until bubbly; add salt, eggs, oil and 1½ c. flour. Knead. Let rise until double. Roll out ¼" thick. Spread with melted butter and sprinkle with cinnamon. Roll like jelly rolls and cut 1½" slices. Place in greased 13" x 9" pan. Let rise. Just before baking, pour hot caramel syrup over it. Bake at 350°. Eat warm or frost when cooled.

Caramel Syrup:
½ c. brown sugar
1 Tbsp. butter
¼ c. water

Boil together.

Cinnamon Sticky Buns
...Mrs. Freeman (Mabel) Yoder

1 c. brown sugar
½ c. corn syrup
½ c. butter or margarine
1 c. coarsely chopped pecans
½ c. sugar
2 tsp. cinnamon
2 (17.3 oz.) tubes large
   refrigerated biscuits

In a saucepan combine brown sugar, corn syrup and butter; cook and stir until sugar is dissolved. Add pecans. Spoon into a greased 9" x 13" x 2" pan. In a bowl combine cinnamon and sugar. Cut each biscuit in half. Dip in cinnamon/sugar. Place cut side down, over brown sugar syrup mixture. Bake at 375° for 25-30 minutes. Invert onto a serving plate. Serve warm. Yield: 12-16 servings.

Cinnamon Rolls
...Mrs. Marcus (Joleen) Marner

½ c. water
2 Tbsp. yeast
¾ c. sugar
2 c. milk
½ tsp. salt
2 eggs, well beaten
¾ c. butter, melted
8 c. flour

Mix ingredients in order given. Mix well. Let dough rise until double in size. Roll out to about 1". Brush with melted oleo. Sprinkle with brown sugar, cinnamon and nuts. Roll up and cut into 1" slices. Place in greased pans. Let rise. Bake at 350° for 15 minutes or until light brown. Ice while warm.

Cinnamon Rolls
...Mrs. Vern (Irene) Schlabach

1 Tbsp. salt
$\frac{1}{2}$ c. sugar
1$\frac{1}{4}$ c. corn oil
4 c. water
2 eggs, beaten
$\frac{1}{4}$ c. yeast
10-12 c. flour

I usually put water with first 3 ingredients. then stir in 5 c. flour. Add eggs and stir well. Put yeast with 5 c. flour; stir well. then I use my hands and add 1-2 c. flour. You'll learn by baking and the texture how much flour to add. This recipe makes 3 dozen rolls. This recipe you don't have to let rise before rolling out and cutting. After rolling out spread with butter, brown sugar and cinnamon. Roll and cut. Bake at 350° until lightly browned 20-25 minutes.

Caramel Roll-Me-Ups
...Mrs. Marcus (Joleen) Marner

2 cans biscuits

Topping:
1 c. brown sugar
$\frac{1}{4}$ c. butter, melted
$\frac{1}{3}$ c. maple syrup
$\frac{1}{3}$ c. chopped nuts

Mix topping and place in bottom of a 9" x 13" pan.

Filling:
1 (8 oz.) pkg. cream cheese
$\frac{1}{4}$ c. powdered sugar
2 Tbsp. butter, softened

Combine filling ingredients. Mix well. Flatten biscuits into oval shape. Place 1 tsp. cream cheese filling on center of each one. Roll biscuit to make "sausage" shape and pinch seam closed. Place in 9" x 13" pan seam side down. Bake until nicely browned at 350°. Turn upside down after baking and serve warm. Delicious with ice cream.

One thing about silence is—no one can go around repeating it.

Easy Crescent Flip-Overs ...Mrs. LaVern (Martha) Yoder

3 tubes of crescent dinner rolls
1 qt. of your favorite pie
   filling, thickened
1 (8 oz.) pkg. cream cheese
1 egg yolk
³/₄ c. powdered sugar

Put crescents on cookie sheets, then mix cream cheese, egg yolk and powdered sugar together. Now put 1 tsp. cream cheese filling on each triangle of crescent rolls and 1 tsp. pie filling on top of cream cheese filling, then flip over end of triangle to cover the filling and pinch all edges shut. Bake at 350° for 20 minutes or until golden brown. Cool slightly then glaze. Glaze with 1 c. powdered sugar and enough cold water to make a nice glaze. Easy and delicious.

Overnight Sweet Rolls ...Mrs. Sam (Viola) Miller

1 c. milk, scalded
1 stick oleo
¹/₃ c. sugar
¹/₂ tsp. salt
2 eggs, beaten
1 pkg. yeast, dissolved in
   ¹/₄ c. warm water
4 c. flour

Keep dough in refrigerator overnight. Then roll out and spread with butter, brown sugar and cinnamon. Let rise until double, then bake at 375° for 15-20 minutes. A quick and easy roll for brunch. Glaze.

Fruit Rolls ...Mrs. Freeman (Mabel) Yoder

2 tsp. salt
³/₄ Tbsp. wheat gluten
6 c. hot water
4 lb. donut mix (slightly over)
6 Tbsp. yeast
1 lb. flour
blueberry pie filling
glaze

In a large bowl stir hot water and salt. Add approximately ¹/₄ of donut mix and gluten and mix well. Add yeast, then gradually the rest of donut mix and flour. Knead until smooth; will be a sticky dough. Let rise 10 minutes. Roll out onto a floured surface. Can divide dough in half. Roll out to desired thickness. Spread blueberry pie filling, not too thick, and roll up and cut. Place on greased cookie sheets or pans and let rise until double. Bake at 375° for approximately 20-25 minutes or until golden. Glaze with your favorite frosting. Variation: Instead of blueberry filling, use butter, brown sugar and cinnamon. Very good.

Soft Bread Sticks
...Mrs. Nathan (Barbara) Lehman

1 c. warm water
1 Tbsp. yeast
3 Tbsp. sugar
1/4 c. oil
1 tsp. salt
3 c. flour

Mix first three ingredients and let yeast rise. Add remaining ingredients. Mix together and knead like bread. Let rise once. Divide dough in 12 portions and roll into sticks. Let rise again. Brush with beaten egg white and sprinkle with garlic salt and parsley. Preheat oven to 400° and bake 15 minutes or less. Place 9" x 13" pan with boiling water on bottom rack. Enjoy with cheese sauce or pizza sauce.

Quick Bread
...Mrs. Freeman (Mabel) Yoder

2 c. flour
1/2 tsp. salt
4 tsp. baking powder
1 egg, beaten
3 Tbsp. vegetable oil or
   softened butter
3/4 c. water

Mix water and egg; beat. Add oil or butter. In another bowl combine flour, salt and baking powder; add liquids and knead lightly. Heat 2 Tbsp. oil in a 12" skillet. Press dough into skillet, then flip it over so the top is greased. Over low heat and loosely covered fry until slightly raised and lightly browned, then turn over and do the other side. Serve warm with butter and honey or jam, or can be used like biscuits and served with gravy. This is one of our favorites.

Bread
...daughter, Charlene Yoder

4 c. warm water
2 Tbsp. yeast (level)
1/3 c. vegetable oil
1/2 c. sugar
4 tsp. salt
1 egg, beaten
4 c. whole wheat flour
approx. 8-10 c. white flour

Put water and yeast in a large bowl. Let set for 5 minutes. Then add oil, sugar, salt, egg, 2 c. whole wheat flour and 4 c. white flour. Stir well with a big spoon. Add remaining whole wheat flour and knead with hands. Gradually add more white flour to form a soft dough. Knead about 20 minutes. Cover and let rise until double; punch down. Let rise again, then divide into 4 loaves. Let rise until double. Bake at 325° for 10 minutes. Increase to 350° and bake for 20-25 minutes longer or until golden brown. This bread keeps a long time without getting rancid or moldy. This is our favorite!

White Bread ...Mrs. Marcus (Joleen) Marner

1 c. lukewarm water
1 Tbsp. brown sugar
2 Tbsp. yeast
1 c. sugar
1 Tbsp. salt
½ c. shortening
1 qt. warm water
13 c. flour

In a small bowl, take 1 c. lukewarm water and mix brown sugar and yeast in it. In a large bowl mix sugar, salt, shortening and 1 qt. warm water. Add 4 c. flour and beat well. Add yeast mixture. Add 3 more cups of flour and beat well. Keep on adding flour 1-2 c. at a time, beating well after each addition. When dough gets too stiff to beat, use your hands and knead in enough flour to make a soft dough. Cover and let rise in a warm place. Punch down at 45 minute intervals 3 times. Form into loaves. Let rise until double in size. Bake at 350° for 30 minutes.

Whole Wheat Bread ...Mrs. Monroe (Mary) Hochstetler

3½ c. warm water
½ c. canola oil
½ c. honey (I use sorghum molasses)
½ c. gluten
¼ c. lecithin
3 Tbsp. yeast
1 Tbsp. salt
1 egg
7 c. flour or more

Let rise 2 times. Bake at 350° for 30 minutes or until done. Yield: 4 loaves. Use organic wheat flour (Prairie Gold).

Whole Wheat Bread ...Mrs. David (Barbara) Wagler

5 c. water
⅔ c. oil
¾ c. honey
2 Tbsp. lecithin granules
¼ c. gluten
½ c. yeast
1 Tbsp. salt
13 c. wheat flour

Use warm water from faucet. Sprinkle yeast and gluten over water. Add oil, honey, salt and lecithin granules. Add 6 c. flour and stir well. Gradually add approximately 7 more cups flour, kneading as you go. Knead well. Let rise 2 times. Then place 1 lb. dough in pans. Let rise until double and bake at 325°-350° for 20-25 minutes.

23

Rye Bread
...Mrs. Melvin (Katie) Miller

2 c. lukewarm water
1 Tbsp. sugar
1 Tbsp. yeast
2 c. white flour
2 Tbsp. caraway seed
1½ tsp. salt
2 Tbsp. shortening, melted
1½ c. white flour
1½ c. rye flour

Mix first four ingredients. Let rise. Add remaining ingredients. Knead. Let rise. Punch down and let rise again. Form into loaf. Let rise and bake at 400° for 30 minutes. Before baking brush top with egg for a shiny crust.

Egg Bread
...Mrs. Freeman (Amanda) Kauffman

¼ stick oleo
½ c. flour
2 c. milk
6 or 8 hard-boiled eggs

Put oleo in a pan and melt. Add flour and stir until light brown, then add milk and stir until smooth. If too thick, add more milk. Add wieners or ham and cheese. Add hard-boiled eggs and put over toast. Also good without the eggs.

Honey Oatmeal Bread
...Mrs. Paul (Mary Ann) Mast

2 qt. hot water
1 lb. oatmeal

Put hot water and oatmeal in bowl. Let set for 5 minutes.

1 doz. eggs, beaten
2¼ c. vegetable oil
2¼ c. honey
½ c. yeast
3 Tbsp. salt
3 c. very warm water (not too hot)

Add and let set for 3-5 minutes.

8-9 lb. white flour
3 lb. wheat flour

Put in bowl and gradually add to above mixture. Once everything is mixed together, knead with your hands for another 8-10 minutes. Let rise 3 times at 30 minute intervals. The fourth time shape into loaves. Bake at 350° for 30 minutes or until done. Yield: 18 loaves at 1½ lb. each. A favorite!

Wheat Bread with Flax Seed
...Mrs. Paul (Mary Ann) Mast

7¹/₂ c. water
4¹/₂ Tbsp. yeast
1¹/₄ c. sugar
1¹/₄ c. vegetable oil
3 Tbsp. salt
6 Tbsp. flax seed
6 c. wheat flour
additional white flour

Combine first six ingredients and mix well. Add 2 c. wheat flour, mix well and add rest of wheat flour and enough white flour to make a nice soft dough that doesn't stick to your hands. Punch down 3 times at 30 minute intervals. The fourth time take dough and shape into loaves. Bake at 350° for 30 minutes. Yield: 8 (1¹/₂ lb.) loaves. A bakery favorite!

Quick Cheese Bread
...Mrs. Freeman (Mabel) Yoder

1 loaf French or homemade bread
2 Tbsp. Parmesan cheese
1 stick butter, softened
¹/₄ tsp. pepper or lemon pepper
¹/₂ tsp. garlic powder
¹/₂ tsp. dried basil
¹/₂ tsp. oregano
3 c. shredded Italian or
    marble cheese

In a small bowl combine seasonings, Parmesan cheese and butter. Spread on 12-14 pieces of bread, divide cheese evenly on bread, place on a cookie sheet and broil 4-6" from flame until cheese is melted and bread is warm. Always a hit at our house.

The glory of the star, the glory of the sun,
We must not lose either in the other.
We must not be so full of the hope of Heaven
That we cannot do our work on the earth.
We must not be so lost in the work of the earth
That we shall not be inspired by the hope of Heaven.

Ranch Cheese Bread   ...daughter, Charlene Yoder

1 c. warm water
1 Tbsp. yeast
1 tsp. sugar
2¹/₂-3 c. flour
1 tsp. salt
1 Tbsp. oil

Mix water and yeast. Add sugar, salt and oil. Knead in flour to make a soft dough. Place in a greased bowl. Cover; let rise 20 minutes in a warm place. Punch dough down and roll on a greased 12" pizza pan.

Topping:
¹/₂ c. prepared Ranch dressing
¹/₄ tsp. salt
¹/₄ tsp. garlic powder
¹/₄ tsp. thyme
1 Tbsp. Parmesan cheese
1 c. mozzarella cheese
1 c. marble cheese
¹/₂ tsp. oregano

Spread Ranch dressing evenly over dough. Combine seasonings and Parmesan cheese and sprinkle over dressing. Bake at 375° approximately 25-30 minutes. Remove from heat and sprinkle mozarella and marble cheese over all. Bake 5 minutes longer. A family favorite!

Ranch Butter Bread   ...Mrs. Freeman (Mabel) Yoder

2 Tbsp. yeast
¹/₂ c. warm water
¹/₂ c. sugar
2 c. warm buttermilk*
¹/₂ c. butter, softened
3 eggs, beaten
1 or 2 env. original Ranch
   salad dressing mix
2 tsp. salt
8-9 c. flour

In a bowl dissolve yeast in warm water. Add sugar; let set 5 minutes, then add buttermilk, butter, eggs and Ranch dressing. Mix salt and 4 c. flour and beat well until smooth. Stir in remaining flour and knead until smooth and elastic. Cover and let rise in a warm place until double. Punch dough down and divide into 4 portions. Roll each one into approximately 14" x 12" rectangle. Roll up jelly-roll style starting with the long end. Pinch seams shut and tuck ends under. Place seam side down on greased baking sheets. With a sharp knife make 5 shallow slashes across the top of each loaf. Cover and let rise until double, 30 minutes or so. Bake at 350° for 20-25 minutes or until golden. Brush with butter. *Heated buttermilk will appear curdled; regular milk may be used. This is great served with soup!

26

Buttery Bubble Bread ...Mrs. Freeman (Mabel) Yoder

1 pkg. or Tbsp. yeast
1 c. warm water
$^1/_2$ c. sugar
$^1/_2$ c. shortening
1 egg
$^1/_2$ tsp. salt
4-4$^1/_2$ c. flour
6 Tbsp. butter or margarine,
   melted

In a large bowl dissolve yeast in warm water. Add sugar, shortening, egg, salt and 1 c. flour. Beat until smooth. Stir in enough flour to form a soft dough. Knead until smooth and elastic. Cover and let rise until double or about 1 hour. Punch dough down and pinch off small pieces and roll into 1$^1/_2$" balls. Dip into melted butter and arrange in a greased tube pan or a large loaf pan. Drizzle with remaining butter. Cover and let rise approximately 45 minutes. Bake at 350° for 30-35 minutes or until golden brown. Cool for 5 minutes before inverting on a serving platter. Serve warm. Yum!

Onion Cheese Bread ...daughter, Amy Yoder

1 c. chopped onion
4 tsp. vegetable oil
3 c. biscuit/baking mix
2 eggs
1 c. milk
1$^1/_2$ c. shredded cheddar
   cheese, divided
6 tsp. dried parsley flakes,
   divided
2 Tbsp. butter or margarine,
   melted

In a skillet, sauté onion in oil until tender. Place biscuit mix in a bowl. Combine eggs and milk; stir into biscuit mix just until combined. Stir in the onion, 1 c. cheese and 4 tsp. parsley. Spread the batter into 2 greased 8" round baking pans. Sprinkle with remaining cheese and parsley. Drizzle with butter. Bake at 400° for 15-20 minutes or until cheese is melted and top of bread is lightly browned. Is good served with butter or pizza sauce.

The only safe and sure way to destroy an
enemy is to make him your friend.

Coffee Raisin Bread   ...Mrs. Freeman (Mabel) Yoder

3/4 c. raisins
3 c. flour
1 c. warm strongly brewed coffee
3 Tbsp. vegetable oil
1 egg, beaten
1 1/2 tsp. salt
1/4 c. sugar
1 tsp. cinnamon
1/4 tsp. allspice
1/4 tsp. cloves
2 1/2 tsp. dry yeast

Glaze:
powdered sugar
milk
vanilla extract

Toss raisins with 1 Tbsp. flour; set aside. In a large bowl, pour coffee, egg and oil together. Dissolve yeast. Mix first mixture, yeast, salt, sugar, spices and 1 c. flour together. Beat well. Add the rest of the flour and knead. When almost done kneading, add raisins and knead until smooth and elastic. Let rise until double. Punch down and place in a greased bread pan. Bake at 350° for 25-30 minutes or until golden brown. Cool slightly and remove from pan. Drizzle glaze over loaf. Very tasty!

Peanut Butter Bread   ...Mrs. Freeman (Mabel) Yoder

2 c. flour
1/2 c. sugar
2 tsp. baking powder
1 tsp. salt
1 egg
1 c. milk
3/4 c. peanut butter

Cream sugar, egg and peanut butter. Add flour, salt and baking powder. Gradually add milk and mix just until combined. Pour into a loaf pan 8" x 4" x 2". Bake for 50-60 minutes at 350° until a toothpick comes out clean. Serve with grape jelly.

Banana Nut Bread   ...Mrs. Paul (Mary Ann) Mast

2 c. sugar
1 c. shortening
6 ripe bananas, mashed
4 eggs
1 tsp. salt
1/2 tsp. vanilla
2 tsp. baking soda
2 1/2 c. flour
1 c. pecans

Cream together sugar and shortening. Add mashed bananas and stir. Add well beaten eggs and stir. Add the rest of ingredients. Bake at 350° for 1 hour or until done. Yield: 3 (1 lb.) loaves.

Pineapple Banana Bread ...Mrs. Freeman (Mabel) Yoder

3 c. flour
2 c. sugar
1 tsp. salt
1 tsp. baking soda
1 tsp. cinnamon
3 eggs
1 1/8 c. vegetable oil
2 tsp. vanilla extract
1 c. crushed pineapple, drained
2 c. (4 or 5 med.) mashed bananas

Combine all dry ingredients. In another beat the eggs; add oil and vanilla. Add pineapple and bananas and mix well. Stir into the dry ingredients just until moistened. Pour into 2 greased 8" x 4" x 2" loaf pans. Bake at 350° for 60-65 minutes or until a toothpick comes out clean. You may drizzle the tops with your favorite glaze.

Batter Bread ...Mrs. Freeman (Mabel) Yoder

1 Tbsp. yeast
1/2 c. warm water
1 c. warm milk (110°-115°)
1/2 c. butter or margarine, softened
1/4 c. sugar
2 tsp. salt
3 eggs
5 1/2-6 c. flour

In a large bowl combine yeast and warm water. Add milk, butter or margarine, sugar and salt; stir well. Then add eggs and 3 c. flour; beat until smooth. Stir in enough remaining flour to form a soft dough (do not knead). Cover and let rise until double. Stir the dough down. Spoon into a greased and floured 10" tube pan or divide into 2 bread pans. Cover and let rise until doubled, about 1 hour. Bake at 375°-400° for 25-30 minutes until golden brown. This bread is good to start in the afternoon and have fresh warm bread for supper. Delicious!

Golden Corn Bread ...Mrs. Jonathan (Naomi) Wagler

1 c. yellow cornmeal
1 c. flour
1/4 c. sugar
1/2 tsp. salt
4 tsp. baking powder
1 egg
1 c. milk
1/4 c. shortening or vegetable oil

Sift together dry ingredients into bowl. Add egg, milk and shortening or oil. Beat thoroughly. Bake in greased 9" square pan at 425° for 15-20 minutes.

29

Bread Bowl

...Mrs. Freeman (Mabel) Yoder

1 (1 lb.) loaf frozen bread dough or use your own	Bake bread in a round 9"-10" bowl. Cool. Then slice the top off and cut the inside out 1" from the side, leaving a hollow shell. Fill with dip and cover the whole loaf with tinfoil and bake at 350° for 20-25 minutes or until dip is warm.
$1/2$ tsp. minced garlic 1 (8 oz.) cream cheese 1 (8 oz.) bacon-flavored cheese or Co-Jack or cheddar 1 pkg. dried beef, cut fine 16 oz. sour cream $1/2$ c. real bacon bits (not imitation)* 1 tsp. (rounded) minced onion or $1/4$ c. finely chopped onions 1 tsp. Worcestershire sauce $1/4$ tsp. liquid hickory smoke salt and Lawry's seasoning to taste	Mix well and fill bread bowl. Place bread bowl on a large platter and surround it with bread pieces, taco chips, etc. Pictured on the front cover of this cookbook. *Use bacon bits only if you are not using bacon-flavored cheese.

A gracious word may smooth the way,
A joyous word may light the day,
A timely word may lessen stress,
A loving word may heal and bless.

Maple Pumpkin Muffins
...Mrs. Freeman (Mabel) Yoder

2 c. flour
³/₄ c. brown sugar
2 tsp. baking powder
1 tsp. cinnamon
¹/₂ tsp. baking soda
¹/₂ tsp. pumpkin pie spice
¹/₄ tsp. salt
2 eggs
1 c. canned pumpkin
³/₄ c. evaporated milk
¹/₄ c. vegetable oil
3 Tbsp. maple syrup
¹/₂ c. chopped pecans
1 (3 oz.) pkg. cream cheese,
  softened

Topping:
¹/₄ tsp. chopped pecans
2 tsp. brown sugar

In a large bowl, combine flour, brown sugar, baking powder, cinnamon, soda, pumpkin pie spice and salt. Whisk the eggs, pumpkin, milk, oil and 1 Tbsp. maple syrup; stir into dry ingredients just until moistened. Fold in pecans. In a small bowl beat cream cheese and 2 Tbsp. brown sugar and remaining maple syrup until smooth. Gently stir into batter until mixture appears swirled. Fill greased or paper-lined muffin cups about ³/₄ full into 12 cups. Combine topping; spread over batter. Bake at 400° for 20-25 minutes or until toothpick inserted comes out clean.

Zucchini Chocolate Chip Muffins
...Mrs. Marvin (Mary Ann) Schrock

³/₄ c. sugar
¹/₂ c. vegetable oil
1 egg
1¹/₂ c. flour
1 tsp. soda
1 tsp. cinnamon
¹/₂ tsp. salt
¹/₄ c. milk
1 Tbsp. lemon juice
1 c. shredded zucchini
¹/₄ c. chocolate chips
¹/₄ c. chopped nuts

Beat together sugar, oil and egg. Then beat in dry ingredients. Add milk and lemon juice. Last add zucchini, chocolate chips and nuts. Fill muffin tins ²/₃ full. Bake at 350° for 20-25 minutes. Yield: 1 dozen.

31

Banana Muffins

...Mrs. Nathan (Barbara) Lehma
...Mrs. Jonathan (Rose) Yoder

1½ c. flour
1 tsp. soda
1 tsp. baking powder
½ tsp. salt
3 large bananas, mashed
¾ c. sugar
1 egg, lightly beaten
⅓ c. melted butter

Mix first five ingredients together. Combine dry ingredients. Mix bananas, sugar, egg and butter. Stir into dry mixture just until moistened. Fill greased or paper-lined muffin cups ¾ full. Bake at 375° for 18-20 minutes. Good served with butter or as a cereal.

Topping:
⅓ c. brown sugar
1 Tbsp. flour
⅛ tsp. cinnamon
1 Tbsp. butter

Combine topping ingredients and sprinkle over muffins before baking.

S'more Muffins

...Mrs. Freeman (Mabel) Yoder

1½ c. flour
¾ c. graham cracker crumbs
¼ c. brown sugar
1 tsp. baking soda
½ tsp. salt
1 egg
1½ c. buttermilk
¼ c. vegetable oil
¾ c. chocolate chips
1¼ c. miniature marshmallows

Mix first five ingredients. Combine egg, buttermilk and oil; mix well. Stir into dry ingredients just until moistened. Fold in chocolate chips and 1 c. marshmallows. Fill greased muffin cups ¾ full. Sprinkle a few marshmallows over each muffin. Bake at 375° for 18-20 minutes or until a toothpick comes out clean. Cool slightly; serve warm.

Bran Muffins

...Mrs. Jonathan (Rose) Yoder

1 c. All Bran*
1 c. milk
2 Tbsp. shortening
¼ c. sugar
1 egg, beaten
1 c. flour
1 Tbsp. baking powder
½ tsp. salt

Add bran to milk and let soak 5 minutes. Cream shortening and sugar. Add beaten egg and beat until smooth. Add bran mixture. Add dry ingredients. Stir only enough to mix. Bake at 400° for 25 minutes.
*You can use Wheaties, grapenuts or bran flakes. A good way to use up grapenuts that are toasted too hard.

32

Easy Doughnuts
...Mrs. Sam (Rachel) Kauffman

4 c. water
1 c. oleo
1 c. sugar
2 Tbsp. salt
¼ c. yeast
3 eggs
12 c. flour

Put oleo, sugar and salt in a bowl and add 4 c. hot water. Combine and add yeast. Put in remaining ingredients. Let rise and punch down and let rise again. Roll out and cut with a doughnut cutter. Let rise slightly then deep fat fry until golden brown.

Grandma's Cake Donuts
...Mrs. Danny (Vanessa) Reeves

2 eggs, well beaten
1 c. sour milk
   (¾ c. milk + ¼ c. lemon juice)
1 c. sugar
2 Tbsp. soft shortening
1 tsp. baking soda
2 tsp. baking powder
1 tsp. cinnamon
½ tsp. nutmeg
½ tsp. salt
3½ c. flour

Mix beaten eggs, milk, sugar and shortening. Blend well. Add flour and other dry ingredients. Stir well. On floured board pat part of dough ⅓" thick. Cut with donut cutter. Fry at 370° until golden brown on one side, then turn over and fry other side. Grandma fries her donuts in Crisco. Drain on paper towels. Shake in a bag with white sugar while still warm. If in a hurry, drop dough in by the teaspoon or with a cookie dough scoop for donut holes.

Soft Pretzels
...Mrs. Steve (Martha) Yoder

4-4½ c. flour
2 Tbsp. yeast
1½ c. warm water
1½ tsp. salt

Dissolve yeast in water. Add flour and salt. Flour can be scant. Let rise for 15 minutes. Knead well and then make pretzels. Dip in ¼ c. water with 2 tsp. soda. Bake at 400° for 15-20 minutes. Dip in melted butter after they are baked. Delicious served warm.

Topping Suggestions:
caramel sauce
pizza sauce
Cheese Whiz
brown sugar and cinnamon
cream cheese and mustard
jam

Measurements

a pinch . . . . $^1/_8$ tsp. or less	4 quarts . . . . .1 gallon
3 teaspoons. . . . . 1 tablespoon	8 quarts . . . . .1 peck
4 tablespoons . . . . $^1/_4$ cup	4 pecks. . . . . 1 bushel
8 tablespoons . . . . $^1/_2$ cup	16 ounces. . . . . 1 pound
12 tablespoons . . . . $^3/_4$ cup	32 ounces. . . . . 1 quart
16 tablespoons . . . . 1 cup	1 ounce liquid . . . . . . 2 tablespoons
2 cups. . . . . 1 pint	8 ounces liquid. . . . . 1 cup
4 cups. . . . . 1 quart	*Use standard measuring spoons and cups. All measurements are level.*

Substitutions

Ingredient	Quantity	Substitute
baking powder	1 tsp.	$^1/_4$ tsp. baking soda plus $^1/_2$ tsp. cream of tartar
catsup or chili sauce	1 c.	1 c. tomato sauce plus $^1/_2$ c. sugar and 2 Tbsp. vinegar (for use in cooking)
chocolate	1 square (1 oz.)	3 or 4 Tbsp. cocoa plus 1 Tbsp. butter
cornstarch	1 Tbsp.	2 Tbsp. flour or 2 tsp. quick-cooking tapioca
cracker crumbs	$^3/_4$ c.	1 c. bread crumbs
dates	1 lb.	1$^1/_2$ c. dates, pitted and cut
dry mustard	1 tsp.	1 Tbsp. prepared mustard
flour, self rising	1 c.	1 c. all-purpose flour, $^1/_2$ tsp. salt and 1 tsp. baking powder
herbs, fresh	1 Tbsp.	1 tsp. dried herbs
milk, sour	1 c.	1 Tbsp. lemon juice or vinegar plus sweet milk to make 1 c. (let stand 5 minutes)
milk, whole	1 c.	$^1/_2$ c. evaporated milk plus $^1/_2$ c. water
min. marshmallows	10	1 lg. marshmallow
onion, fresh	1 small	1 Tbsp. instant minced onion, rehydrated
sugar, brown	$^1/_2$ c.	2 Tbsp. molasses in $^1/_2$ c. granulated sugar
sugar, powdered	1 c.	1 c. granulated sugar plus 1 tsp. cornstarch
tomato juice	1 c.	$^1/_2$ c. tomato sauce plus $^1/_2$ c. water

When substituting cocoa for chocolate in cakes, the amount of flour must be reduced. Brown and white sugars usually can be interchanged.

The Little Things

It really is the little things
That mean the most of all...
The "let me help you with that" things
That may seem very small,
The "I'll be glad to do it" things
That make your cares much lighter,
The "laugh with me, it's funny" things
That make your outlook brighter...

The "never mind the trouble" things,
The "yes, I understand,"
The interest and encouragement
In everything you've planned...
It really is the little things,
The friendly word or smile,
That add such happiness to life
And make it more worthwhile.
—*Mary Dawson Hughes*

Cookies & Bars

The Lord is my shepherd...
That's relationship!

I shall not want...
That's supply!

He maketh me to lie down in green
pastures...
That's rest!

He leadeth me beside the still
waters...
That's refreshment!

He restoreth my soul...
That's healing!

He leadeth me in the paths of
righteousness...
That's guidance!

For his name's sake...
That's purpose!

Yea, though I walk through the
valley of the shadow of death...
That's challenge!

I will fear no evil...
That's comfort!

For thou art with me...
That's faithfulness!

Thy rod and thy staff they comfort
me...
That's security!

Thou preparest a table before me in
the presence of mine enemies...
That's hope!

Thou anointest my head with oil...
That's consecration!

My cup runneth over...
That's abundance!

Surely goodness and mercy shall
follow me all the days of my life...
That's blessing!

And I will dwell in the house of the
Lord forever.

Chocolate Chip Cookies …Mrs. Glen (Pollyanna) Hochstetler

3 sticks butter or oleo
1 c. Crisco
1 1/2 c. white sugar
1 1/2 c. brown sugar
1 1/3 c. instant pudding
4 eggs
2 tsp. salt
2 tsp. soda
4 tsp. vanilla
6 c. (scant) flour
2 1/2 c. chocolate chips

Blend oleo, Crisco, sugars and eggs. Add rest of ingredients. Bake 8 minutes at 350°. Don't overbake!

Chocolate Bit Cookies …Mrs. David (Emma) Hershberger

2 c. brown sugar
1 c. white sugar
2 c. shortening
6 eggs
1 Tbsp. vanilla
2 tsp. salt
4 tsp. soda
4 tsp. cream of tartar
7 c. flour
2-3 pkg. chocolate chips

Cream together sugars and shortening. Add eggs and beat well. Then add rest of ingredients. We like these since they don't take so much sugar.

Bulk Chocolate Chip Cookies
…Mrs. Danny (Vanessa) Reeves

9 c. flour
4 tsp. baking soda
2 tsp. salt
3 c. sugar
3 c. brown sugar
4 c. shortening (butter-flavored
  is good)
4 c. nuts (optional)
4 pkg. chocolate chips (I use only 3)

Cut all ingredients together except chocolate chips. Add the chocolate chips. Store in airtight container. Yield: 4 batches.
To bake: Mix 7 full cups of cookie mix with 2 eggs and 1 tsp. vanilla. Bake at 375° for 8-10 minutes. Delicious!

Choc-Oat-Chip Cookies...Mrs. Edward (Lizzie Ann) Schrock

1 c. margarine or butter, softened
1¼ c. firmly packed brown sugar
½ c. white sugar
2 eggs
2 Tbsp. milk
2 tsp. vanilla
1¾ c. flour
1 tsp. soda
½ tsp. salt
2½ c. quick oats
1 (12 oz.) pkg. chocolate chips
1 c. nuts

Beat margarine and sugars until creamy. Add eggs, milk and vanilla; beat well. Add flour, soda and salt; mix well. Stir in oats, chips and nuts. Drop by rounded tablespoon onto ungreased cookie sheet. Bake at 375° for 9-10 minutes for a chewy cookie, 12-13 minutes for a crisp cookie.

Whole Wheat Chocolate Chip Cookies
...Mrs. Aaron (Mary Ada) Yoder

8 sticks butter
2½ c. fructose*
2½ c. brown sugar
8 eggs
2 Tbsp. vanilla
10 c. Prairie Gold wheat flour
2⅔ c. instant vanilla pudding
4 tsp. soda
4 tsp. salt
6 c. chocolate chips

Mix butter, fructose, brown sugar, eggs and vanilla together. In separate bowl combine flour, instant vanilla pudding, soda and salt. Gradually add flour mixture to first mixture. Add chocolate chips. Bake at 350°. This recipe can be made in half. Enjoy!
*White sugar can be used instead of fructose.

What lies behind us and what lies before us, are tiny matters compared to what lies within us.

Peanut Butter Chocolate Cookies

...Mrs. David (Rachel) Plank

½ c. oleo
½ c. sugar
¼ c. brown sugar
¼ c. peanut butter
1 egg
1 tsp. vanilla
½ c. (scant) cocoa
½ tsp. baking soda
1½ c. flour

Filling:
¾ c. peanut butter
¾ c. powdered sugar

Mix together in order given, then make a pattie with chocolate dough. Place a teaspoon of filling in middle and bring edges over to completely cover it. Flatten each cookie with a glass. Bake at 375° for 7-9 minutes.

Chewy Chocolate Chip Peanut Butter Cookies

...Mrs. Paul (Mary Ann) Mast

2 c. butter or margarine, softened
2 c. peanut butter
3 c. brown sugar
½ c. white sugar
6 eggs
6 Tbsp. corn syrup
6 Tbsp. water
1 Tbsp. soda
1½ tsp. salt
2 Tbsp. vanilla
8 c. flour
3½ c. chocolate chips

Cream together first 4 ingredients. Add eggs and whip well. Add the next 5 ingredients and mix well. Add flour and chocolate chips. Bake at 325° for approximately 10-12 minutes. Do not overbake!

Norma's Oatmeal Cookies ...Mrs. Lonnie (Norma) Bontrager

2 c. brown sugar
2 c. white sugar
1 c. butter
1 c. shortening
2 tsp. baking powder
2 (3³/₈ oz.) boxes instant
  vanilla pudding
3 c. chocolate chips
6 c. quick oatmeal
4 eggs
4 c. flour
1 tsp. salt
2 tsp. baking soda
2 tsp. vanilla

Blend sugars, butter and shortening. Add eggs. Add rest of ingredient. Stir in chocolate chips last. Bake at 375° until light brown, about 8 minutes. Our favorite!

Triple Chocolate Caramel Cookies
...daughter, Charlene Yoder

1¹/₂ c. butter, softened
1 c. sugar
1 egg
1 tsp. vanilla
3 c. flour
¹/₂ c. cocoa
1¹/₂ c. chocolate chips
1 c. pecans
1 (12¹/₂ oz.) bottle caramel
  ice cream topping
6 oz. dark or milk chocolate
  coating, melted

Combine butter, sugar, egg and vanilla. Beat well. Combine flour and cocoa; add to creamed mixture. Stir in chocolate chips and pecans. Roll into 1" balls and place 2" apart on ungreased cookie sheets. Using a wooden spoon handle make a ¹/₂" deep dent in the center of each ball; fill half full of caramel topping. Bake at 350° for 15-18 minutes or until caramel is bubbly and cookies are set. Cool then remove and drizzle with chocolate coating. These are more like candy than cookies.

The secret of life is not to do what one likes,
but to try and like what one has to do.

Pumpkin Chip Cookies
...Mrs. Edward (Lizzie Ann) Schrock

2 c. sugar
1 c. lard
2 eggs, beaten
2 tsp. vanilla
2 Tbsp. milk
2 c. pumpkin
4 c. flour
4 tsp. baking powder
2 tsp. baking soda
1 tsp. salt
2 tsp. cinnamon
1 (6 oz.) pkg. chocolate chips
1 c. nuts

Mix sugar, lard and eggs until creamy. Add vanilla, milk and pumpkin. Mix well. Sift dry ingredients and add gradually; mix well. Stir in chips and nuts, then drop by spoonfuls onto cookie sheets. Bake at 375° about 14 minutes. Very moist cookies!

Raisin-Filled Cookies
...Mrs. Melvin (Katie) Miller

1/2 c. white sugar
1/2 c. brown sugar
3/4 c. shortening
1 egg
1/2 c. sweet milk
1 Tbsp. baking powder
1/2 tsp. soda
3 c. flour

Sift soda with flour to make a soft dough. Chill dough. Roll and cut. Place filling between two cookies. Cut a hole in the top cookie so filling stays in. Bake cookies for 8-10 minutes in 350° oven.

Filling:
1 1/2 c. ground-up raisins
1 c. sugar
1 1/2 c. (scant) boiling water
2 Tbsp. flour

Boil until it thickens.

Molasses Crinkle Cookies ...Mrs. Jonathan (Rose) Yoder

2¼ c. shortening
3 c. brown sugar
3 eggs
¾ c. molasses
6¾ c. flour
2 Tbsp. soda
¾ tsp. salt
1½ tsp. cloves
1 Tbsp. cinnamon
1 Tbsp. ginger

Mix first 4 ingredients, then add the remaining ingredients. Chill several hours or overnight. Roll in balls; dip tops into sugar. Bake at 375° for 10-12 minutes. Do not overbake. Very good!

Molasses Cookies ...Mrs. Edward (Lizzie Ann) Schrock

½ c. butter
½ c. shortening
1½ c. sugar
½ c. molasses
2 eggs
4 c. flour
½ tsp. salt
2¼ tsp. baking soda
2¼ tsp. ginger
1½ tsp. cloves
1½ tsp. cinnamon

Beat butter, shortening, sugar and eggs. Add molasses and stir well. Add rest of ingredients, stirring well. Roll into balls, then roll in sugar. Flatten and bake for 11 minutes at 350°.

Keep on smiling. It makes everyone
wonder what you've been up to.

Maple Leaf Cookies   …Mrs. Melvin (Katie) Miller

1 lb. butter
8 eggs
1 tsp. salt
4 c. brown sugar
2 Tbsp. cream
1/4 c. maple flavoring
6 tsp. soda
10 1/2 c. flour

Cream butter and sugar together. Add eggs, beating well. Blend in remaining ingredients. Bake 8-10 minutes at 350°. When cool, put icing between two cookies and enjoy!

Icing:
2 egg whites, beaten
1 tsp. cream
1/2 c. Crisco
2 c. powdered sugar
1 Tbsp. vanilla
2 Tbsp. flour
3/4 c. marshmallow creme

Toffee Chip Cookies   …Mrs. Freeman (Mabel) Yoder

1/2 c. butter or margarine, softened
1 (14 oz.) can sweetened condensed milk
3/4 c. flour
2 c. graham cracker crumbs (approx. 32 squares)
2 tsp. baking powder
2 c. chocolate chips
1 1/2 c. English toffee bits
1 c. coconut (optional)
1/4 tsp. salt

Combine butter and milk; mix well. Add flour, crackers, baking powder and salt. Mix gently, then add all other ingredients and mix well. Drop by teaspoon on greased cookie sheets. Bake at 350°. The best!

43

Buttermilk Cookies
...Mrs. Steve (Linda) Kauffman

2 c. brown sugar
2 tsp. vanilla
2 tsp. baking powder
4 c. flour
$^{1}/_{2}$ c. chopped nuts, if desired
1 c. shortening or lard
2 eggs
1 c. buttermilk
$^{1}/_{2}$ tsp. soda
1 tsp. salt

Mix sugar and shortening. Add vanilla and eggs. Dissolve soda in buttermilk. Add baking powder to the flour. Add liquid and flour alternately. Add nuts if desired. Store in the refrigerator overnight. Can be dropped. Bake in 400° oven. They are delicious frosted with caramel icing.
Optional: Sprinkle chopped nuts on frosting.

Orange Cookies
...Mrs. Sam (Rachel) Kauffman

1 c. solid shortening (Crisco)
2 eggs
$^{1}/_{2}$ c. sugar
$^{1}/_{2}$ c. orange juice
1 c. sour milk or buttermilk
1 tsp. vanilla
$^{1}/_{2}$ tsp. salt
1 Tbsp. baking powder
1 tsp. soda
4 c. flour

Cream shortening and eggs together. Add sugar, orange juice, sour milk and vanilla. Add dry ingredients. Mix well. Bake at 350° for 10 minutes or until bottom is slightly brown. Cool and frost.

Frosting:
$^{1}/_{2}$ c. orange juice
1 lb. powdered sugar
3 Tbsp. butter, at room temperature

Just when a woman thinks her work is done, she
becomes a grandmother. What a great reward!

Lemon Zucchini Drops

...Mrs. Freeman (Mabel) Yoder

½ c. butter or margarine,
   softened
1 c. sugar
1 egg
1 c. finely shredded zucchini
1 tsp. grated lemon peel or
   2 tsp. lemon flavoring
2 c. flour
1 tsp. baking soda
1 tsp. baking powder
1 tsp. cinnamon
½ c. raisins
½ c. nuts

In a bowl cream butter, sugar and egg. Add zucchini and lemon peel or flavoring. Gradually add the rest of ingredients. Drop by teaspoon on greased cookie sheets. Bake at 375° for 8-10 minutes or until lightly browned.

Lemon Glaze:
2 c. powdered sugar
2-3 Tbsp. lemon juice

Combine powdered sugar and lemon juice until thin spreading consistency. Spread or drizzle over cooled cookies. Delicious!

Zucchini Cookies

...Mrs. Marvin (Mary Ann) Schrock
...Mrs. Freeman (Mabel) Yoder

1 c. butter, softened
2 c. sugar
2 eggs
4 c. flour
2 tsp. soda
1 tsp. cloves or allspice
2 tsp. cinnamon
1 tsp. salt
2 c. chocolate chips
2 c. chopped nuts
2 c. shredded zucchini

Cream together sugar, butter and eggs until fluffy. Add sifted dry ingredients alternately with zucchini. Add chocolate chips and nuts. Drop by teaspoonful on greased cookie sheet. Bake at 375° for 12-15 minutes. Do not overbake.
Note: If your zucchini has a dry texture, use less flour.
Mabel adds 4 slightly rounded Tbsp. cocoa and uses nutmeg instead of cloves.

Cranberry Chip Cookies ...Mrs. Freeman (Mabel) Yoder

1/2 c. butter or margarine,
  softened
1/2 c. shortening
3/4 c. sugar
3/4 c. brown sugar
2 eggs
2 1/2 c. flour
1 tsp. baking soda
1/2 tsp. salt
1 c. chocolate chips
1 c. vanilla chips
1 c. dried cranberries
1 c. chopped pecans

Cream butter, shortening, sugars and eggs. Beat well. Combine and add the rest of ingredients. Add cranberries, chips and nuts last. Drop on greased cookie sheets. Bake at 375° for 9-11 minutes. Cool for a few minutes before removing from pans.

Pumpkin Whoopie Pies

...Mrs Marvin (Mary Ann) Schrock

3/4 c. vegetable oil
1 1/2 c. brown sugar
2 eggs
2 c. precooked pumpkin
1 tsp. vanilla
3 c. flour
1 tsp. cloves
1 tsp. cinnamon
1 tsp. ginger
1 tsp. salt
1 tsp. soda

Cream together oil, sugar and eggs, then add pumpkin and vanilla. Beat well, then add dry ingredients. Bake at 350° for 10-12 minutes. Do not overbake!

Filling:
3 egg whites
3 tsp. vanilla
3 Tbsp. milk
3 Tbsp. flour
4 c. powdered sugar
1 1/2 c. Crisco

Beat egg whites, then add all ingredients except Crisco. Beat until creamy. Now add Crisco and beat until fluffy. Spread some on a cookie. Put another one on top to make a sandwich cookie.

Chocolate Mint Whoopie Pies

...Mrs. James (Ida) Lehman

1 c. sugar
6 Tbsp. canola oil
2 eggs
2 c. flour
$\frac{1}{2}$ c. cocoa
1 tsp. baking soda
$\frac{1}{2}$ tsp. salt
$\frac{1}{2}$ c. milk, divided
4 Tbsp. butter or margarine,
  softened
2-3 c. powdered sugar
$\frac{1}{4}$ tsp. mint extract
6-8 drops green food coloring
  (optional)

In a bowl combine sugar, eggs and oil. Beat well. Add dry ingredients. Gradually add 6 Tbsp. milk; mix well. Drop by teaspoon on greased cookie sheets. Bake at 375°-400° until edges are set and top is cracked. Cool. Then mix butter, powdered sugar, extract and food coloring with remaining milk. Add more milk if needed. Then spread on the bottom of half the cookies and top with the rest for a great sandwich cookie.

Christmas Cut-Outs

...Mrs. Freeman (Mabel) Yoder

2 c. butter
3 c. white sugar
5 eggs
1 c. sour cream
1 tsp. salt
1 tsp. soda
1 tsp. vanilla
1 tsp. baking powder
$\frac{1}{4}$ c. boiling water
7 c. flour

Cream butter and sugar. Add other ingredients. Mix well. Chill dough. Roll and cut out. Bake at 375° for 8 minutes. Don't overbake. The longer they sit the better.

The best relationship is the one in which your love for
each other exceeds your need for each other.

Butterscotch Cookies
...Mrs. Freeman (Mabel) Yoder

4 eggs, beaten
4 c. brown sugar
1 c. butter
1 c. lard
2 tsp. vanilla
1½ Tbsp. baking soda dissolved in
   2 Tbsp. water
2 Tbsp. cream of tartar
7¼ c. flour
18 oz. butterscotch chips

Mix in order given. Dough will be stiff so you may need to use your hands to finish up. Roll in balls and bake at 350° until light brown. Good luck and enjoy!

Gift in a Jar Cookies
...Mrs. James (Ida) Lehman

1½ c. all-purpose flour
1 c. brown sugar
¾ c. M&Ms
½ c. coarsely chopped salted
   peanuts
½ c. raisins
¼ c. cocoa
¾ tsp. soda
¼ tsp. salt

On card:
⅔ c. butter, softened
2 eggs
1½ tsp. vanilla

Layer ingredients attractively in any order into 1 qt. jar with tight-fitting lid. Pack ingredients down slightly before adding another layer. Cover lid with fabric, attach card with remaining ingredients with a ribbon. An attractive gift for birthdays or to cheer a sick person.

Preheat oven to 350°. Beat butter in large bowl until smooth. Add eggs and vanilla. Add cookie mix into butter mixture. Stir until blended. Drop heaping tablespoonsful dough 2" apart onto ungreased cookie sheets. Bake 12 minutes or until almost set. Yield: 2 dozen cookies.

We are shaped and fashioned by what we love.

Fruit Squares

...Mrs. Wayne (Ruth) Raber

1 c. oleo or butter
1³/₄ c. white sugar
4 eggs
1 tsp. vanilla
1 tsp. almond extract
3 c. flour
1 tsp. baking powder
1 tsp. salt

Cream together butter, sugar and eggs and add the rest of the ingredients and stir. Spread ²/₃ of the batter on a greased 15" x 10" pan. Cover with 1 qt. pie filling (any kind) and drop spoonfuls of batter over filling. Bake at 350° for 45 minutes. Drizzle with glaze if you wish.

Squash Bars

...Mrs. Marcus (Joleen) Marner

4 eggs
1²/₃ c. sugar
1 c. oil
2 c. cooked and mashed squash
2 c. flour
2 tsp. baking powder
2 tsp. cinnamon
1 tsp. salt
1 tsp. baking soda

Mix all ingredients well and bake on a cookie sheet pan at 350°. Bake for 30 minutes. Top with cream cheese frosting.

Frosting:
1 (8 oz.) pkg. cream cheese
1 tsp. butter, softened
1-1¹/₂ c. powdered sugar

Add powdered sugar until frosting is easy to spread.

People are like stained glass windows. They sparkle and shine
when the sun is out, but when the darkness sets in, their true
beauty is revealed only if there is a light from within.

Granola Bars
...Mrs. David (Rachel) Plank

½ c. light corn syrup
1 c. brown sugar
⅔ c. peanut butter
½ c. oleo or butter, melted
2 tsp. vanilla
3 c. quick oats
½ c. coconut
½ c. sunflower seeds
½ c. raisins
½ c. wheat germ
1 c. chocolate chips

In a large bowl combine all ingredients down to vanilla and blend well. Stir in remaining ingredients. Press mixture firmly into cake pan. A double batch makes one large cookie sheet. Bake for 15-20 minutes or until edges are slightly brown. Best if not overbaked. I usually omit the coconut, raisins, wheat germ and sunflower seeds.

Chewy Granola Bars
...Mrs. Jonathan (Rose) Yoder
...Mrs. Melvin (Mary) Stutzman

¾ c. brown sugar
⅔ c. peanut butter*
¼ c. light corn syrup or honey
½ c. margarine or butter, melted
2 tsp. vanilla
3 c. oatmeal
½ c. coconut
⅓ c. whole wheat flour
1 c. raisins
⅓ c. wheat germ
½ c. chocolate chips (optional)

Mix the first 5 ingredients together until well blended. Add the remaining ingredients. Press firmly into 9" x 13" pan. Bake at 350° for 10-15 minutes or until lightly browned. Bake for the least amount of time possible, since the longer they bake, the drier they tend to become.
*A good way to use up leftover church peanut butter. Use 2 c. as a substitute for the first 3 ingredients. Church peanut butter keeps very well frozen.

Chewy Granola Bars
...Mrs. Robert (Miriam) Graber

5 c. quick oats
4$\frac{1}{2}$ c. Rice Krispies
1 c. coconut
1 c. chocolate chips
1 c. graham cracker crumbs
1$\frac{1}{2}$ lb. marshmallows
$\frac{1}{4}$ c. butter
$\frac{1}{4}$ c. oil
$\frac{1}{2}$ c. peanut butter
$\frac{1}{2}$ c. honey

Melt butter and oil over low heat. Add marshmallows. When melted, remove from heat and add peanut butter and honey. Mix into well-mixed dry ingredients. Press into buttered large cookie sheet.

Chewy Granola Bars
...Mrs. Gerald (Rosanna) Schrock

$\frac{1}{2}$-1 c. brown sugar
$\frac{2}{3}$ c. peanut butter
$\frac{1}{2}$ c. light corn syrup or honey
$\frac{1}{2}$ c. margarine, melted
2 tsp. vanilla
3 c. uncooked oatmeal
$\frac{1}{3}$ c. whole wheat flour
$\frac{1}{2}$ c. raisins
2 Tbsp. sesame seeds, optional
$\frac{1}{2}$ c. coconut
$\frac{1}{2}$ c. sunflower seeds
$\frac{1}{3}$ c. wheat germ
$\frac{1}{2}$ c. chocolate or butterscotch chips

Mix first 5 ingredients together until well blended, then add remaining ingredients. Press mixture into greased 9" x 13" pan. Bake at 350° for 15-20 minutes or until lightly browned.

Some people, no matter how old they get, never lose their beauty—they merely move it from their faces to their hearts.

Sour Cream Raisin Bars   ...Mrs. Daniel (Fannie) Hershberger

Crumbs:
1¾ c. oatmeal
1¾ c. flour
1 c. brown sugar
1 tsp. soda
1 c. oleo

Preheat oven to 350°. Put ⅔ of crumb mixture in jelly roll pan. Bake for 15-20 minutes. Cool. I use 1½ recipes for crumbs.

Filling:
4 egg yolks
1¼ c. sugar
1 Tbsp. cornstarch
2 c. sour cream
2 c. raisins

In saucepan combine yolks, sugar, cornstarch, sour cream and raisins. Boil 5-10 minutes. Stir often. Pour over crumb crust. Cover with remaining crumbs and bake 20 minutes. Cool and cut into bars.

Chocolate Peanut Butter Pizza
...Mrs. Ray (LeEtta) Yoder

½ c. sugar
½ c. brown sugar
½ c. margarine, softened
½ c. peanut butter
½ tsp. vanilla
1 egg
1½ c. flour
2 c. miniature marshmallows
1 c. chocolate chips

Combine sugars, margarine, peanut butter, vanilla and egg. Stir in flour. Press dough evenly over bottom of pizza pan, forming rim. Bake 10 minutes at 375°. Remove and sprinkle with marshmallows and chips. Continue to bake until marshmallows are brown and fluffy, 5-8 minutes. Cool; cut into wedges. Store in tightly covered container.

Ginger Cremes   ...Mrs. Melvin (Katie) Miller

1 c. Karo
1¼ c. brown sugar
1 c. shortening
1 c. hot water or coffee
1 Tbsp. soda
1 tsp. ginger
1 tsp. cloves
1 tsp. cinnamon
3 eggs, beaten
4½ c. flour

Stir syrup, sugar, shortening and eggs together. I use spices scantly. Add flour and water or coffee last. Spread on greased cookie sheet and bake 20 minutes or until done at 350°. Ice with a brown sugar icing and enjoy! One of my mother's favorite recipes!

Halfway Bars
...Mrs. Freeman (Amanda) Kauffman

1 c. oleo
1¼ c. brown sugar, divided
pinch of salt
½ c. white sugar
2 eggs, separated
1½ tsp. soda
2 c. flour
1 c. chocolate chips

Mix oleo, ½ c. brown sugar, salt, white sugar, egg yolks, soda and flour. Pat in cake pan, then press chocolate chips on top. Beat egg whites until stiff and add ¾ c. brown sugar and pour over mixture. Bake at 325° for 20 minutes.

Chocolate Caramel Bars
...Mrs. David (Emma) Hershberger

2¼ c. flour
2 c. quick oats
1½ c. brown sugar
1 (12 oz.) jar caramel ice
   cream topping
1 tsp. baking soda
½ tsp. salt
1½ c. butter
2 c. chocolate chips

In a bowl combine flour, oats, brown sugar, baking soda and salt. Cut in butter until crumbly. Set half aside for topping. Press remaining crumb mixture into greased 9" x 13" pan. Bake at 350° for 15 minutes. Sprinkle with chocolate chips; whisk the caramel topping with a little flour until smooth and drizzle on top of chocolate chips, then sprinkle with remaining crumb mixture. Bake 18-20 minutes. Cool 2 hours before cutting.

Quick Bars
...Mrs. Richard (Verna Kay) Stutzman

2 c. flour
1 c. sugar
¾ c. brown sugar
1 tsp. salt
1 tsp. baking soda
2 c. quick oats
2 eggs, beaten
1 c. (scant) vegetable oil
½ tsp. vanilla
1½ c. chocolate chips

Combine sugars with oil, then add eggs. Sift in dry ingredients. Add quick oats and chocolate chips. Press into ungreased 15" x 10" x 1" pan. Bake at 350° for 20 minutes. Do not overbake.

Peanut Butter Oat Bars

...daughter, Amy Yoder

⅔ c. butter or margarine, melted
¹/₄ c. peanut butter
1 c. packed brown sugar
¹/₄ c. light corn syrup
¹/₄ tsp. vanilla
4 c. quick oats

In a mixing bowl combine the butter, peanut butter, brown sugar, corn syrup and vanilla; gradually stir in the oats. Press into a greased 9" x 13" pan. Bake at 400° for 12-14 minutes or until edges are golden brown. Cool.

Topping:
1 c. milk chocolate chips
¹/₂ c. butterscotch chips
¹/₃ c. peanut butter

Meanwhile, for topping melt chips and peanut butter in a saucepan over low heat. Stir until blended; spread over warm bars. Cool completely; refrigerate for 2-3 hours before cutting. Note: This recipe does not contain flour.

Frosted Cinnamon Zucchini Bars

...Mrs. Marvin (Mary Ann) Schrock ...Mrs. Freeman (Mabel) Yoder

³/₄ c. butter or margarine, softened
¹/₂ c. sugar
¹/₂ c. brown sugar
2 eggs
1 tsp. vanilla
1³/₄ c. flour
1¹/₂ tsp. baking powder
2 c. shredded zucchini
1 c. coconut
³/₄ c. chopped nuts, optional

Cream butter and sugars. Add eggs, beating well. Add vanilla and zucchini. Stir, then add the rest of the ingredients. Spread in a greased 15" x 10" x 1" pan. Bake at 350° for 25-30 minutes or until toothpick near the center comes out clean. Frost cooled bars.

Frosting:
2 c. powdered sugar
1 tsp. cinnamon
2 Tbsp. butter, melted
1 tsp. vanilla
2-3 Tbsp. milk

Stir all together and spread over cooled bars. May garnish with chopped nuts.

Zucchini Bars

...Mrs. Edna Slabaugh

3 c. flour
1/2 tsp. soda
1 Tbsp. baking powder
1 tsp. salt
1/8 tsp. nutmeg
1/8 tsp. cloves
3/4 c. butter
1 c. brown sugar
1/2 c. white sugar
1 tsp. vanilla
2 eggs
2 c. peeled and grated zucchini
1/2 c. chopped walnuts
1/2 c. butterscotch chips or raisins

Sift flour, soda, baking powder, salt, nutmeg and cloves together. Cream butter, sugars, vanilla and eggs together. Combine both mixtures. Gradually add zucchini, walnuts and chips or raisins. Pour into greased and floured 10" x 15" pan. Bake at 375° for 20-25 minutes. Frost.

Caramel Frosting:
1/2 c. butter
1/4 c. milk
1 c. brown sugar
1-1 1/2 c. powdered sugar

Melt butter. Add brown sugar and bring to a boil for 2 minutes. Add milk and bring to second boil. Remove from heat; add powdered sugar.

Pecan Squares

...Mrs. Richard (Verna Kay) Stutzman
...Mrs. Leland (Orpha) Yoder

Crust:
3 c. flour
1/2 c. white sugar
1 c. butter or margarine, softened
1/2 tsp. salt

Blend together flour, sugar, butter and salt until mixture is coarse crumbs. Press firmly into a greased 15" x 10" x 1" pan. Bake at 350° for 20 minutes.

Filling:
4 eggs
1 1/2 c. corn syrup
1 1/2 c. white sugar
3 Tbsp. butter or margarine, melted
1 1/2 tsp. vanilla
2 1/2 c. chopped pecans

Meanwhile combine first 5 filling ingredients. Stir in pecans. Spread evenly over hot crust. Bake at 350° for 25 minutes or until set. Cool. Yield: about 4 dozen.

Frosted Banana Bars

...Mrs. Sam (Viola) Miller
...sister, Elvesta Bontrager

1/2 c. butter, softened
2 c. white sugar
3 eggs
1 1/2 c. mashed ripe bananas
1 tsp. vanilla
2 c. flour
1 tsp. baking soda
pinch salt

In a mixing bowl cream butter and sugar. Beat in eggs, bananas and vanilla. Combine the flour, baking soda and salt; add to creamed mixture and mix well. Pour into a greased baking pan. Bake at 350° for 25 minutes or until toothpick comes out clean.

Frosting:
1/2 c. butter, softened
1 (8 oz.) pkg. cream cheese, softened
4 c. powdered sugar
2 tsp. vanilla

Cream butter and cream cheese in a mixing bowl. Gradually add powdered sugar and vanilla; beat well. Spread over bars. Keep in refrigerator.

Twinkies

...Mrs. Jonathan (Naomi) Wagler

1 box yellow cake mix
1 (2/3 c.) sm. box instant vanilla pudding
1/2 c. Crisco
1 c. water
4 eggs

Cut Crisco into dry ingredients; add eggs and water. Mix well. Line 2 large cookie sheets with wax paper and divide dough. Bake at 350° for 15-20 minutes.

Filling:
10 Tbsp. flour
2 c. milk
2 c. powdered sugar
1 c. Crisco (a must)
1/2 tsp. salt
2 tsp. vanilla

Cook flour and milk together. Let cool thoroughly, also stirring occasionally before adding remaining filling ingredients. Spread filling on top of one cake and top with the other cake. Remove wax paper and cut into squares.

Pear Custard Bars
...Mrs. Mervin (Emma) Yoder

Crust:
1/2 c. butter, softened
1/4 c. sugar
1 c. flour
1/4 tsp. vanilla
2/3 c. nuts
pinch salt

Bake crust in 8" square pan at 325° for 15-20 minutes. Cool. Top with filling. Sprinkle with sugar and cinnamon. Bake at 375° for 25-30 minutes or until set.

Filling:
1 (8 oz.) pkg. cream cheese
1/2 c. sugar
1 egg
1/2 tsp. vanilla
1 1/2 c. chopped pears

Butterscotch Bars
...Mrs. Freeman (Mabel) Yoder

1/2 c. margarine, softened
1 c. brown sugar
1/2 c. white sugar
1 tsp. vanilla
2 tsp. baking powder
2 c. flour
1 tsp. salt
1 c. coconut
1 1/2 c. butterscotch or
   chocolate chips
1/2 c. chopped nuts
2 eggs

Combine sugars, eggs, vanilla and margarine. Cream together well then add flour, salt, baking powder and coconut. Mix well. Add nuts. Spread in a greased 9" x 13" pan. Sprinkle chips over the top and bake at 350° for approximately 30 minutes.

When I have nothing left but God, then I become aware that God is all I need.

Rhubarb Custard Bars

...Mrs. Glen (Pollyanna) Hochstetler

Crust:
1 1/2 c. flour
1/2 c. sugar
1/8 tsp. salt
9 Tbsp. chilled butter, cut into
small pieces

Preheat oven to 350°. Combine flour, sugar and salt in a bowl. Cut in butter with a pastry blender until mixture resembles coarse meal. Press mixture into a 13" x 9" baking dish coated with cooking spray. Bake at 350° for 15 minutes or until crust is golden brown.

Filling:
1/3 c. flour
1 1/2 c. sugar
1 1/2 c. milk
3 large eggs
5 c. sliced fresh or frozen
rhubarb

Combine flour and sugar in a large bowl; add milk and eggs, stirring with a whisk until well blended. Stir in rhubarb. Pour rhubarb mixture over crust. Bake at 350° for 40 minutes or until set. Cool to room temperature.

Topping:
1/2 c. sugar
1 (8 oz.) pkg. cream cheese
1/2 tsp. vanilla
1 c. frozen whipped topping,
thawed

Place sugar, cheese and vanilla in a bowl; beat with a mixer at medium speed until smooth. Gently fold in whipped topping; spread evenly over baked custard. Cover and chill at least 1 hour. We love these bars!

If there be any virtue, and if there be
any praise, think on these things.
—Philippians 4:8

Salted Peanut Chews ...Mrs. Jonathan (Rose) Yoder

1 1/2 c. flour
1/2 tsp. baking powder
1/4 tsp. soda
1/2 tsp. salt
1/2 c. brown sugar
1/2 c. butter
2 egg yolks
1 tsp. vanilla
4 c. miniature marshmallows

Mix first 5 ingredients. Cut in butter. Beat egg yolks and vanilla together and stir into flour mixture until crumbly. Pat into 13" x 9" pan. Bake 12-15 minutes at 350°. Sprinkle on marshmallows and put back in oven 1-2 minutes. Cool while preparing topping.

Topping:
2/3 c. corn syrup
1/4 c. butter
12 oz. peanut butter chips
2 tsp. vanilla
2 c. Rice Krispies
2 c. salted peanuts

In a large saucepan heat corn syrup, butter, chips and vanilla until chips are melted, stirring constantly. Remove from heat and stir in cereal and peanuts. Immediately spoon over marshmallows and spread. Chill and cut into bars.

Cappuccino Muffin Bars ...Mrs. Freeman (Mabel) Yoder

2 c. flour
3/4 c. sugar
2 1/2 tsp. baking powder
1/2 tsp. salt
1 tsp. cinnamon
2 Tbsp. instant coffee granules
1 c. milk
1/2 c. butter, melted
1 egg
1 tsp. vanilla
1 c. mini chocolate chips

In a bowl dissolve coffee in milk until dissolved. Add butter, egg and vanilla; mix well. Combine dry ingredients and mix with liquid just until moistened. Fold in chocolate chips. Spread into a greased 9" x 13" pan. Bake at 350° for 20-25 minutes. Cool and spread with frosting. Yummy! Can also be baked in muffins pans.

Frosting:
1 (8 oz.) pkg. cream cheese, softened
1 tsp. instant coffee granules
1 tsp. vanilla
2 c. powdered sugar
2 Tbsp. milk
1/2 c. mini milk chocolate chips

Mix coffee granules and milk. Add cream cheese and other ingredients and spread.

59

Blond Brownies
...Mrs. Monroe (Mary) Hochstetler

2 c. flour
1 tsp. baking powder
²/₃ c. butter
2 eggs
¹/₄ tsp. soda
1 tsp. salt
2 c. brown sugar
2 tsp. vanilla
1 c. chocolate chips
¹/₃ c. nuts

Mix flour, soda, baking powder and salt. Melt butter in pan; add sugar. Blend in eggs and vanilla. Add flour mixture. Spread in ungreased 9" x 13" pan. Sprinkle with chips and nuts; bake at 350° for 30 minutes.

Double-Decker Confetti Brownies
...Mrs. Jonathan (Wilma) Hochstetler

³/₄ c. butter, softened
1 c. white sugar
1 c. brown sugar, packed
3 large eggs
1 tsp. vanilla
2¹/₂ c. flour, divided
2¹/₂ tsp. baking powder
¹/₂ tsp. salt
¹/₃ c. baking cocoa
1 Tbsp. butter, melted
1 c. M&Ms, divided

Cream ³/₄ c. butter and sugars until light and fluffy; beat in eggs and vanilla. Add 2¹/₄ c. flour, baking powder and salt. Divide batter in half. Blend together baking cocoa and 1 Tbsp. melted butter; stir into half of the dough. Spread cocoa dough evenly into greased 9" x 13" baking pan. Stir remaining ¹/₄ c. flour and ¹/₂ c. M&Ms into remaining dough. Spread evenly over cocoa dough in pan. Sprinkle with remaining ¹/₂ c. M&Ms. Bake at 350° for 25-30 minutes or until edges start to pull away from sides of pan.

Chocolate Peanut Butter Brownies
...Mrs. David (Lydia) Schwartz

1 c. margarine
2 c. sugar
3 eggs
1¹/₂ tsp. vanilla
¹/₄ c. (rounded) cocoa
1¹/₂ c. flour
¹/₄ tsp. salt
³/₄ c. chopped nuts
1 c. peanut butter chips

Cream margarine and sugar. Beat in eggs and vanilla. Add cocoa, then flour, salt, nuts and chips. Mix well. Pour into a buttered 9" x 13" pan, pushing plenty of batter into the corners so it bakes evenly. Bake at 350° for approximately 30 minutes or until done. Cool and sprinkle with powdered sugar.

Tri-Level Brownies   ...Mrs. Samuel (Susie) Hochstetler

½ c. flour
¼ tsp. baking soda
¼ tsp. salt
1 c. oatmeal
½ c. brown sugar
6 Tbsp. butter
3 Tbsp. cocoa
¾ c. white sugar
⅔ c. flour
¼ tsp. baking powder
¼ c. milk
5 Tbsp. butter, melted
1 egg
½ tsp. vanilla

Mix flour, baking soda, salt, oatmeal, brown sugar and butter. Press into 11" x 7½" pan and bake at 350° for 10 minutes. Combine cocoa, white sugar, flour and baking powder. Add milk, melted butter, egg and vanilla. Pour over crust and bake another 25 minutes. Spread glaze on bars while hot. Cut when cooled.

Glaze:
1½ c. powdered sugar
1 tsp. vanilla
2 Tbsp. hot water (add a
   little more if too thick)
3 Tbsp. butter
2 Tbsp. cocoa

Combine until smooth.

Maple Butterscotch Brownies
...Mrs. Dennis (Mary) Bontrager

1¼ c. brown sugar
½ c. butter, melted
1½ tsp. maple flavoring
2 eggs
1½ c. flour
1 tsp. baking powder
1 c. walnuts (optional)
½ c. butterscotch chips
powdered sugar (optional)

In a medium sized bowl, mix first 3 ingredients. Beat in the eggs, one at a time. Combine flour and baking powder; add to egg mixture. Stir in walnuts if desired and chips. Pour into a greased 9" square cake pan. Bake at 350° for 30 minutes or until toothpick inserted comes out clean. Cool. Dust with powdered sugar if desired. Delicious!

Notes

God Bless

This Nest

Enter into his gates with thanksgiving,
and into his courts with praise: be
thankful unto him, and bless his name.

Psalm 100:4

Cakes & Frostings

Springtime

Springtime is a time of new life,
　A time of new leaves on the trees,
And it is also a time of flowers,
　Wherein you can sometimes find bees.

Springtime is a time to rejoice,
　In all that is bright and fair,
In the sun, the moon, and the stars so bright,
　And the birds that fly in the air.

And springtime is also a time
　To praise Jesus Christ, our Lord,
For all His mercies, anew each day,
　That abundantly from Heaven are poured.
　　—written and submitted by daughter, LuAnn Yoder

Turtle Cake

...Mrs. Orva (Marietta) Yoder

1 chocolate cake mix
14 oz. caramels or 14 oz. tub
   caramel apple dip*
1 c. chocolate chips
³/₄ c. butter
¹/₂ c. evaporated milk
1 c. nuts

Prepare cake according to directions on package (or use your favorite recipe). Pour half into a 9" x 13" pan and bake at 350° for 15 minutes. Melt caramels, butter and milk and mix on low heat, stirring constantly. Pour over baked cake. Top with chocolate chips and nuts. Pour on rest of cake batter. Bake another 20 minutes or until done. Best while cake is still warm. Very good with ice cream.
*Using caramel apple dip is much easier than melting caramels.

Chocolate Upside Down Cake

...Mrs. Marcus (Joleen) Marner ...Mrs. Aaron (Mary Ada) Yoder

2¹/₂ c. cake flour
1¹/₂ c. sugar
4 tsp. baking powder
¹/₂ tsp. salt
¹/₄ c. cocoa
4 Tbsp. butter
1 c. milk
2 tsp. vanilla
1 c. nuts (optional)

Sift and measure flour. Then sift flour, sugar, cocoa, salt and baking powder together into a mixing bowl. Melt butter and mix with milk and vanilla. Stir into dry ingredients. Add nuts and blend thoroughly. Pour into a well greased 9" x 13" cake pan.

Topping:
¹/₄ c. cocoa
1 c. brown sugar
1 c. granulated sugar
2 c. boiling water

Mix together the cocoa and sugars. Spread this over the top of the cake batter. Over all pour the 2 c. of hot water and place in a moderate oven (350°) to bake an hour. This is a rich chocolate cake with chocolate sauce underneath. Joleen uses half this recipe. It is best served slightly warm with whipped cream or ice cream. Delicious! Variation: May omit the cocoa in the batter and use only 2 c. flour and use 3 c. water in the topping.

Upside Down Chocolate Cake

...Mrs. Freeman (Mabel) Yoder

1 c. brown sugar
¹/₂ c. butter or margarine
1 c. chopped pecans or halves
1 c. coconut
¹/₂ c. evaporated milk

In a saucepan over low heat cook and stir brown sugar and butter until sugar is dissolved and butter is melted. Pour into a greased 9" x 13" pan. Sprinkle with pecans and coconut; drizzle with evaporated milk. Set aside.

Cake:
²/₃ c. butter or margarine, softened
1³/₄ c. sugar
3 Tbsp. cocoa
3 eggs
2 tsp. vanilla
3 c. flour
1 tsp. baking soda
1 tsp. baking powder
1 tsp. salt
1¹/₂ c. buttermilk

Cream butter and sugar. Beat in eggs and vanilla. Add dry ingredients, alternating with buttermilk. Pour over topping in pan. Bake at 350° for 40-45 minutes or until done. Cool 5 minutes, then invert onto a large serving plate. May serve with whipped cream if desired.

Moist Chocolate Cake   ...Mrs. Freeman (Mabel) Yoder

1³/₄ c. sugar
2 c. flour
¹/₄ c. cocoa
2 tsp. baking soda
1 tsp. baking powder
1 tsp. salt
2 eggs
1 c. brewed coffee
1 c. buttermilk or sour milk*
¹/₂ c. vegetable oil
1 tsp. vanilla

In a large bowl combine eggs, sugar, oil and vanilla. Stir well. Add flour, soda, baking powder, cocoa and salt. Gradually add coffee and buttermilk or sour milk. Bake at 350° for approx. 45-50 minutes.
*To make sour milk: Use 1-2 Tbsp. vinegar to 1 c. milk.

Mayonnaise Chocolate Cake ...Mrs. Freeman (Mabel) Yoder

1 c. flour
³/₄ c. sugar
¹/₄ c. cocoa
1 tsp. baking powder
1 tsp. baking soda
1 c. mayonnaise
1 c. water

In a large bowl combine sugar and mayonnaise. Mix well and add dry ingredients. Add water a little at a time. Pour into a 9" x 13" pan and bake at 350° for 20-25 minutes or until a toothpick comes out clean. A moist cake and great to make when you're out of eggs. Frost with your favorite frosting. Cake does not get very high.

Zucchini Chocolate Cake

...Mrs. Marvin (Mary Ann) Schrock

1 c. margarine or vegetable oil
1¹/₂ c. white sugar
2 eggs
¹/₂ c. buttermilk or sour milk
2 c. grated zucchini
2¹/₂ c. flour
¹/₄ c. cocoa
¹/₂ tsp. baking powder
1 tsp. soda
¹/₂ tsp. cinnamon
¹/₂ tsp. cloves

Cream together oil and sugar, then beat very well after each ingredient before adding dry ingredients. Pour into a 9" x 13" cake pan. Sprinkle with 1 c. chocolate chips and bake at 350° for 40-45 minutes. Do not overbake as it will become very dry.

Zucchini Cake

...Mrs. Freeman (Mabel) Yoder

¹/₂ c. butter
¹/₂ c. vegetable oil
1³/₄ c. sugar
2 eggs
2 tsp. vanilla
1 tsp. salt
1 tsp. baking powder
1 tsp. baking soda
2¹/₂ c. flour
1 tsp. cinnamon
1 tsp. cloves
2 c. peeled, shredded zucchini
¹/₂ c. nuts
¹/₄ c. water

Beat eggs, sugar, butter, vanilla and oil. Add dry ingredients, water and zucchini. Bake at 350° for 40 minutes or until toothpick comes out clean.

Rich Strawberry Shortcake
...Mrs. Freeman (Amanda) Kauffman

2 c. flour
2 Tbsp. sugar
1 Tbsp. baking powder
1/2 tsp. salt
1/2 c. butter
1 egg, beaten
2/3 c. light cream

Sift dry ingredients. Cut in butter until mixture is like coarse crumbs. Combine egg and cream; add all at once to dry ingredients. Stir to moisten. Spread in greased pie pan. Sprinkle sugar over top. Bake at 375° for 20-25 minutes or until golden brown. Serve with strawberries and milk.

Mexican Wedding Cake
...Mrs. Robert (Miriam) Graber

2 eggs
2 c. sugar
2 c. flour
2 tsp. soda
1 tsp. salt
2 c. crushed pineapple and juice
1 c. nuts

Mix all together and bake in a 9" x 13" pan for 30-40 minutes at 350°.

Frosting:
1 (8 oz.) pkg. cream cheese
1 stick oleo or butter
3 c. powdered sugar
1 tsp. vanilla

Beat until well blended. Cool cake and frost.

Peaches and Cream Coffee Cake
...Mrs. David (Emma) Hershberger

3/4 c. flour
1 tsp. baking powder
1/2 c. milk
1/2 tsp. salt
1 egg
2 Tbsp. oleo
1 (16 oz.) can sliced peaches, drained (save juice)
1 (8 oz.) pkg. cream cheese
1/4 c. peach juice
1/2 c. sugar

Beat together first 6 ingredients. Grease an 8" x 8" pan. Pour mixture into pan. Place slices of peaches on top of pie mixture. Beat together cream cheese, peach juice and sugar. Spread on top of mixture about 1" from sides. Sprinkle 1 Tbsp. sugar and 1 Tbsp. cinnamon over top. Bake at 350° for 30-35 minutes.

Carrot Cake

...Mrs. Steve (Linda) Kauffman

2 c. sugar
4 eggs
2 tsp. soda
2 tsp. baking powder
3 c. ground raw carrots
1 c. cooking oil
2 c. flour
1 tsp. salt
2 tsp. cinnamon
^{1}/$_2$ c. chopped nuts

Cream sugar and cooking oil. Add eggs and beat well. Sift flour, soda, baking powder and cinnamon together. Add the creamed mixture. Fold in carrots and nuts. Bake in a 350° oven.

Carrot-Pineapple Cake

...Mrs. Melvin (Katie) Miller

1 c. salad oil
3 eggs
2 c. sugar
2^1/$_2$ c. flour
1 tsp. soda
^{1}/$_2$ tsp. salt
1 tsp. cinnamon
1 tsp. vanilla
1 c. chopped nuts
1 c. grated carrots
1 c. crushed pineapple, drained
1 c. coconut

Place oil, eggs and sugar in a large bowl and beat well. Add flour, soda, salt and cinnamon; beat well. Add vanilla, nuts, carrots, pineapple and coconut. Bake in a greased 13" x 9" pan for 40-50 minutes in 350° oven. Yummy!

He giveth power to the faint; and to them that
have no might he increaseth strength.
—Isaiah 40:29

Sunshine Carrot Pineapple Cake

...Mrs. Wayne (Ruth) Raber

2 c. all-purpose flour
1½ c. brown sugar
2 tsp. baking soda
1 tsp. salt
2 c. grated carrots
1 c. coconut
1 c. chopped nuts
¾ c. vegetable oil
2 Tbsp. lemon juice
1 tsp. vanilla
1 (20 oz.) can crushed pineapple

In a large bowl combine the first 7 ingredients. Combine oil, lemon juice and vanilla. Drain pineapple, reserving juice. If necessary add enough water to juice to measure ¾ c. Add oil mixture and pineapple juice mixture to dry ingredients. Stir just until moistened. Fold in pineapple. Place in greased 9" x 13" baking pan. Bake at 350° for 40-50 minutes.

Frosting:
1 (8 oz.) pkg. cream cheese, softened
3 Tbsp. powdered sugar
1 (12 oz.) pkg. whipped topping
flaked coconut (optional)

Beat cream cheese and sugar until smooth. Fold in whipped cream. Spread over cake. Sprinkle with coconut if desired.

Rather than ask God, "Why?" in the face of trial we should ask, "What would You have me to learn from this?"

Coconut-Banana Cake   ...Mrs. Allen (Elsie) Bontrager

³/₄ c. butter
1¹/₂ c. sugar
¹/₂ tsp. salt
2 eggs, beaten
1 tsp. vanilla
¹/₂ c. buttermilk
1 c. mashed bananas
2 c. flour
1 tsp. soda
1 tsp. baking powder
¹/₂ c. chopped nuts (optional)
1 c. flaked coconut

Cream butter, sugar and salt together. Add beaten eggs, vanilla, buttermilk and mashed bananas. Stir just until mixed, then add dry ingredients. Mix well. Bake at 375° for 25-30 minutes. Cool and spread with filling or use cream cheese frosting.

Creamy Nut Filling:
¹/₂ c. sugar
2 Tbsp. flour
¹/₂ c. cream
2 Tbsp. butter
¹/₂ c. pecans
¹/₄ tsp. salt
1 tsp. vanilla

Combine sugar, flour, cream and butter in heavy saucepan. Cook until thickened. Add pecans, salt and vanilla. Cool and spread.

Banana Cake   ...Mrs. Edward (Lizzie Ann) Schrock

1 c. white sugar
1 c. brown sugar
¹/₂ c. butter
2 egg yolks
3 bananas, mashed
1 c. sweet milk
2³/₄ c. flour
1 Tbsp. baking powder
1 tsp. soda
2 egg whites, stiffly beaten

Cream butter and sugars. Add mashed bananas and egg yolks. Mix well. Add milk and stir. Add dry ingredients, stirring well. Add egg whites last. Bake in 350° oven.

Pistachio Cake
...Mrs. Willis (Mary Esther) Wagler

1 yellow cake mix
1 pkg. instant pistachio
   pudding mix
1 c. sour cream
1/2 c. cooking oil
4 eggs
1 tsp. butter flavor

Add all the ingredients together, except eggs, and mix well. Add eggs one at a time and mix well. Pour half of mixture in greased and floured tube pan. Add half of nut mixture (recipe below) then rest of batter, then rest of nut mixture on top. Bake at 350° for 50-60 minutes.

Nut Mixture:
1/2 c. chopped nuts
1/2 c. brown sugar
1 tsp. cinnamon

Mix and add to cake as suggested above.

Pineapple Upside Down Cake
...Mrs. Edward (Lizzie Ann) Schrock

3 Tbsp. butter
1 c. brown sugar
pineapple slices or 1 can crushed pineapple, reserve juice
yellow cake mix
whipped topping

Melt butter in cake pan. Add brown sugar and let dissolve. Lay in slices of pineapple. Stir together a yellow cake mix using pineapple juice with the water. Pour batter on top of pineapples. Bake at 350°. When cake is done, flip upside down onto a cookie sheet. When cake is cooled, add whipped topping.

Overnight Coffee Cake
...Mrs. David (Lydia) Schwartz

Batter:
3/4 c. sugar
1/4 c. shortening
1 tsp. vanilla
1 egg
1 1/2 c. self-rising flour*
1 c. milk

Cream together the sugar, shortening and vanilla. Add the egg, sifted dry ingredients and the milk. Pour half of the batter into a greased 8" x 8" square pan. Cover with half of topping. Add remaining batter, then top with remaining topping. Can be baked now or refrigerated overnight. Bake at 350° for 25 minutes. Ice while warm with the following icing: powdered sugar, milk and vanilla. *Self-rising flour: 2 c. flour, 1 Tbsp. baking powder, 1 tsp. salt.

Topping:
1/2 c. brown sugar
2 Tbsp. butter, melted
2 Tbsp. flour
1/2 c. chopped nuts
2 tsp. cinnamon

Pumpkin Pecan Layer Cake

...Mrs. Willis (Mary) Bontrager

2 c. crushed vanilla wafers
1 c. chopped pecans
$^3/_4$ c. melted butter, divided
carrot cake mix
3 eggs
2 Tbsp. water
1 c. pumpkin

Mix crushed wafers, pecans and $^1/_2$ c. melted butter. Press evenly in 3 layer pans. Combine cake mix, eggs, water, $^1/_4$ c. melted butter and pumpkin. (I just use a carrot cake recipe and add 1 c. pumpkin, or pumpkin bar recipe.) Mix together and divide on crumbs in 3 pans. Bake at 350° for 30 minutes.

Filling:
4 c. powdered sugar
$^2/_3$ c. butter, softened
1 (8 oz.) pkg. cream cheese
2 tsp. vanilla
$^1/_4$ c. caramel topping
1 c. pecan halves

Spread filling between layers., nut side down. With $^3/_4$ c. filling, spread between layers. Frost only sides of cake. Spread caramel topping over top of cake, drizzling some over frosted sides. Arrange pecan halves on top.

Pumpkin Roll

...Mrs. John (Susan) Lehman

3 eggs, beaten
1 c. sugar
$^2/_3$ c. pumpkin
1 tsp. lemon juice
$^3/_4$ c. flour
1 tsp. baking powder
2 tsp. cinnamon
1 tsp. ginger
$^1/_2$ tsp. nutmeg

Add sugar gradually to eggs. Mix in pumpkin and lemon juice. Fold in dry ingredients. Bake at 375° for 15 minutes in a greased and floured cookie sheet. While still warm roll up in dish towel sprinkled with powdered sugar. Unroll when cool and add filling.

Filling:
1 c. powdered sugar
1 (8 oz.) pkg. cream cheese
4 Tbsp. butter
1 tsp. vanilla

Mix until smooth and spread on roll. Roll back to original shape minus the towel! Freeze or keep in refrigerator.

Delicious Coffee Cake   ...Mrs. Sam (Mary) Hershberger

1 c. sugar
1 c. shortening
1 tsp. soda
1 tsp. baking powder
$^{1}/_{2}$ tsp. salt
2 eggs
2 c. flour
1 c. sour cream

Cream sugar and shortening. Add eggs and sour cream, then dry ingredients. Bake in 2 pie pans. Sprinkle crumbs on top. Bake at 350° until golden brown. Then cut cake in half horizontally. Fill with filling.

Crumbs:
$^{1}/_{3}$ c. brown sugar
$^{1}/_{4}$ c. white sugar
$^{1}/_{3}$ c. mini chocolate chips
cinnamon

Filling:
2 egg whites, beaten
2 tsp. vanilla
1 (8 oz.) pkg. cream cheese
2 c. powdered sugar
$^{1}/_{4}$ c. butter

Out of This World Coffee Cake
...Mrs. Nathan (Barbara) Lehman

Batter:
$^{1}/_{2}$ c. butter
1 c. white sugar
2 eggs
$1^{1}/_{2}$ tsp. vanilla
1 c. cream
2 c. flour
1 tsp. baking powder
1 tsp. soda
$^{1}/_{2}$ tsp. salt

Mix butter, sugar, eggs and vanilla, then add cream and dry ingredients. Spread half of batter in 9" x 13" cake pan. Sprinkle half of topping on, then layer with rest of batter. Top with topping. Bake at 345° for 40-45 minutes.

Topping:
$^{1}/_{3}$ c. brown sugar
$^{1}/_{2}$ c. white sugar
1 tsp. cinnamon
1 c. chopped pecans

74

Sweet Potato Cake

Mrs. Freeman (Mabel) Yoder

³/₄ c. vegetable oil
2 c. sugar
4 eggs
1¹/₂ c. finely shredded
   uncooked sweet potatoes
¹/₄ c. hot water
1 tsp. vanilla
2¹/₂ c. flour
3³/₄ tsp. baking powder
1 tsp. salt
1 tsp. cinnamon
1 c. sliced almonds or walnuts

Beat oil, sugar and eggs. Beat well. Add sweet potatoes and vanilla. Next add flour, cinnamon, baking powder and salt. Add water gradually. Add nuts. Pour into greased 9" x 13" pan. Bake at 350° for 40-45 minutes.

Frosting:
¹/₂ c. butter or margarine
1 c. brown sugar
1 c. evaporated milk
3 egg yolks, beaten
1¹/₂ c. coconut
¹/₂ c. sliced almonds
1 tsp. vanilla
dash salt

Melt butter; whisk in sugar, milk and egg yolks until smooth. Bring to a boil and boil gently for 2 minutes. Remove from heat. Stir in coconut, almonds and vanilla. Spread over warm cake. A very moist cake.

Christmas Fruitcake

Mrs. Freeman (Mabel) Yoder

3 c. peeled, chopped apples
2 c. sugar
¹/₂ c. apple juice
3 eggs
³/₄ c. vegetable oil
1 tsp. vanilla
3 c. flour
2 tsp. apple pie spice
1 tsp. baking soda
1 tsp. salt
2 c. coarsely chopped pecans
¹/₂ lb. each red and green halved candied cherries
¹/₂ lb. diced candied pineapple

Line 3 loaf pans 8" x 4" x 2" with wax paper. Grease and set aside. In a large bowl combine apples, sugar and apple juice. Let set for 15 minutes. Add eggs, oil and vanilla; mix well. Combine flour, spice, baking soda and salt. Fold in pecans, cherries and pineapple. Pour into prepared pans. Bake at 350° for 55-65 minutes or until a toothpick comes out clean. Cool.

Toffee Mocha Cake …Mrs. Freeman (Mabel) Yoder

1 c. butter or margarine, softened
1³/₄ c. sugar
2 eggs
2 tsp. vanilla extract
2²/₃ c. flour
3 Tbsp. (heaping) cocoa
2 tsp. baking soda
¹/₂ tsp. salt
1 c. buttermilk or sour milk*
2 tsp. instant coffee granules
1 c. boiling water

In a mixing bowl cream butter and sugar. Beat in eggs and vanilla. Add dry ingredients alternately with buttermilk or sour milk. Dissolve coffee in hot water. Add to batter. Pour into a greased 9" x 13" pan. Bake at 350° for 35-40 minutes or until toothpick comes out clean.
*To make sour milk: Place 1-2 Tbsp. vinegar in a cup and fill with milk. It will appear curdled.

Topping:
¹/₂ tsp. instant coffee granules
1 tsp. hot water
2 c. whipping cream or
   Rich's topping
3 Tbsp. brown sugar
6 Heath candy bars, crushed

Dissolve coffee in hot water. Mix brown sugar and whipped topping. Mix with coffee mixture. Spread over cooled cake and sprinkle toffee over everything.

Rhubarb Custard Cake …Mrs. Orlie (Mary) Troyer

1 yellow cake mix
5 c. diced rhubarb
1¹/₂ c. sugar
2 c. whipping cream,
   not whipped

Mix cake according to directions. Pour into a 9" x 13" pan. Mix rhubarb and sugar together. Sprinkle over cake mix batter. Pour cream over all. Bake at 350° for 45-55 minutes. Cake will rise to the top and cream will form custard on the bottom. Serve warm with milk or ice cream.

Faith makes things possible, not easy.

Homemade Chocolate Cake ...Mrs. Melvin (Mattie) Yoder

3 c. all-purpose flour
2 c. sugar
1/3 c. baking cocoa
2 tsp. baking soda
1 tsp. salt
2 c. water
3/4 c. vegetable oil
2 tsp. vanilla
2 tsp. vinegar

In a mixing bowl combine first 5 ingredients. Add the water, oil, vanilla and vinegar. Mix well. Batter will be thin. Pour in to a greased 9" x 13" pan. Bake at 350° for 25-30 minutes or until toothpick comes out clean. Cool before frosting.

Chocolate Cream Cheese Frosting:
3 oz. cream cheese, softened
1/4 c. butter or margarine, softened
2 c. confectioners' sugar
1/3 c. baking cocoa
dash of salt
3 Tbsp. milk
1/2 tsp. vanilla extract

Better Than Almost Anything Cake
...Mrs. Orlie (Mary) Troyer

1 German chocolate cake mix
1 can Eagle Brand milk
1 c. caramel ice cream topping
12 oz. Cool Whip
1-2 Butterfinger or Heath
   candy bars

Prepare cake mix according to directions. Bake in a jelly roll pan. As soon as cake is done poke holes in cake with a wooden spoon handle. Pour Eagle Brand milk over the cake. Cool slightly then spread on the caramel topping. Cool completely and top with whipped topping and sprinkle with crushed candy bars.

77

Ho Ho Cake

...Mrs. Monroe (Mary Hochstetler

2 c. flour
1¹/₂ c. sugar
³/₄ c. cocoa
2 tsp. baking powder
1 tsp. soda
¹/₂ tsp. salt
³/₄ c. oil
2 eggs, beaten
1 c. milk
1 tsp. vanilla
1 c. hot coffee

Sift dry ingredients together. Then add liquids, all but coffee. Last add hot coffee. Batter will be very thin. A very moist cake. Bake at 325° for 35 minutes or until center of cake springs back when lightly touched.

5 Tbsp. (level) flour
1¹/₄ c. milk
1 c. sugar
¹/₂ c. shortening
¹/₂ c. margarine

Cook flour and milk until thick. In a separate bowl mix sugar, shortening and margarine. Beat until fluffy. Then beat in cooled flour-milk mixture and spread over cooled cake. Must be cold.

Topping:
¹/₂ c. margarine, melted
3 c. powdered sugar
¹/₄ c. cocoa
1 tsp. vanilla
1 egg, beaten
2 Tbsp. hot water

Mix together and beat until fluffy. Add more water if needed to make a spreading consistency. Very good! Takes some practice with the middle part.

Cowboy Cake

...Mrs. Orva (Marietta) Yoder

Crumbs:
2 c. brown sugar
2 c. flour
¹/₂ c. shortening

Mix crumbs together.

1 c. sour milk
1 tsp. soda
1 egg
2 Tbsp. vanilla
¹/₂ tsp. salt

In another bowl mix the rest of ingredients together; take out ²/₃ c. of crumbs. Mix the rest with the batter. Put in a cake pan; sprinkle the crumbs you've kept out on top. Put nuts on top of crumbs. Bake at 325° for 30 minutes.

Fruit Cocktail Cake
...Mrs. Melvin (Katie) Miller

2 eggs, beaten
1 1/2 c. white sugar
1 c. oil
1 (24 oz.) can fruit cocktail
2 c. flour
1/2 tsp. salt
2 tsp. soda

Beat eggs until light; beat in sugar. Add some oil to egg mixture, then alternate with dry ingredients. Last fold in fruit, juice and all. May sprinkle 1/3 c. coconut on top after batter is in pan. Bake at 350° for 35-40 minutes. A delicious moist cake!

Sour Cream Pound Cake
...Mrs. Melvin (Katie) Miller

1/4 c. margarine or butter
2 1/2 c. powdered sugar
3 large eggs
1 1/2 c. sour cream
1 1/2 c. flour
1 tsp. baking powder
1 Tbsp. vanilla

Beat margarine and powdered sugar until fluffy. Add eggs one at a time, beating just until yellow disappears. Add flour and baking powder alternately with sour cream. Stir in vanilla. Pour into a greased and floured loaf or bundt pan. Bake at 325° for one hour. Cool in pan for 10 minutes. Remove from pan and cool on wire rack. Serve with whipped cream. Delicious!

Silver White Cake
...Mrs. Sam (Rachel) Kauffman
...Mrs. Freeman (Amanda) Kauffman

2 1/4 c. flour
1 1/2 c. sugar
3 1/2 tsp. baking powder
1 tsp. salt
1/2 c. soft shortening
1 c. milk
1 tsp. flavoring
4 egg whites
1/2 c. sugar in egg whites

Sift together dry ingredients. Add shortening, milk and flavoring. Beat egg whites and 1/2 c. sugar. Fold into first mixture. Bake at 350° for 30-35 minutes.

Oatmeal Cake

...Mrs. Allen (Elsie) Bontrager

1¼ c. boiling water
1 c. quick oats
½ c. butter
1 c. white sugar
1 c. brown sugar
2 eggs
1½ c. flour
1 tsp. soda
1½ tsp. cinnamon
½ tsp. salt
1 tsp. vanilla

Pour boiling water over oats; let cool. Cream butter and sugars. Add eggs. Next, add the oats. Sift dry ingredients together and add next. Bake at 350° for about 40 minutes. Use a 9" x 13" pan.

Topping:
2 Tbsp. butter
¼ c. brown sugar
¼ c. milk or cream
1 tsp. vanilla
½ c. chopped nuts
½ c. coconut

Mix together in a saucepan and cook for 2-3 minutes. Spread on cake as soon as removed from oven. A very moist and delicious cake!

Amazing Corn Cake

...Mrs. Monroe (Mary) Hochstetler

1 (17 oz.) can cream style corn
½ c. brown sugar
½ c. white sugar
3 eggs
1 c. vegetable oil
1 tsp. soda
1 tsp. salt
1 tsp. cinnamon
1 Tbsp. baking powder
2 c. all-purpose flour
½ c. raisins
½ c. nuts

Combine corn and sugars. Add eggs and oil. Beat until well blended. Combine dry ingredients and add to batter. Mix well. Last stir in raisins and nuts. Pour in greased 13" x 9" pan. Bake at 350° for 30-35 minutes.

Caramel Frosting:
4 Tbsp. butter
½ c. brown sugar
¼ c. milk
2-3 c. powdered sugar

Bring butter and sugar to a boil. Remove and stir in milk. Stir in powdered sugar until desired consistency. Frost cooled cake. Something different but very good.

Fresh Apple Cake

...Mrs. Marvin (Mary Ann) Schrock

1³/₄ c. sugar
1¹/₂ c. oil
1 tsp. vanilla
2 eggs
2¹/₂ c. flour
¹/₂ tsp. salt
1¹/₂ tsp. soda
3 c. chopped apples
¹/₂ c. coconut (optional)
¹/₂ c. chopped nuts

Cream together sugar, oil, eggs and vanilla. Beat well, then add rest of ingredients. Pour into 9" x 13" pan. Bake at 350° for 1 hour.

Topping:
1 c. brown sugar
1¹/₂ Tbsp. cornstarch
1 Tbsp. margarine
³/₄ c. water

Stir all together and cook until it's thick or until it looks clear. Put on cake immediately. Cake may still be warm.

Chocolate Chip Date Cake

...Mrs. Richard (Verna Kay) Stutzman

1 c. dates
1 tsp. soda
1¹/₄ c. boiling water
³/₄ c. shortening
1 c. sugar
2 eggs
¹/₂ tsp. vanilla
¹/₄ tsp. salt
2 tsp. cocoa
1¹/₂ c. flour

Mix dates, soda and boiling water. Let cool. Cream together shortening and sugar. Add vanilla and eggs. Add cooled date mixture alternately with flour, cocoa and salt. Put in 9" x 13" pan and top with topping.

Topping:
¹/₃ c. sugar
¹/₃ c. nuts
6 oz. chocolate chips

81

Strawberry Rhubarb Coffee Cake
...Mrs. John (Susan) Lehman

Filling:

3 c. sliced fresh or frozen rhubarb
1 qt. fresh strawberries, mashed
2 Tbsp. lemon juice
1 c. sugar
1/3 c. cornstarch

In a saucepan combine rhubarb, strawberries and lemon juice. Cook on medium heat for 5 minutes. Combine sugar and cornstarch. Stir into fruit, stirring constantly until thickened.

Cake:

3 c. all-purpose flour
1 c. sugar
1 tsp. baking powder
1 tsp. soda
1/2 tsp. salt
1 c. butter
1 1/2 c. buttermilk
2 eggs
1 tsp. vanilla

Mix dry ingredients and cut in butter until mixture resembles coarse crumbs. Beat buttermilk, eggs and vanilla. Stir into crumb mixture. Spread half of batter into a greased 9" x 13" pan. Carefully spread filling over top. Drop remaining batter onto filling. Sprinkle topping over batter. Bake at 350° for 40-45 minutes.

Topping:

1/4 c. butter
3/4 c. flour
3/4 c. sugar

Dirt Cake
...Mrs. Freeman (Amanda) Kauffman

1 (16 oz.) pkg. Oreo cookies, crushed
1/2 c. butter or margarine, melted
1 (8 oz.) pkg. cream cheese, softened
16 oz. Cool Whip
1 lg. box instant chocolate pudding

Mix crushed cookies and melted butter. Save 1 1/2 c. cookie crumbs for top and pat the rest in bottom of 13" x 9" pan. Cool until set. Blend half of Cool Whip with cream cheese and spread over cookie crumbs. Mix chocolate pudding according to package directions. Use slightly less milk for a firmer pudding. Spread over layers and cool. Top with remaining Cool Whip and rest of cookie crumbs. Delicious!

Carrot Cupcakes ...Mrs. Freeman (Mabel) Yoder

4 eggs
2 c. sugar
3/4 c. vegetable oil
2 c. flour
2 tsp. cinnamon
1 tsp. baking soda
1 tsp. baking powder
1 tsp. allspice
1/2 tsp. salt
3 c. shredded carrots

In a mixing bowl beat eggs, sugar and oil. Gradually add dry ingredients, then add carrots last. Fill greased or paper-lined muffin cups two-thirds full. Bake at 325° for 25-30 minutes. Cool.

Chunky Frosting:
1 (8 oz.) pkg. cream cheese, softened
1/4 c. butter or margarine
2 c. powdered sugar
1/2 c. coconut
1/2 c. chopped pecans
1/2 c. raisins

Beat cream cheese and butter. Add powdered sugar. Stir in coconut, pecans and raisins. Frost the cupcakes. Yield: 24 cupcakes. Delicious!

Caramel Icing ...Mrs. Steve (Linda) Kauffman

1/2 c. butter
1 c. brown sugar
1/4 c. milk
1 3/4-2 c. powdered sugar, sifted

Melt butter and add brown sugar. Cook over low heat, stirring constantly, about 3-4 minutes. Add milk. Stir until mixture comes to a boil. Remove from heat. Slowly add powdered sugar, beating well after each addition until thick enough to spread. Enough for a large cake.

In making others happy, you will be happy too,
For the happiness you give away returns to shine on you.

General Food Hints

- An apple cut in half and placed in the cake box will keep cake fresh several days longer.
- To keep hard cheese fresh, cover with cloth moistened in vinegar; or grate the cheese and store in a tightly covered jar in the refrigerator.
- To keep sour cream fresh longer, store upside down in the refrigerator so that air cannot enter the container.
- Fresh tomatoes keep longer if stored in the refrigerator with stems down.
- Parsley will keep a long time in the refrigerator if, after washing it, you place it in a covered jar while still slightly damp.
- If soup is too salty, place a piece of raw potato in cooking pot to absorb the salty taste. If soup is too greasy, drop a lettuce leaf in pot. When grease has been absorbed, remove lettuce.
- Citrus fruit yields nearly twice the amount of juice if it is dropped into hot water a few minutes or rolled beneath your hand before squeezing.
- To peel a tomato easily, spear it with a kitchen fork and plunge it into boiling water 30 seconds. The skin will slide right off.
- Tomatoes cut vertically "bleed" less.
- Before measuring syrup, jelly, molasses, honey or other sticky substances, grease the measuring cup.
- To ignite alcohol, brandy, rum, etc., you must first heat it gently to allow the alcohol vapors to rise. If you boil the liquid, the alcohol will evaporate and never ignite.
- Before using the pulp of citrus fruits, grate the peel, being careful not to include the bitter-tasting inner white rind. Place in a tightly covered container and freeze until needed.
- For a ready supply of bread crumbs, save the heels from all your bread plus any stale bread. Place in a plastic bag and freeze until needed. Make crumbs by putting the frozen slices in a blender or food processor. you can also make crumbs first, then freeze for use in any recipe calling for fresh crumbs.
- Fried or baked chicken is especially delicious when it has first been marinated in the refrigerator overnight in buttermilk, sour milk or sour cream.
- To keep honey from clinging to inside of measuring cup, first coat inside of cup with oil.
- You can get more juice from a dried-up lemon if you heat it for five minutes in boiling water before you squeeze it.
- When making cracker crumbs, put the crackers in a clear bag and use the rolling pin to crush them. This doesn't make a mess on the counter or the rolling pin and the crumbs can easily be poured from the bag into a measuring cup. Then shake the bag out and save it to be used again.

Unto thee, O God, do we give thanks, unto thee do we give thanks, for that thy name is near thy wondrous works declare.

Psalm 75:1

Pies

THE PROVERBS 31 WOMAN

A virtuous woman who can find?
O men, will ye take heed?
Of rubies fair, wilt thou compare
Her price doth far exceed.

Her husband safely trusteth her;
His heart with hers is bound.
No need of spoil, amid life's toil,
With him—shall then be found.

This woman, she will do him good,
Each day of all her life.
No evil seeds or wicked deeds—
A true and faithful wife.

She seeketh wool and flax and such,
Then worketh willingly.
Her hands so worn, from all they've
   borne
Will never idle be.

Like merchants' ships, she brings her
   food
From lands both far and near.
She looketh well unto her house,
Spreading warmth and cheer.

She riseth also while 'tis night,
Her household she must feed.
This woman tends to make amends
To each and every need.

A field is seen, she buyeth it,
But first considers well.
The woman plans and with her hands
A vineyard she must build.

The poor and needy take no thought
Should snow or storms arise.
They all are safe, they do not chafe,
For she has much supplies.

All men may know, how can they
   tell—
Her husband in the gates?
The elders of the land thereof
All know at any rates.

Strength and honor are her clothing;
She shall rejoice in time to come.
She is the kind in whom you'll find
The law of kindness in her tongue.

When morning comes, her children
   rise
And call her blessedness.
Her husband, too, he praiseth her
Beauty of holiness!

But favor is deceitful
And beauty all is vain.
The woman who the Lord will fear
She shall then be praised.

—Mrs. John (Susan) Lehman

Sour Cream Cherry Pie...Mrs. Sam (Mary) Hershberger

2¹/₂ c. cherry pie filling
1 c. sugar
1 c. sour cream
3 oz. cream cheese
3 Tbsp. flour

Crumbs:
1 c. flour
¹/₂ c. sugar
¹/₄ c. butter

Combine sugar and flour. Add sour cream and cream cheese. Blend well. Put fruit in unbaked pie shell. Pour mixture over fruit. Top with crumbs. Bake at 425° for 15 minutes. Reduce heat to 350°. Bake for 25 more minutes. Delicious!
Note: Always have cream cheese and sour cream at room temperature before using.

Ground Cherry Pie ...Mrs. Melvin (Katie) Miller

1 qt. ground cherries
2¹/₂ c. white sugar
1 tsp. vinegar
¹/₂ tsp. salt
1 qt. water
approx. ¹/₂ c. clear jel

Heat ground cherries, sugar, water, vinegar and salt. Make a paste with clear jel and water and add to above mixture once it comes to a boil. Boil till it gets clear. Yield: 2 pies. Make a top crust and bake approx. 20-25 minutes in 425° oven.

Azar's Strawberry Pie ...sister, Elvesta Bontrager

3 c. sugar
3 c. water
1 tsp. salt
6 Tbsp. light corn syrup
2 Tbsp. Perma-Flo
6 Tbsp. (rounded) strawberry Jell-O
strawberries

Place 2¹/₂ c. water, sugar, salt, corn syrup and Jello-O in a saucepan. Bring to a boil. Combine Perma-Flo and remaining water in a small bowl until it makes a smooth paste. Add slowly to boiling water and cook until thick, 1-2 minutes. Cool. Add sliced strawberries to desired amount and pour into baked pie shells. Serve with dollops of Cool Whip.

Rosy Rhubarb Pie
...Mrs. Owen (Treva) Yoder

1 c. sugar
3 Tbsp. (heaping) Perma-Flo
2 Tbsp. strawberry Jell-O
¼ tsp. salt
1 c. boiling water
2 Tbsp. Karo
2 Tbsp. butter
2 c. chopped rhubarb
2 c. fresh halved strawberries

Mix sugar, Perma-Flo, strawberry Jell-O and well salt in saucepan. Add boiling water and Karo. Stir immediately. Heat and stir until thickened. Add butter. Cool, then add rhubarb and strawberries. Filling should be thick, will be thinner after baking. Put in unbaked pie crust. Moisten edges, cover with top crust, press down, seal well and crimp edges. Bake at 400° for 10 minutes, then at 350° until golden brown.

Sweet Cream Rhubarb Pie
...Mom, Rosa Bontrager

2 c. diced rhubarb
1¼ c. sugar
1 Tbsp. flour
1 egg, separated
1 c. heavy whipping cream
⅛ tsp. salt

Mix flour and sugar. Add salt and cream, then add beaten egg yolk. Stir well. Beat egg white. Fold into mixture. Spread rhubarb into a 9" unbaked pie shell. Pour cream mixture over rhubarb and bake at 350° until golden brown. Always a family favorite in the spring.

French Rhubarb Pie
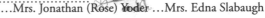
...Mrs. Jonathan (Rose) Yoder ...Mrs. Edna Slabaugh

1 egg
¾ c. sugar
1 tsp. vanilla
2 Tbsp. flour
2 c. raw, chopped rhubarb

Mix and pour into unbaked pie shell. Yield: 1 pie.

Topping:
¾ c. flour
½ c. brown sugar
⅓ c. butter

Bake at 400° for 10 minutes. Reduce to 350° and bake for 30 minutes. Edna uses 1 c. sugar. Freezes well.

Grape Pie

...Mrs. Reuben (Martha) Yoder

3 c. Concord grapes
1 c. sugar
3 Tbsp. flour
1 Tbsp. butter
1 Tbsp. lemon juice

Wash, drain and stem grapes. Remove and grind skins and set aside. Simmer pulp for 5 minutes. (Don't add water to pulp.) While hot, press pulp through sieve to remove seeds. Combine steamed pulp with ground skins. Combine sugar and flour and add to grapes. Blend in lemon juice and butter. Put into 1 – 9" pie crust. Top with crumb topping.

Crumbs:
1 c. flour
$^1/_2$ c. sugar
$^1/_4$ c. butter

Mix until crumbly. Bake at 350° for 40 minutes.

Key Lime Pie

...Mrs. Sam (Rachel) Kauffman

4 eggs, separated
1 can sweetened condensed milk
$^1/_2$ c. lime juice (fresh key limes if possible)
6 Tbsp. sugar
$^1/_2$ tsp. cream of tartar

Preheat oven to 350°. Beat 4 egg yolks; add condensed milk and lime juice. Beat until thick and pour into baked pie shell. For topping beat 4 egg whites. Blend in sugar and cream of tartar. Beat until stiff and forms peaks. Bake in moderate oven until egg whites are golden brown. Also good with Cool Whip.

Lemonade Pie

...Mrs. Danny (Vanessa) Reeves

1 (16 oz.) container Cool Whip
1 can sweetened condensed milk
1 (6 oz.) can frozen lemonade or pink lemonade
2 graham cracker crusts (store-bought or homemade)

Beat all ingredients until well mixed. Pour into crust. Chill about 1 hour. Sprinkle a few graham cracker crumbs on top of pies. Easy and delicious!

Chewy Banana Pie
...Mrs. Freeman (Mabel) Yoder

Crust: (or 1 baked pie shell)
3/4 c. butter or margarine, softened
2 c. vanilla wafers (about 60)
3/4 c. powdered sugar

Melt 1/2 c. butter; toss with wafer crumbs. Press into a 9" pie plate. In small bowl cream remaining butter, beat in powdered sugar until mixed and spread over crust.

Filling:
1 c. whipping cream or topping
1/4 c. sugar
2 Tbsp. cocoa
1 c. chopped walnuts
1 large firm banana, thinly sliced
1/3 c. maraschino cherries, cut up
additional whipped topping
chocolate curls
cherries

Beat topping, sugar and cocoa until stiff peaks form. Fold in the walnuts, banana and cherries. Spoon into crust. Refrigerate 8 hours or overnight. Garnish the edges with topping chocolate curls and cherries. This tastes similar to a banana split.

Green Tomato Pie
...Mrs. David (Lydia) Schwartz

1 c. white sugar
1/2 c. brown sugar
2 Tbsp. flour
1/4 c. vinegar
1 Tbsp. butter
1 tsp. cinnamon
1/4 tsp. cloves

Fill an unbaked pie shell with very thinly sliced, peeled green tomatoes. Remove seeds if you wish. Pour mixture over tomatoes. Put crust on top. Bake at 425° for 15 minutes, then at 350° until done, 30-40 minutes.

Walnut Pie
...Mom, Elsie Yoder

4 eggs, separated
1 c. white Karo
3/4 c. white sugar
3/4 c. brown sugar
5 Tbsp. flour
1 1/2 c. chopped walnuts
3 unbaked pie crusts

Mix all together except nuts. Fold in beaten egg whites last. Put 1/2 c. walnuts in each unbaked pie shell. Divide liquids in 3 pans.

Kentucky Pecan Pie ...Mrs. Edward (Lizzie Ann) Schrock

1 c. corn syrup
¹/₂ c. brown sugar
¹/₃ c. butter, melted
3 eggs, slightly beaten
1 tsp. vanilla
¹/₃ tsp. salt
1 c. pecans

Combine syrup, sugar, salt, butter and vanilla. Add eggs. Pour into 9" pie shell. Sprinkle pecans over all. Bake in heated oven at 350° for 45 minutes. Walnuts may also be used or ²/₃ c. oatmeal or 1 c. Rice Krispies or 1 c. coconut for a coconut pie.

Zucchini Pie  ...Mrs. Glen (Pollyanna) Hochstetler

7 c. zucchini
1¹/₄ c. sugar
1¹/₂ Tbsp. flour
1¹/₂ tsp. cream of tartar
1¹/₂ tsp. cinnamon
dash salt and nutmeg
1-2 tsp. lemon juice

Peel and slice zucchini lengthwise. Remove seeds and slice like apples. Add a little water and bring to a boil in a large saucepan. Simmer for a few minutes until tender. Drain well and cool. Add rest of ingredients. Place in an unbaked pie shell.

Crumbs:
1 c. flour
¹/₄ c. sugar
¹/₂ tsp. cinnamon
¹/₄ c. margarine

Mix all crumb ingredients and spread over the top. Bake at 350° for 1 hour. Tastes almost like apple pie and is delicious!

Words of wisdom—persist, persevere and be consistent and you will find that most things are possible.

Caramel Cinnamon Apple Pie

...Mrs. Freeman (Mabel) Yoder

1 – 9" unbaked pie shell
1 qt. apple pie filling

Topping:
(lattice crust top, optional)
²/₃ c. crushed graham crackers
¹/₄ c. brown sugar
3 Tbsp. (level) flour
¹/₃ c. butter
dash salt

Garnish:
2 c. whipped topping or
    caramel pecan whipped cream
¹/₂ c. butterscotch caramel
    ice cream topping
pecans, coarsely chopped

Pour apple pie filling into pie shell. Mix topping ingredients and spread evenly over pie filling. At this point you may add a lattice top crust over the crumb topping. This is optional. Bake at 375° for 30-40 minutes or until crust is done. While pie is still warm cover the crumbs or lattice crust with ice cream topping. Cool. Then before serving, spread whipped cream over all and sprinkle with pecans. This is a great way to spruce up plain apple pie.

Pumpkin Pie

...Mrs. John (Susan) Lehman

1 c. pumpkin
1 c. sugar
1 c. brown sugar
3 Tbsp. flour
3 eggs, separated
1 tsp. salt
¹/₂ tsp. nutmeg
¹/₂ tsp. cinnamon
3 c. milk
¹/₂ tsp. lemon flavoring
1 tsp. vanilla

Mix pumpkin, flour, sugars, spices and salt. Add egg yolks, milk, lemon and vanilla. Beat egg whites and fold into mixture. Bake at 350° until firm. Yield: 2 pies.

Double Layer Pumpkin Pie

...Mrs. Freeman (Mabel) Yoder

9" baked pie shell or
   graham cracker crust
1½ pkg. (12 oz.) cream
   cheese, softened
1 Tbsp. milk
2 Tbsp. sugar
1 c. cold milk
1 (3 oz.) sm. box instant
   vanilla pudding
1 (16 oz.) can pumpkin
2 tsp. pumpkin pie spice*
2 c. whipped topping
additional whipped topping

Mix cream cheese, milk and sugar until smooth. Fold in topping and spread on bottom of crust. Pour milk and pudding in a bowl. Mix well. (Mixture will be thick.) Stir in pumpkin and spices with wire whisk. Spread over cream cheese layer. Garnish with topping, a dollop on each piece. Refrigerate a few hours before serving.
*A substitute for pumpkin pie spice is 1 tsp. cinnamon, ½ tsp. ground ginger and ¼ tsp. cloves.

Pumpkin Custard Pie

...Mrs. David (Fannie) Miller

4 c. brown sugar
8 eggs, separated
1 pt. pumpkin
8 Tbsp. (slightly rounded) flour
2 tsp. pumpkin pie spice
1 c. Carnation milk or cream
pinch salt
2 qt. scalded milk

Mix everything together except egg whites. Beat those stiffly and beat in with remaining ingredients last with wire whip. Pour into unbaked pie shells. Sprinkle cinnamon on top. Bake at 425° for 10 minutes and then turn oven temperature down to 350° until done. Yield: 4 pies.

Triple Layer Mud Pie...Mrs. Freeman (Mabel) Yoder

1 c. milk chocolate chips
½ c. sweetened condensed milk
½ c. chopped pecans
2½ c. cold milk
1 lg. box or ⅔ c. instant
   chocolate pudding
8 oz. Cool Whip
9" baked pie shell or
   Oreo cookie crust

Melt chocolate chips over low heat, then add sweetened condensed milk. Pour into crust; sprinkle with pecans. Mix cold milk and instant pudding until well blended and pour onto pecans. Top with topping. Garnish with chocolate syrup or chocolate curls.

Creamy Peanut Butter Pie …Mrs. Sam (Mary) Hershberger

baked 9" pie shell
Cool Whip

Crumbs:
½ c. peanut butter	Mix together.
¾ c. powdered sugar	

Filling:
1 box instant vanilla pudding	Mix pudding and milk. Beat, then add ice
1 c. milk	cream and Cool Whip. Top with Cool Whip
1 c. ice cream	and crumbs. Also put crumbs on bottom of
1 c. Cool Whip	crust.

Frozen Peanut Butter Pie …Mrs. Dennis (Mary) Bontrager

Crust:
24 peanut butter sandwich cookies	Crush cookies and mix with butter. Press in 1
5 Tbsp. butter, melted	– 9" pie pan.

Filling:
1 (8 oz.) pkg. cream cheese, softened	Mix cream cheese, peanut butter, sugar and vanilla until well blended. Gently stir in
1 c. creamy peanut butter	1½ c. whipped topping; spoon into crust.
¾ c. white sugar	Garnish with remaining whipped topping and
1 Tbsp. vanilla	additional cookies if desired. Delicious!
1 (8 oz.) tub whipped topping, divided	

Raisin Pie …Mrs. Orva (Marietta) Yoder

1 c. raisins	Cook raisins and water, then add sugar, salt,
1 c. water	butter and lemon juice. Cook until raisins are
½ tsp. lemon juice	soft, approximately 2 minutes. Take 2 Tbsp.
1 c. sugar	Perma-Flo with a small amount of cold water;
1 Tbsp. butter	stir into the boiling raisin mixture. Cook until
pinch salt	thickened. Pour into a pie crust, then put a
	crust on top yet. Bake at 400° for 30 minutes.

Raisin Cream Pie
...Mrs. Sam (Mary) Hershberger

1 c. raisins
1/2 c. water
1 (8 oz.) pkg. cream cheese
1/4 c. powdered sugar
1 c. Rich's topping
1 box instant vanilla pudding
3/4 c. milk

Cook raisins and water until water is used up. Cool. Cream powdered sugar and cream cheese together. Whip Rich's topping (save enough for a dollop on each piece). Beat vanilla pudding with milk. Mix all together and put in baked pie shell. Delicious!

Cream Pies
...Mrs. Daniel (Fannie) Hershberger

2 c. milk
2 Tbsp. butter
1/4 c. white sugar
2 egg yolks
1 Tbsp. flour
2 Tbsp. cornstarch
1/2 tsp. vanilla
1/4 tsp. salt

Melt butter in saucepan. Add milk and sugar. Mix rest of ingredients with a little milk and add to milk in saucepan. Bring to a boil. Use this as your basic vanilla pudding for all your cream pies.

Cream Cheese Vanilla Crumb Pie
...Mrs. Simon (Esta) Miller

2 c. water
1 c. brown sugar
1 c. Karo
2 Tbsp. flour
2 eggs, divided
1 tsp. vanilla
1 (8 oz.) pkg. cream cheese
1/2 c. white sugar
1/2 tsp. salt

Heat water, brown sugar and Karo. Thicken with 2 Tbsp. flour and enough water to make paste. Stir in 1 beaten egg and vanilla. Let cool before dividing in 2 unbaked pie shells. Mix cream cheese, white sugar, 1 egg and salt. Drizzle this over caramel mixture in pie shells.

Crumbs:
2 c. flour
1/2 c. brown sugar
1/2 c. butter, softened
1/2 tsp. cinnamon
1/2 tsp. cream of tartar
1 tsp. baking soda

Divide crumbs on 2 pies. Bake in 375° oven for 30 minutes.

Chocolate Pie Filling
...Mrs. Melvin (Mary) Stutzman

1 qt. water
1 pt. cream
²/₃ c. Mira Clear or Therma-Flo
¹/₄ c. cocoa
1¹/₄ c. sugar
vanilla

Heat cream and 2 c. water. Mix dry ingredients and remaining 2 c. water. Add chocolate mixture to hot cream. Heat until thick, stirring constantly. Remove from heat and cool slightly before pouring into baked pie shell. Yield: 2 – 9" pies. This is a smooth silky pudding. Serve with whipped topping on top.

Cappuccino Chocolate Pie
...Mrs. Freeman (Mabel) Yoder

1 c. chocolate chips
¹/₃ c. whipping cream
1 Tbsp. corn syrup
1 tsp. vanilla
pinch salt
9" baked pie shell or graham
    cracker crust
1 c. pecans, chopped
4 oz. cream cheese, softened
1¹/₂ c. milk
2 Tbsp. brewed coffee
1 (6 oz.) lg. box or ²/₃ c.
    instant vanilla pudding
2 Tbsp. instant coffee granules
8 oz. whipped topping

In a saucepan melt chocolate chips, cream, syrup, vanilla and salt over low heat. Stir until smooth. Spoon into crust and sprinkle with pecans. Beat cream cheese until smooth; gradually add milk and brewed coffee. Mix well. Add pudding and instant coffee. Beat well. Fold in 1¹/₂ c. topping and spoon over pecans in the crust. Spread remaining topping over all. Garnish with chocolate curls if desired. Yummy!

He shall cover thee with his feathers, and
under his wings shalt thou trust.
—Psalm 91:4

Caramel Chocolate Pie   ...Mrs. Freeman (Mabel) Yoder

3 (8") baked pie crusts
18 oz. caramel apple dip
2 Tbsp. cream or milk
3 (3 oz.) boxes instant
  chocolate pie filling*
1 c. chopped pecans
1 c. milk chocolate toffee bits
whipped topping

Mix caramel and milk, then spread evenly in the 3 pie crusts. Fix pie filling according to directions. Set aside. Divide pecans on top of caramel. Spread pie filling over the pecans. Sprinkle toffee bits evenly over the chocolate filling. Spread whipped topping around the outer part of the pile leaving the middle open. Swirl with caramel and chocolate ice cream syrup.
*I use the chocolate pie filling found in this section by Mrs. Melvin (Mary) Stutzman. It's delicious!

Caramel Custard Pie   ...Mrs. Steve (Martha) Yoder
...Mrs. John (Mary) Hochstetler

³/₄ c. white sugar
1 Tbsp. (heaping) flour
1 c. milk
1 c. cream
2 eggs, separated
¹/₂ tsp. maple flavoring
pinch of salt

Mix together flour, sugar and salt. Add beaten egg yolks and flavoring and enough milk to make a smooth batter. Bring milk to boiling. Add batter and 2 stiffly beaten egg whites. Pour in pie shell. Sprinkle chopped nuts on top. Bake at 375° for 10 minutes, then at 300° until done. Yield: 1 pie. Variation: Mary uses 2 c. milk and no cream. Our family's favorite!

Cloud 9 Pie   ...Mrs. Daniel (Fannie) Hershberger
...Mrs. Melvin (Mattie) Yoder

1 c. sugar
¹/₄ tsp. salt
1 Tbsp. unflavored gelatin
³/₄ c. milk
3 egg yolks, slightly beaten
1 tsp. orange peel, shredded
³/₄ c. orange juice
¹/₂ tsp. lemon peel, shredded
¹/₄ c. lemon juice
1 c. whipped topping
9" baked pastry shell

Combine sugar, gelatin and salt in saucepan. Add milk and egg yolks. Cook over medium heat, stirring until mixture thickens slightly. Remove from heat. Add juices and peels. Chill until partially set. Fold in whipped topping. Chill until mixture mounds. Pile in baked pie shell. This pie can be frozen.

Cherry Pie Filling
...Mrs. Roy (Lovina) Yoder

1 qt. sour cherries
$^1/_2$ qt. water
$^1/_2$ c. brown sugar
$^1/_2$ c. white sugar
1 tsp. red food coloring
1 Tbsp. almond flavoring
$^1/_2$ tsp. salt
1 tsp. vanilla
$^1/_4$ c. cherry Jell-O
$^3/_4$ c. clear jel
$1^1/_2$ c. water

Heat everything except clear jel and $1^1/_2$ c. water. Add clear jel to water to make a thin paste. Add to hot cherries, stirring until boiling. Recipe can be doubled or tripled, and then canned as pie filling.

Strawberry Pie Filling
...Mrs. Marvin (Mary Ann) Schrock

3 oz. strawberry Jell-O
$^1/_2$ c. white sugar
$^1/_8$ tsp. salt
$^1/_2$ c. water or strawberry juice
$^1/_4$ c. cornstarch
$^1/_2$ c. water
4 c. sliced strawberries

Put Jell-O, sugar, salt and water or juice together and bring to a boil. Dissolve. Mix cornstarch with water. Add to first 4 ingredients. Cook until thickened. Add strawberries. Stir only enough to coat the berries evenly.

Pie Crust
...Mrs. Melvin (Mary) Stutzman

2 c. shortening
3 c. flour
2 tsp. baking powder
pinch of salt

Crumble together. Put an egg in 1 c. measure. Fill with water. Mix with 1 c. flour. Add to crumb mixture and stir until just moistened. This recipe has always turned out good for me.

Never-Fail Pie Crust   ...Mrs. Freeman (Mabel) Yoder

4 c. flour
1½ tsp. salt
1 Tbsp. baking powder
1¾ c. lard

Mix together with a pastry cutter or fork until it is mealy and crumbly. If you are using a home-rendered lard use as directed but if you use pre-creamed shortening use 2 c. Beat 1 egg, 1 Tbsp. vinegar and ½ c. cold water. Then add all at once to flour mixture. Fold together gently, then press to form a ball. Handle as little as possible. Let set 15-20 minutes, then roll and use.

A good glaze for your pie tops: 1 egg, beaten, and ¼ c. milk stirred together. Brush or spoon over the top and sprinkle with sugar. Makes them golden brown and slightly shiny. These will not get soggy.

Helpful Hint: Pie dough does not like to be handled a lot. The less it is worked after the liquid has been added the flakier the crust.

Pie Crumbs-The Best   ...Mrs. Simon (Esta) Miller

20 c. Flaky pie flour (pastry)
½ c. white sugar
2½ Tbsp. salt
1 Tbsp. baking powder
1 can butter Crisco

Mix gently as for pie crumbs. Store in tight container. Moisten with cold milk just so you can handle it.

Mix:
2 c. pie crumbs
⅓ c. white sugar

Sprinkle on top lid of fruit pies.

There is no better exercise for the heart than
reaching down and lifting people up.

Hints for Meats

- Heat the frying pan before adding oil or butter to prevent sticking.
- Sprinkle salt in the bottom of a frying pan to prevent food from sticking.
- When you want a crisp, brown crust on chicken, rub mayonnaise over it.
- Try basting meat with ½ c. brown sugar, 1 Tbsp. dry mustard, ½ c. tomato juice, 1½ c. chili sauce and ½ c. pineapple juice for a delicious flavor.
- Grate an apple into hamburger, then shape into patties to add moistness.
- A large roast or turkey can be carved easily after it stands for 30 minutes.
- To remove the wild flavor, soak game birds 3 hours in 1 Tbsp. baking soda and 1 Tbsp. salt to 1 gal. of water. Basting in 7-Up helps take away the game taste.
- Add leftover coffee to ham, beef or pork gravy for a beautiful color.
- Use a small amount of baking powder in gravy if it seems greasy. The grease will disappear.
- Use an ice cream dipper to make meat balls.
- To make a fluffy meat loaf, beat an egg white stiff and add it after all other ingredients have been mixed.
- When making hamburgers, mix a little flour with the meat and they will stay together better.
- For smooth brown gravy, brown the flour well in meat drippings before adding the liquid. Another way to brown flour is by placing it in a custard cup beside meat in oven. When meat is done, the flour will be brown and ready to make a nice, brown gravy.
- Raw meats, especially liver, grind easily if frozen, not stone hard, but just firm.
- To prevent splashing when frying meat, sprinkle a little salt into the pan before putting the fat in.
- The odor from baking or boiling salmon may be eliminated by squeezing lemon juice on both sides of each salmon steak or on the cut surface of the salmon and letting it stand in the refrigerator for one hour before cooking.

Bacon
- Bacon will lie flat in the pan if you prick it thoroughly with a fork as it fries.
- Bacon dipped in flour will not shrink, or pinch a fold in the middle of a bacon slice to help prevent curling. Soaking in ice water a few minutes also works.
- A quick way to separate frozen bacon: Heat a spatula over the stove burner, then slide it under each slice to separate it from the others.

Beatitudes for a Housewife

Blessed is she whose daily tasks are a labor of love; her willing hands and happy heart translate duty into privilege, and all her labor becomes a service to God and to mankind.

Blessed is she who opens the door to welcome both stranger and well-loved friend; her gracious hospitality is a test of brotherly love.

Blessed is she who mends stockings and toys and broken hearts; her patience and understanding is a balm to humanity.

Blessed is she who scours and scrubs; for well she knows that cleanliness is one true expression of godliness.

Blessed is she who sings while she works; for music lightens the heaviest load and brightens the dullest chore.

Blessed is she who dusts away doubt and fear, and polishes each task with prayer; her faith will triumph over all adversity.

Blessed is she who serves laughter and smiles with every meal; her buoyancy of spirit is an aid to both mental and physical digestion.

Blessed is she who thanks God for all her many blessings, and has made Him her honored guest in every activity of the home.

Blessed is she who preserves the sanctity of the home; hers is a sacred trust that crowns her with honor and with dignity.

—*Author Unknown*

Meats & Main Dishes

Mealtime

When it's almost mealtime
There is work to do;
We must peel potatoes,
Wash the carrots, too.
Fetch a jar of meatballs,
Put them in a pan,
Then we set the table
Neatly as we can.

Sister makes a pudding,
Mother cuts the bread,
I fill up the fruit bowl,
Then the table's spread.
When the men come, hungry,
We all find our place.
Then when we are seated
We have silent grace.

We enjoy our mealtimes,
Good food, talk and fun,
Everyone together
Till the meal is done.
Then it's time for dishes,
Clearing all away,
Ready for another
Mealtime in this way.

Pot Roast

...Mrs. Marcus (Joleen) Marner

1 beef roast (about 2½ lb.)
4 or 5 potatoes, quartered
2 or 3 large carrots
2 celery sticks
1 med. onion, sliced
salt and pepper
2 tsp. Worcestershire sauce
2 tsp. soy sauce
1 or 2 dashes liquid smoke

Cut beef and vegetables into serving size pieces. Arrange in roaster. Pour 2-3 c. water in bottom of roaster. Sprinkle seasonings over beef. Add salt and pepper. Bake at 350° for 2½-3 hours or until beef is fork-tender.

Grilled Pork Steaks

...Mrs. John (Mary) Hochstetler

pork steaks
soy sauce
garlic salt
olive oil

Lay pork steaks on cookie sheets, the amount you need for your family. Sprinkle soy sauce on top. Then sprinkle garlic salt on top. Let marinate for 30-45 minutes. Put on hot grill, side down with soy sauce. Spread other side evenly with 1 tsp. or more olive oil. Grill both sides until done, not too well done. In winter I use oven broiler to grill the steaks which is also delicious.

Barbecued Ribs

...Mrs. Freeman (Mabel) Yoder

1½ c. brown sugar
1 tsp. salt
2 c. ketchup
½ c. white Karo syrup
1 tsp. liquid smoke
3-5 lb. pork spareribs
½ tsp. Tabasco sauce (optional)
1 c. water
1 Tbsp. Worcestershire sauce

Combine sugar, salt, ketchup, Karo, water, Worcestershire sauce and liquid smoke. Stir until sugar is dissolved. Add ribs and stir until coated. Transfer to a large roasting pan and bake at 350° for 2 hours. These go really good with Holiday Mashed Potatoes.

Spaghetti

...Mrs. Sam (Mary) Hershberger

1½ lb. hamburger
2 tsp. salt
1 tsp. pepper
1 tsp. garlic salt
½ c. onions
5 c. tomato juice
3 Tbsp. brown sugar
2 tsp. (rounded) flour
1 c. shredded cheese

Fry hamburger. Add salt, pepper, garlic salt and onions. When browned add flour, tomato juice and brown sugar. Simmer for 1 hour. Pour over cooked spaghetti. Top with cheese. Eat with garlic bread. Delicious!

Tasty Spaghetti

...Mrs. Steve (Martha) Yoder

3 qt. water
1 tsp. salt
1 lb. spaghetti, broken up
1¼ c. milk
⅔ c. flour
2 lb. hamburger
onions
salt
pepper
1 qt. spaghetti sauce
3 Tbsp. brown sugar

Heat water and salt to boiling. Add broken up spaghetti. Cook slowly until spaghetti is tender. In a gravy shaker mix milk and flour and add to spaghetti. Heat until boiling, then add Velveeta cheese until nice and cheesy. In another skillet fry hamburger with onions, salt and pepper. Add spaghetti sauce and brown sugar. Heat until bubbly. Serve as gravy on the spaghetti. A pan of fresh warm bread sticks are a great complement with this meal.

Spaghetti Carbonara

...Mrs. Danny (Vanessa) Reeves

8 oz. spaghetti
½ lb. bacon
⅔ c. chopped onions
1 can mushrooms
3 egg yolks, slightly beaten
¼ c. butter
1½ c. cheddar cheese
⅛ tsp. salt
a lot of pepper

Cook spaghetti and drain. Cook bacon and break up. Sauté mushrooms and onions in 2 Tbsp. bacon grease. Remove mushrooms and onions and melt butter with bacon grease. Add everything in the pan and toss with a fork lightly. Add egg yolks gradually and mix well. Serve immediately. My mother lived in Italy for a time and acquired this recipe while there.

Easy Beef Stroganoff
...Mrs. Steve (Martha) Yoder

2 lb. ground beef
1 lg. onion, chopped
1 pt. sour cream
2 cans cream of mushroom soup
1 can cream of celery soup
1 pkg. dry onion soup mix

Brown beef. Add remaining ingredients, adding sour cream last. Serve over rice or noodles.

Appetizer Meatballs
...Mrs. Monroe (Mary) Hochstetler

2 lb. ground beef
1 lb. ground sausage
1 c. evaporated milk
2 c. oatmeal
$^1/_2$ tsp. pepper
2 tsp. chili powder
$^1/_2$ tsp. garlic powder
2-3 tsp. salt
2 eggs
$^1/_2$ c. chopped onion

Mix all meatball ingredients together. Shape into small 1" balls. Place in baking dish in single layer.

Sauce:
2 c. catsup
$1^1/_2$ c. brown sugar
1 tsp. liquid smoke
$^1/_2$ tsp. garlic powder
$^1/_2$ c. chopped onion
barbecue sauce (optional)

Combine sauce ingredients and pour over meatballs. Bake at 350° for 1 hour. Yield: 9 dozen meatballs.

Sausage Supreme
...Mrs. Edna Slabaugh

2 c. fried sausage
2 c. uncooked macaroni
1 can cream of mushroom soup
2 c. milk
$^1/_2$ med. onion, chopped
$^1/_2$ tsp. salt
$^1/_2$ tsp. pepper
3 Tbsp. butter
1 c. cheese

Melt cheese and soup in milk. Combine all ingredients. Refrigerate overnight. Bake at 350° for $1^1/_2$ hour. Bake longer if you double recipe.

Taco Potato Stack

...Mrs. Richard (Verna Kay) Stutzman

baked potatoes
hamburger
lettuce, chopped
tomatoes, chopped
sour cream
med. cheese sauce
mashed nacho chips

Brown hamburger with onions and taco seasoning. Cut baked potatoes in half. Add remaining ingredients in layers as listed. This can be made in amounts to fit your family or a crowd. An easy favorite to take camping!

Hamburger Rice Casserole

...Mrs. Orlie (Mary) Troyer

1½ lb. hamburger
½ c. onion
1 c. rice
3 c. water
seasoning salt
salt
pepper
1 can cream of mushroom soup
1 can cream of chicken soup
1½ c. frozen peas, thawed

Brown hamburger and onion together. Season with salt and pepper. Boil rice in water until tender. Mix rest of ingredients together and put in a 9" x 13" pan.

Topping:
12 oz. sour cream
2 c. cornflakes, crushed
¼ c. oleo, melted

Cover with 12 oz. sour cream and the cornflakes mixed with melted oleo. Bake at 350° until hot. Do not overbake.

Rice Casserole

...Mrs. Marvin (Mary Ann) Schrock

1 lb. hamburger
1 lg. onion
1 c. chopped celery
1 c. uncooked rice
3 Tbsp. soy sauce
1 qt. chicken broth
1 can cream of mushroom soup
1½ soup cans water
⅛ tsp. salt

Fry meat. Add celery and onion. Cook rice in chicken broth, then add the rest of the ingredients. Pour into a 2 qt. casserole dish and bake for 45 minutes at 350°.

Rice Pizza
...Mrs. Sam (Viola) Miller

1½ c. rice
3 c. water
4 Tbsp. butter
1 lb. hamburger
1 qt. spaghetti sauce
2-3 c. shredded cheese

Cook rice, water and butter for 10 minutes. Let set for 10 minutes. Meanwhile fry hamburger until brown. Add spaghetti sauce and heat thoroughly. Pour over rice. Top with cheese. This can also be made ahead of time by layering the cooked rice, hamburger, spaghetti sauce and cheese. Place in a casserole dish or cake pan. Cover and bake at 350° for 30 minutes.

Taco Rice Casserole
...Mrs. Lonnie (Norma) Bontrager

1½ c. rice
1½ lb. ground beef
1 pkg. taco seasoning
1 qt. pizza sauce
1 c. sour cream
1 c. mayonnaise
¼ c. chopped onion
1 c. shredded cheddar cheese

Heat oven to 350°. A cake pan works well. Cook rice in 3 c. water. Cook ground beef until browned; mix taco seasoning with meat. Mix together sour cream, mayonnaise, onion and cheese. Put in layers: rice, pizza sauce, meat and top with sour cream mixture. Bake 25 minutes or until cheese is melted.

Taco Rice
...Mrs. Andrew (Joanna) Hostetler

1 lb. hamburger
1 med. onion
½ pkg. taco seasoning
1 (16 oz.) chunk tomatoes
1 c. rice
1 c. mayonnaise
1 c. sour cream
1 c. shredded cheese
2 c. Bisquick mix
¾ c. milk

Fry hamburger and onions until brown. Add taco seasoning and tomatoes. Cook rice with reserved tomato juice. Add enough water to make 2½ c. When rice is soft, mix it with the hamburger mixture. Pour into a 9" x 13" pan. Mix together mayonnaise, sour cream and cheese. Spread over hamburger mixture. Make a thin batter of Bisquick and milk and pour over top of sour cream mixture. Bake at 400° for 30 minutes.
Suggestion: If I don't have shredded cheese, I add a layer of Velveeta on top of sour cream mixture.

Mexican Casserole ...Mrs. Simon (Esta) Miller

$^1/_2$ c. flour
$^1/_2$ tsp. baking powder
2 Tbsp. oleo
$^1/_2$ c. sour cream
1 egg, beaten
5 lb. hamburger fried with
   1 onion, seasoned with taco
   seasoning
3 cans refried beans
1 lb. fried bacon, crumbled
4 c. minute rice, prepared
2 c. chopped green pepper
Velveeta cheese
3 c. sour cream

Stir flour, baking powder, oleo, sour cream and beaten egg together. Spread dough in bottom of large roaster. Layer hamburger and onion, beans, bacon, rice, green pepper, cheese and sour cream in roaster. Bake in 350° oven for $2^1/_2$ hours or until heated through. Top with lettuce and chopped tomato and serve with salsa on the side.

Taco Crescent Bake ...Mrs. David (Fannie) Miller

1 (8 oz.) tube refrigerated
   crescent rolls
2 c. crushed corn chips, divided
$1^1/_2$ lb. ground beef
1 (15 oz.) can tomato sauce or
   pizza sauce
1 env. taco seasoning
1 c. (8 oz.) sour cream
1 c. (4 oz.) shredded cheddar
   cheese

Unroll crescent dough into a rectangle; press onto the bottom and 1" up the sides of a greased 13" x 9" baking dish. Sprinkle with 1 c. chips; set aside. In a large skillet cook beef until brown. Stir in tomato sauce and taco seasoning. Bring to a boil. Reduce heat and simmer uncovered for 5 minutes. Spoon over chips. Top with sour cream, cheese and remaining chips. Bake uncovered at 350° for 25-30 minutes or until crust is lightly browned.

We make a living by what we get.
We make a life by what we give.

Chili Skillet

...Mrs. David (Barbara) Wagler

1 lb. ground beef
1 c. chopped onion
½ c. chopped green pepper
1 garlic clove, minced
1 c. tomato juice
1 (8 oz.) can kidney beans,
  undrained
4 tsp. chili powder
1 tsp. dried oregano
1 tsp. salt
½ c. uncooked long grain rice
1 c. canned or frozen corn
½ c. (4 oz.) shredded cheddar
  or Monterey Jack cheese
olives, optional

In a large skillet over medium heat cook beef, onion, green pepper and garlic until meat is brown and vegetables are tender. Drain fat. Add tomato juice, kidney beans, chili powder, oregano, salt and rice; cover and simmer about 25 minutes or until tender. Stir in corn and olives; cover and cook 5 more minutes. Sprinkle with cheese; cover and cook only until cheese melts, about 5 minutes. The best! Good served with potato salad.

Pizza Potato Casserole

...Mrs. Nathan (Barbara) Lehman

4 lb. sausage, browned
  with onions
2 onions
1 c. green peppers
2 cans mushrooms, drained
4 cans mushroom soup
peeled, cooked and chopped potatoes, enough to fill 6 qt. kettle
2 qt. pizza sauce
1 qt. salsa
2 tsp. basil
1 sm. pkg. pepperoni
½ box Velveeta cheese
salt to taste
pepper to taste

Mix all together and bake at 350° for 1½ hours. Enough for 1 roaster.

Pizza Casserole

...Mrs. Roy (Lovina) Yoder

1 lb. noodles
3-4 lb. hamburger or sausage
1 Tbsp. salt
$^1/_2$ c. onions and peppers
1 qt. tomato juice
$^1/_2$ c. sugar
2 tsp. salt
$1^1/_2$ tsp. oregano
$1^1/_2$ tsp. sweet basil
1 c. flour
2 cans cream of mushroom soup
2 c. Velveeta cheese
2 cans mushrooms
$^1/_2$-1 c. pepperoni

Cook and drain noodles. Fry hamburger. Add salt, onions and peppers. Heat tomato juice. Mix sugar, flour and spices. Add water to make a thin paste. Add paste to hot tomato juice, stirring until boiling. Remove from burner. Add cream of mushroom soup and Velveeta cheese. Stir until cheese is mostly melted. Put noodles, hamburger and tomato sauce together in roaster. Add mushrooms and pepperoni and mix. Bake at 300° for 45 minutes or until hot.

Pizza Casserole

...Mrs. Allen (Elsie) Bontrager

1 lb. hamburger or seasoned sausage
1 onion, chopped
2 (16 oz.) cans pizza sauce
1 (10 oz.) pkg. mozzarella cheese
1 (7 oz.) pkg. elbow macaroni, cooked
4 oz. pepperoni, thinly sliced
1 can mushrooms

Brown meat and chopped onion together and season with salt and pepper, unless you are using seasoned sausage. (Sausage is the best.) Grease a casserole dish; mix and bake at 350° for 45 minutes. Top with more cheese and pepperoni, about 15 minutes before it's finished, if you wish.

Delicious Casserole

...Mrs. John (Mary) Hochstetler

$1^1/_2$ lb. hamburger
1 c. chopped onion
1 sm. can pimentos
1 can mushroom soup
1 can cream of chicken soup
1 (1 lb.) pkg. noodles (large wide kind)
1 can peas
1 can corn
$^1/_2$ pt. sour cream
salt to taste

Brown hamburger and onions. Boil noodles until soft. Mix everything together and put in 4 qt. baking dish. Bake at 350° until bubbly or about 45 minutes.

Penny Supper Casserole

...Mrs. Andrew (Joanna) Hostetler

6 hot dogs, sliced
4 med. potatoes, cooked and diced
1 c. cooked or frozen peas, drained
2 Tbsp. diced onion
1 can mushroom soup
1/4 c. butter, softened
1 Tbsp. mustard

Combine in order given and pour into casserole dish. Bake at 350° for 45 minutes. Stir and top with grated cheese and bake for 5 more minutes.

Suggestion: If it's too thick, you can add a little milk.

Hobo's Delight

...Mrs. Lonnie (Norma) Bontrager

2 lb. ground beef, browned
2 onions, chopped
2 (6 oz.) cans tomato paste
2 (8 oz.) cans tomato sauce
4 c. water
1/4 c. sugar
4 cloves garlic, crushed
2 tsp. Accent
2 tsp. chili powder
2 tsp. oregano
2 tsp. cumin
2 tsp. salt
1/2 c. rice
15 1/4 oz. can chili beans, drained
corn chips

After ground beef is cooled and drained, add all other ingredients except corn chips. Simmer until rice is tender (about 20 minutes). To serve on plate put a handful of corn chips, a ladle or two of meat mixture on top of chips, some grated cheese, some chopped tomatoes and shredded lettuce and top all with some Ranch dressing.

Shipwreck Casserole

...Mrs. Melvin (Mattie) Yoder

1 1/2 lb. hamburger
1 qt. potatoes
1 pt. carrots
1 pt. peas
1 can mushroom soup
1 can celery soup

Fry hamburger with onions, salt and pepper. Cook vegetables separately for 5 minutes. Put in layers in casserole dish. Add Velveeta cheese. Add enough milk to suit your taste. Bake at 350° for 1 hour or until done.

Meatball Sub Casserole ...Mrs. Sam (Mary) Hershberger

1 lb. hamburger
3 c. onions
salt and pepper
1 loaf homemade bread, sliced
   1" thick
1 (8 oz.) pkg. cream cheese or
   sour cream
1/2 c. salad dressing
1 tsp. Italian seasoning
2 c. mozzarella cheese or
   your favorite
1 (28 oz.) jar spaghetti or
   pizza sauce
1 c. water
dash garlic powder

Fry hamburger, onions, salt and pepper. Set aside. Arrange bread in a baking dish. Mix cream cheese, salad dressing and Italian seasoning. Spread over bread slices then top with 1 c. cheese. Mix spaghetti sauce, water and garlic powder; mix with hamburger. Pour this over cheese mixture. Top with rest of cheese. Bake at 350° for 30 minutes. Very good.

Curly Fry Tortilla Casserole ...Mrs. Simon (Esta) Miller

6 lb. hamburger
1 onion, chopped
3 cans mushroom soup
2 cans chicken soup
24 oz. sour cream
2 lg. bags tortillas, cut up
1 qt. pizza sauce or salsa
4 c. shredded cheddar cheese
Velveeta cheese
2 bags curly fries, frozen
seasoning salt

Fry hamburger and onion. Mix mushroom soup, chicken soup, sour cream, tortillas, pizza sauce or salsa and shredded cheese. Mix in with hamburger and put in large roaster. Bake at 325°-350° until heated through approximately 2 hours. Remove from oven and top with Velveeta cheese. Then put curly fries on top and bake another 30 minutes at 400°. Sprinkle top with seasoning salt. This recipe fills a large roaster to the brim.

A word of encouragement during a failure is worth more than an hour of praise after success.

112

Cheesy Tortillas
...Mrs. Freeman (Mabel) Yoder

10 flour tortillas
2 lb. sausage
2 c. chopped tomatoes
1 c. chopped onion
1 pepper, finely chopped
1 c. sour cream
3 c. chopped lettuce
1 lb. shredded mozzarella cheese

Preheat oven to 325°. Brown sausage and drain. Divide sour cream onto 10 tortillas and spread evenly. More or less may be used. Spoon sausage evenly down the middle of each tortilla. Then do the same with tomatoes, onions, peppers, lettuce and cheese. Fold tortillas and overlap, secure with toothpicks and stack side by side on a 10" x 15" cookie pan. Cover with tinfoil and bake until heated through, approximately 15-20 minutes. May serve with additional sour cream.

Baked Chicken
...Mrs. Monroe (Mary) Hochstetler

5 chicken breasts or thighs
1 can whole cranberry sauce
1 pkg. onion soup mix
8 oz. French dressing

Place chicken in baking pan. Mix the remaining ingredients and pour over chicken. Bake at 350° for 1 hour. Is absolutely delicious!

Grilled Chicken Breast
...Mrs. Nathan (Barbara) Lehman

Italian dressing
chicken breast slices, as much you need

Marinate breasts in dressing for 3 hours. Grill on medium heat, 5 minutes on each side. Very tasty. It's our family's favorite.

Barbecued Chicken
...Mrs. Nathan (Barbara) Lehman

1 pt. vinegar
1 pt. water
2 Tbsp. salt
1 Tbsp. black pepper
1/4 c. Worcestershire sauce

Bring to a boil. Four times this recipe is just right for 3 chickens. Soak chicken in brine for 1 hour. Bring to a boil. Simmer for 15 minutes. Grill chicken for 45 minutes, turning and basting with brine every 5 minutes on medium heat. Put in roaster and bake 1 hour at 300°.

Chicken Fajitas

...Mrs. Gerald (Rosanna) Schrock

4 chicken breasts, cooked
3 bell peppers
1 onion
3 Tbsp. cooking oil
1 pkg. soft tortillas, warmed
salsa
sour cream
shredded cheese
tomatoes (optional)

Chop chicken, peppers and onion. Stir fry in a pan with cooking oil until tender. Spoon desired amount into warmed tortilla. Top with desired amounts of remaining ingredients and roll up.

Cheesy Chicken Pizza

...Mrs. Freeman (Mabel) Yoder

1 c. diced, cooked chicken
1 sm. onion, sliced
$\frac{1}{2}$ c. chopped green pepper
$\frac{1}{4}$ c. chopped sweet red pepper
$\frac{1}{4}$ c. mushrooms
1 c. shredded cheddar cheese
1 c. mozzarella cheese
$1\frac{1}{2}$ c. pizza sauce
your favorite pizza dough or
   1 (10 oz.) tube refrigerated
   pizza crust dough

Roll out dough into a 12" circle on a large pizza pan. Spread with pizza sauce. Top with chicken, onion, pepper, mushrooms and cheeses. Bake on lowest rack at 400° for approximately 20 minutes if using store-bought dough. Homemade may take 30-35 minutes.

Zucchini Patties

Mrs. Danny (Vanessa) Reeves

4 c. shredded zucchini
2 eggs
$\frac{1}{2}$ c. flour
1 small onion, chopped
salt and pepper

Beat eggs, then add all other ingredients and mix well. Fry in oil over medium-high heat until golden brown. Serve with mayonnaise and tomatoes on buns or bread.

Barbecue Chicken Pizza

...daughter, Amy Yoder

4 lg. boneless chicken breasts
1 c. chopped green peppers
1/2 c. chopped onion
1 c. chopped ham
2 (8 oz.) pkg. mozzarella cheese
prepared mustard
1/2 c. barbecue sauce
1 c. pizza sauce
pizza dough
2 Tbsp. oil

Prepare your favorite pizza dough. Cut chicken in bite-size pieces and sauté chicken and onions in oil until chicken is tender. Place pizza dough in 15" x 10" x 1" pan. Spread a thin layer of prepared mustard on dough. Combine barbecue sauce and pizza sauce and spread evenly over mustard. Bake at 375° approximately 20 minutes, then spread chicken, ham, peppers and cheese over dough and bake an additional 15 minutes or until pizza dough is lightly browned on the bottom. A unique and different pizza. Delicious! My specialty!

Potluck Chicken Casserole

...Mrs. John (Susan) Lehman

1/2 c. mushrooms
3 Tbsp. finely chopped onions
2 garlic cloves, minced
4 Tbsp. butter
3 Tbsp. flour
1 1/4 c. milk
3/4 c. mayonnaise
4 c. cooked chicken
3 c. cooked rice
1 c. chopped celery
1 c. frozen peas, thawed
2 tsp. lemon juice
1 tsp. salt
1/2 tsp. pepper
3/4 c. coarsely crushed cornflakes

Sauté mushrooms, onion and garlic in 3 Tbsp. butter until tender. Stir in flour, gradually add milk and bring to a boil. Cook and stir for 2 minutes or until thickened. Remove from heat and add mayonnaise. Add rest of ingredients, mixing well. Melt 1 Tbsp. butter and toss with cornflake crumbs. Sprinkle over casserole. Bake uncovered at 350° for 30-35 minutes.

Chicken Potato Bake ...Mrs. Freeman (Mabel) Yoder

3 lb. chicken	Place chicken in a greased 9" x 13" pan.
1 lb. red potatoes, chunked	Arrange potatoes around chicken. Drizzle
³/₄ c. Italian salad dressing	with dressing; sprinkle with Italian seasoning
1 Tbsp. Italian seasoning	and Parmesan cheese. Cover and bake at 400°
³/₄ c. grated Parmesan cheese	for 20 minutes. Uncover; bake for 20-30
	minutes longer or until potatoes are tender
	and chicken juices run clear.
	*Pictured on the front cover of this cookbook.

Chicken Supreme Casserole
...Mrs. Harry (Edna Mae) Bontrager

2 c. cooked and diced chicken	Mix all ingredients together except cheese. Put
2 c. milk	in greased casserole dish and refrigerate
1 med. onion, diced	overnight. Remove from refrigerator several
¹/₄ tsp. pepper	hours before baking. Bake at 350° for 1¹/₂
2 c. uncooked macaroni	hours. Top with cheese during the last part of
2 cans cream of chicken soup	baking. You can cook macaronis and drain
¹/₂ tsp. salt	water off. Mix everything together and bake
3 Tbsp. cheese, melted	for only 45 minutes to an hour. Takes less
	milk if macaronis are cooked.

Chicken in Foil Dinner
...Mrs. Jonathan (Naomi) Wagler

1 chicken leg or thigh	Place chicken in center of 18" x 15" piece of
1 med. potato, cut into fourths	foil; place potato on side of chicken and the
1 med. carrot, cut into ¹/₄" slices	carrots on the other. Mix instant soups with
1 individual serving instant	water until thickened and spoon over chicken.
cream of chicken soup	Top with green beans. Wrap securely and
1 individual serving instant	place on ungreased cookie sheet. Bake at 450°
onion soup	for 50 minutes.
¹/₂ c. water	Note: This could be doubled for 2 people and
¹/₂ c. green beans	you could substitute round steak for chicken.

Chicken Casserole

...Mrs. Danny (Vanessa) Reeves

3 c. diced cooked chicken
$^1\!/_2$ c. celery
$^1\!/_2$ c. green peppers
$^1\!/_2$ c. salad dressing
1 tsp. pepper
$^1\!/_2$ c. chopped onion
1 tsp. salt
8 slices bread
$^1\!/_2$ c. milk
2 to 3 eggs
1 can cream of mushroom soup
$^1\!/_4$ c. cheese

Mix the first 7 ingredients. Cut bread into cubes and put half of it into a greased 13" x 9" dish. Add chicken mixture. Put remaining bread on top. Mix the milk and eggs well and pour over casserole. Refrigerate overnight. Before baking, top with cream of mushroom soup and cheese. Bake at 350° for 30-40 minutes.

Chicken Casserole

...Mrs. Andrew (Joanna) Hostetler

6-8 med. raw potatoes, shoestring
16 oz. mixed vegetables
3 c. chopped chicken
salt and pepper to taste
1 pt. chicken broth
1 can cream of chicken soup
1 tsp. minced onion
1 c. shredded cheese

Put first 3 ingredients in layers in a baking dish. Add salt and pepper. Heat broth, soup and onion. Pour over layers. Bake for 1 hour at 350° or until potatoes are done. Add the cheese when almost done baking. Also add crushed potato chips if desired.

Rice and Chicken

...Mrs. Samuel (Susie) Hochstetler

1 c. rice
1 c. chopped celery
$^3\!/_4$ c. chopped onion
2 tsp. parsley
$^1\!/_2$ tsp. salt
$^1\!/_4$ tsp. pepper
1 can cream of mushroom soup
$^3\!/_4$ c. salad dressing
2 c. water
cut-up chicken

Place rice in a buttered casserole dish. Mix everything else, except chicken. Pour half of mixture over rice, then place a layer of chicken on top and cover with the rest of the mixture of soup and salad dressing. You may use chicken broth instead of water and recipe may be doubled. This casserole is tops!

Roasted Turkey

...Mrs. Freeman (Mabel) Yoder

12 lb. turkey (whole)
2 lb. bacon
4 c. ice cubes
2 tsp. Lawry's seasoning salt
heavy-duty tinfoil

Place 7 layers of aluminum foil on a large surface. Spread out 1 lb. bacon on foil. Place turkey on top. Sprinkle with seasoning salt. Drape the other 1 lb. of bacon over turkey. Fill turkey cavity with ice cubes. Cover with 7 more layers of foil. Wrap completely tight; place in a large roaster with 1 c. water. Roast slowly in oven at 200° for 8 hours, then turn temperature up to 300° for a few more hours or until done. This works great to pop in the oven the evening before Thanksgiving, and wake up to the wonderful aroma of turkey. Keep checking for doneness after 8 hours and adjust oven temperature accordingly. This can also be done in a fire pit in a bed of coals and completely covered with coals then enclosed with dirt. Leave in coals overnight; ice cubes and the foil keep the moisture in. Wonderful smoked flavor!

Turkey Tacos

...Mrs. Allen (Elsie) Bontrager

8 taco shells or tortillas
   (I use tortillas)
1 Tbsp. vegetable oil
1 lb. ground turkey
¹/₂ c. chopped onion
1 (16 oz.) bag frozen broccoli,
   carrots, cauliflower, thawed
1 (10 oz.) can tomatoes with
   green chilies
1 tsp. ground cumin
1 tsp. garlic salt
1 tsp. dried oregano
shredded cheddar cheese
fresh cilantro leaves (optional)

Warm taco or tortilla shells. In a large skillet over medium-hot heat, heat oil until hot. Fry turkey and add onion. Cook and stir until meat is done and onion tender. Drain. Stir in vegetables, tomatoes, cumin, garlic salt and oregano. Cook and stir until veggies are tender and mixture is hot. Spoon into warm tortilla shells. Garnish with cheddar cheese and cilantro, if desired. Delicious!

Cheesy Turkey Meat Loaf ...Mrs. Freeman (Mabel) Yoder

2 lb. ground turkey
1½ c. crushed soda crackers
¼ c. quick oats
2 eggs
½ c. milk
1¼ tsp. salt
½ tsp. pepper
1 c. shredded cheddar or
   marble cheese
2 smoked sausage links or 4
   regular hot dogs, chopped finely

Sauce:
6 Tbsp. ketchup
2 tsp. mustard
2 Tbsp. brown sugar
⅛ tsp. liquid smoke

Combine eggs, crackers, quick oats, milk, salt and pepper. Add turkey and sausage or hot dogs. Mix well. Add cheese and mix gently. Press firmly into a greased 9" x 13" pan. Bake at 350° for 1 hour. Combine sauce and spread on meat loaf the last 20 minutes of baking, uncovered.

Ham Bake ...Mrs. Willis (Mary Esther) Wagler

½ c. chopped onion
½ c. chopped green pepper
2 Tbsp. butter
1 (10¾ oz.) can cream of
   mushroom soup
1 c. sour cream
1 (8 oz.) pkg. noodles, cooked
2 c. (8 oz.) shredded Swiss cheese
3 c. cubed cooked ham
1 c. bread crumbs
¼ c. butter, melted

In medium skillet sauté onions and green peppers in butter. Stir in soup and sour cream. In 3 qt. buttered casserole, layer ⅓ of noodles, ⅓ of cheese, ⅓ of ham and ½ of sauce; repeat layers one more time. The third layer will have noodles, ham and cheese only. Sauté bread crumbs in ¼ c. butter and sprinkle over casserole. Bake 30-45 minutes in 350° oven.

Taking time for Love is more important
than getting things accomplished.

Barbecued Hot Dogs   ...Mrs. Freeman (Mabel) Yoder

1 c. chopped onion
2 Tbsp. vegetable oil
1 c. ketchup
1/2 c. water
1/2 c. vinegar
2 Tbsp. Worcestershire sauce
3 Tbsp. honey
2 tsp. ground mustard
2 tsp. paprika
1 tsp. salt
2 Tbsp. lemon juice
dash pepper
3 lb. hot dogs or smoked
   sausage links

In a large skillet heat oil; sauté onions until tender. Stir in the next 10 ingredients; simmer. Place hot dogs in a roaster. Pour sauce over all and stir to coat. Bake uncovered at 350° for 20-25 minutes. Serve with hot dog buns.

Wiener Salad Bake   ...Mrs. Ray (LeEtta) Yoder

3 Tbsp. butter
3 Tbsp. flour
1 tsp. salt
1/4 tsp. dry mustard
1/4 tsp. pepper
1 1/2 c. milk
3/4 c. mayonnaise
6 med. size potatoes, cooked
   peeled and diced
1 can cut green beans, drained
1 med. onion, chopped
6 wieners, sliced 1/4" thick
1/2 c. buttered coarse bread
   crumbs

Melt butter in small saucepan. Blend in flour, salt, pepper and mustard. Slowly stir in milk. Cook over medium heat, stirring constantly, until mixture thickens. Remove from heat. Blend in mayonnaise. Measure 1/4 c. sauce and save for later. Fold potatoes, green beans, onion and 3/4 of wiener slices into remaining sauce. Spoon into 10 c. size baking dish. Arrange remaining wieners in a ring on top. Spoon reserved 1/4 c. sauce over wieners; sprinkle with buttered bread crumbs. Bake at 350° for 45 minutes or until bubbly hot.

The will of God will not lead you where the
grace of God cannot keep you.

Ham and Potato Puffs
...Mrs. Jonathan (Naomi) Wagler

3 c. mashed potatoes
1-2 c. chopped ham
2 eggs
parsley
seasonings to taste

Reserve 1 egg white and mix remainder of ingredients together. Form into balls. Brush with beaten egg white and roll in flour. Bake at 350° until brown or fry in deep fat. A good way to use up leftover ham and mashed potatoes.

Sausage and Potato Casserole
...Mrs. Freeman (Mabel) Yoder

Bottom Part:
6-8 qt. potatoes
16 oz. sour cream
$^{1}/_{2}$ c. butter
8 oz. cream cheese
2 tsp. salt
1 c. milk

Boil potatoes until tender, then drain and mash. Add butter, sour cream, cream cheese and salt. Mash thoroughly. Add milk; may need to add more or less. Place in a large roaster.

Top Part:
4 lb. medium pork sausage
2 cans cream of mushroom soup
1$^{1}/_{2}$ lb. Velveeta cheese
6 oz. can French-fried onions
2 pt. whole kernel corn, drained
1 med. pepper, cut up
1 med. onion, chopped
1 c. milk

Fry sausage, onions and pepper. Drain, then add corn, cream of mushroom soup, milk and cheese. Mix well, then place on top of mashed potatoes. Bake at 350° for 30 minutes. Just before serving, sprinkle with French-fried onions. This is always a big hit at potlucks!

Egg and Sausage Casserole
...Mom, Elsie Yoder

8 slices of bread, crumbled
2 lb. sausage, browned and drained
2 c. cubed American cheese
4 eggs, beaten
2$^{1}/_{2}$ c. milk
$^{3}/_{4}$ tsp. prepared mustard
1 c. cream of mushroom soup
$^{1}/_{2}$ c. milk

Place bread crumbs in greased 9" x 13" pan. Sprinkle with cheese. Add browned sausage. Blend eggs, 2$^{1}/_{2}$ c. milk and mustard. Pour over ingredients in pan. Refrigerate several hours or overnight. Blend soup and $^{1}/_{2}$ c. milk. Pour over egg mixture in pan and bake at 350° for $^{3}/_{4}$ hour. Cover while baking.

Baked Egg Omelette ...Mrs. Dennis (Mary) Bontrager

7 slices American cheese
1/2 c. meat (cubed ham, bacon or sausage)
12 eggs
1 1/2 c. milk
1 tsp. salt
dash pepper

Grease bottom of 9" x 13" cake pan and line with cheese slices. Add your choice of meat. Beat remaining ingredients with egg beater. Pour on top of meat and cheese. Bake at 350° for 30-45 minutes or until set. Serve with toast and juice. We enjoy this as a Sunday brunch dish.

Open-Faced Omelette ...Mrs. John (Susan) Lehman

1 c. broccoli florets
1/2 c. chopped sweet red pepper
1/4 c. thinly sliced onions
1 Tbsp. butter
1 1/2 c. cubed fully cooked ham
1 c. shredded potatoes (may use hash browns)
10 eggs
1/4 tsp. pepper
1/2 tsp. salt
1/2 c. shredded cheddar cheese

Sauté veggies in butter in skillet until crisp-tender. Add ham and hash browns. Cook for 2 minutes, stirring frequently. Beat the eggs with pepper and salt. Pour over vegetable mixture. Reduce heat. Cover and cook for 10-12 minutes or until set. Remove from heat and sprinkle on the cheese. Cover to melt cheese, then serve immediately.

Skier's French Toast ...Mrs. Freeman (Mabel) Yoder

1/4 c. light Karo syrup
3/4 c. butter and margarine
1 c. (heaping) brown sugar
1/4 c. water
12 slices bread
8 eggs, beaten
1 1/2 c. milk
1 tsp. vanilla
1/2 tsp. salt
1 lb. sausage, fried, crumbled and drained

Bring first 4 ingredients to a boil in a medium saucepan. Pour into a 9" x 13" cake pan. Place 6 slices bread on top of syrup, then spread sausage on top of bread. Place remaining 6 slices bread on top of sausage. Mix beaten eggs, milk, vanilla and salt and pour over all. Bake at 375° for 45 minutes to 1 hour until set. This is good to fix ahead of time and refrigerate overnight and bake the next morning. When toast is done flip it into a cookie sheet with sides, so the syrup side is up. It's the best!

Chicken Noodles
...Mrs. Christy (Anna) Bontrager

2 qt. chicken pieces
1½ qt. chicken broth
2½ gal. water
1¾ c. chicken soup base
5 lb. noodles
4 cans cream of chicken soup
1 c. water
1 lb. butter, browned

Bring chicken pieces, broth, 2½ gal. water and chicken soup base to a boil, then add noodles. Boil for 5 minutes. Mix cream of chicken soup with 1 c. water. Pour that over the top. Brown butter and pour over top. Do not stir! Put lid on and let set for 1 hour before serving. Yield: 1 (20 qt.) stockpot full. Use this recipe for large crowds, etc. as they do not get mushy and stay delicious. Is best if made with homemade noodles or something very similar.

Cooking Noodles
...Mom, Rosa Bontrager

4½ qt. chicken broth
1½ lb. homemade noodles
4-6 tsp. salt or to suit taste
chicken base or bouillon cubes
   to taste

You may use part water to replace some of the broth. Place broth and salt in a large kettle and bring to a boil. Reduce to a simmer and add noodles. Continue simmering for 5 minutes. Take from heat and let set covered until noodles are tender. Add chicken base to taste. When using store-bought noodles, use slightly more noodles.

Zucchini Casserole ...Mrs. Freeman (Mabel) Yoder

3 eggs
½ c. flour
½ tsp. salt
1 c. grated cheese or Velveeta
3 Tbsp. butter, softened
1½ tsp. baking powder
¼ c. chopped onion
2 c. shredded zucchini
2 c. fried meat of your choice (optional)

Beat eggs and butter; add flour, salt, baking powder, onion and cheese. Mix well. Fold in zucchinni and meat. Pour into a greased 7" x 11" pan. Sprinkle with pepper and parsley flakes. Bake at 350°.

Dressing Noodle Casserole

...Mrs. Lonnie (Norma) Bontrager

Dressing:

1 c. chopped celery
1/2 c. chopped carrots
1 sm. onion, chopped
1 med. potato, chopped
1 qt. chicken broth
1 1/2 loaf bread, cubed
8 eggs, beaten
1 1/2 tsp. sage (optional)
salt to taste
2 Tbsp. chicken base

Cook celery, carrots and potato. Mix dressing and put in large roaster.

1 lb. noodles, cooked
1 1/2 lb. Velveeta cheese
3 cans cream of chicken soup
3 cans cream of mushroom soup
3 cans cream of celery soup

Next put cooked noodles on top of dressing, then cheese. Mix and heat soups together. Pour over top.

Seven Layer Hot Dish

...Mrs. Ray (LeEtta) Yoder

3/4 c. potato buds
1 (5 oz.) can chunk chicken
1/4 c. chopped onions
1 c. frozen peas, boiled for 1 minute, then drained
1 can cream of chicken soup
3/4 c. milk
1/2 c. bread crumbs
1 c. grated American cheese

Put potato buds in a well buttered casserole dish. Add chicken, onion, peas, soup and milk. Mix bread crumbs and grated cheese together and put on top. Bake at 350° for 1 hour.

Garden Scramble

...Mrs. Freeman (Mabel) Yoder
...Mrs. James (Ida) Lehman

1 med. zucchini, peeled and cubed
1 sm. butternut squash, peeled and cubed
2 lg. potatoes, cubed
2 lg. red potatoes, cubed
1 med. green pepper
1 med. sweet red pepper
1 sm. onion, sliced
3 med. carrots, chopped
4 garlic cloves, peeled
1 tsp. dried basil and oregano
2 tsp. salt
1 tsp. garlic salt
$^1/_2$ tsp. pepper
$^1/_2$ c. olive or canola oil

In a large bowl toss all ingredients until well coated. Arrange in single layers in 15" x 10" pans. Bake uncovered at 425° for 25-30 minutes or until veggies are tender, stirring occasionally. Truly a Harvest special. Ida does not add carrots and uses a little less oil.

Five Veggie Casserole

...Mrs. Freeman (Mabel) Yoder

2 c. fresh or frozen cut green beans
2 c. chopped celery
$1^1/_2$ c. baby carrots or chopped
$1^1/_2$ c. sliced onions
$^3/_4$ c. chopped green pepper
2 c. diced tomatoes
$^1/_4$ c. butter, melted
3 Tbsp. quick-cooking granulated tapioca or flour
1 Tbsp. sugar
1 tsp. salt
$^1/_2$ tsp. pepper
1 (2.8 oz.) can French-fried onions

In a large bowl combine the beans, celery, onions, carrots, green peppers and tomatoes. Add butter, tapioca or flour, sugar, salt and pepper; mix well. Pour into a 9" x 13" pan or casserole dish. Cover and bake at 350° for 50 minutes. Uncover and sprinkle French fried onions on top. Bake 5 minutes longer or until veggies are tender. May add American cheese too.

Vegetable and Biscuit Casserole

...Mrs. Simon (Esta) Miller

Gravy:
1 qt. chicken broth
1 env. onion soup mix
1/4 c. chicken base
1 can mushroom soup
1 env. brown gravy mix
1 env. mushroom gravy mix
2 Tbsp. Worcestershire sauce

Make gravy with first 7 ingredients. Season with salt, pepper and a dash of garlic. Thicken slightly with 1/2 c. flour and enough water to make paste. Bring to a boil and add Velveeta cheese. Melt. Set aside and cook vegetables separately.

1 lg. bag baby carrots
10 potatoes, peeled and cut up
2 cans mushrooms (optional)
2 qt. frozen peas
3 cans tube biscuits

Pour gravy over carrots, potatoes and mushrooms and put in large roaster. Bake at 350° until heated through. Remove from oven and stir in frozen peas. Now top with biscuits. I cut biscuits in smaller pieces. Bake at 400° until biscuits are browned and baked through. Brush with butter and sprinkle with garlic salt. Very tasty.

Salsify Fritters

...Mrs. Willis (Mary Esther) Wagler

2 c. salsify, cooked and drained
1 c. flour
1 1/2 tsp. baking powder
1/2 tsp. salt
1 Tbsp. sugar
1 egg, beaten
1/2 c. + 1 Tbsp. milk

Combine flour, baking powder, salt, sugar, egg and milk to mashed salsify. Drop in hot oil, then drain on paper towel. Yield: 12-15 fritters. Salsify is a vegetable. A root crop lighter in color than carrots and has its own distinctive flavor.

> Gratitude is not only the greatest of virtues,
> but the parent of all others.
> —Cicero

Potato Ranch Casserole

...Mrs. Freeman (Mabel) Yoder

2-3 lb. hamburger
1 med. onion, chopped
2 cans cream of mushroom soup
4 qt. cooked and shredded
   potatoes
16 oz. sour cream
2 c. Ranch dressing
16 oz. mozzarella or marbled
   cheese
1 lb. bacon, fried and crumbled

Brown hamburger and onions. Add a dash of salt and pepper. Drain. Mix soups and hamburger and place in a large roaster. Place potatoes on top of hamburger. Mix sour cream and Ranch dressing. Spread evenly over potatoes. Bake at 325° for 45 minutes or until heated through. Sprinkle cheese and bacon on top. Bake until cheese melts. Pepperoni may be placed on top instead of bacon.

Country Potato Casserole

...Mrs. Melvin (Mary) Stutzman

4 lb. Country seasoned sausage, fried
16 c. cooked, shredded potatoes
2 peppers, chopped

Sauce:
6 c. water
2 c. milk
1¼ c. flour
3 Tbsp. parsley flakes
3 tsp. celery salt
2 Tbsp. chicken base
3 Tbsp. sour cream and
   onion powder
2 tsp. seasoning salt
2 Tbsp. Worcestershire sauce
1 lb. Velveeta cheese

Heat water and thicken with milk and flour. With wire whisk mix in spices and cheese. Mix all together and bake until hot. Yield: 30 servings.

Scalloped Potatoes ...Mrs. Roy (Lovina) Yoder

6-7 qt. potatoes, cooked, sliced or shoestring

Sauce:
1 c. butter, browned
$2^1/_2$ qt. milk
1 c. chopped onion
3 Tbsp. ham seasoning
1 Tbsp. salt
2 c. flour
3 cans cream of chicken soup
2 c. Velveeta cheese
16 oz. sour cream (optional)

Brown butter. Add milk and onion. Heat and add ham seasoning and salt. Add milk to flour to make a thin paste. Add to mixture, stirring until boiling. Remove from heat. Add chicken soup, Velveeta and sour cream if desired. Mix together and bake at 300° for 45 minutes or until heated.

Crusty Baked Potatoes
...Mrs. Samuel (Susie) Hochstetler

6 med. potatoes
4 Tbsp. butter, melted
$^1/_2$ c. cracker crumbs
1 tsp. salt

Wash and pare potatoes. Cut in halves and roll in melted butter, then in cracker crumbs with salt added. Place in greased pan. Bake at 350° for 1 hour.

Grilled Potato Fans ...Mrs. James (Ida) Lehman

6 med. baking potatoes
2 med. onions, finely chopped
6 Tbsp. butter, cubed
$^1/_4$ c. celery, finely chopped
2 tsp. salt
1 tsp. dried oregano
1 tsp. onion powder
1 tsp. black pepper

With sharp knife make cuts $^1/_2$" apart in each potato, leaving slices attached at bottom. Fan the potatoes slightly. Place each on a piece of heavy-duty foil. Insert onions and butter between potato slices. Sprinkle with celery, salt, oregano, onion powder and pepper. Fold foil around potatoes and seal tightly. Grill over medium-hot heat for 40-45 minutes. Yield: 6 servings. To cut down on grilling time, cook potatoes 7 minutes before slicing them.

Holiday Mashed Potatoes

...Mrs. Sam (Mary) Hershberger ...Mrs. Andrew (Joanna) Hostetler

12 med. potatoes
8 oz. cream cheese
1/2 c. butter
1/2 c. sour cream
2 eggs, beaten
1/2 c. milk
1 tsp. salt
pepper
1 tsp. baking powder

Cook and mash potatoes. Add cream cheese in small bits to hot potatoes. Add butter and sour cream. Mix well. Combine milk and eggs. Add and mix well. Add salt and pepper to taste. Add baking powder. Beat until light and fluffy. Place in 9" round casserole or 9" x 13" pan. Bake at 375° for 30-40 minutes. Can be refrigerated overnight. Joanna does not use eggs and baking powder and adds 1/2-1 tsp. minced garlic or salt.

Caramel Sweet Potatoes

...Mrs. Jonathan (Wilma) Hochstetler

5 med. sweet potatoes or
   #2 1/2 can
1 tsp. salt
1 c. brown sugar
2 Tbsp. butter
3 Tbsp. flour
8 marshmallows
1 c. cream

Cook potatoes until tender. Cut in half lengthwise and arrange in greased baking dish. Mix salt, sugar and flour. Pour over potatoes. Dot with butter and add marshmallows. Pour cream over all. Bake at 350° for 40-45 minutes.

Taco Filled Peppers

...Mrs. Orlie (Mary) Troyer

1 lb. hamburger
1 pkg. taco seasoning mix
1 (8 oz.) can kidney beans,
   drained
1 c. salsa or pizza sauce
4 med. green peppers
1 med. tomato, diced
1/2 c. shredded cheddar cheese
1/2 c. sour cream

In large skillet brown hamburger. Drain. Stir in taco seasoning, kidney beans and salsa. Bring to boil, then simmer for 5 minutes. Cut peppers in half lengthwise. Remove stems and seeds. Immerse peppers in boiling water for 3 minutes. Drain. Spoon about 1/2 c. meat mixture in each half. Bake at 350° for 15-20 minutes. Top each with a dollop sour cream, tomatoes and cheese. Serve immediately.

Garden Ranch Pizza

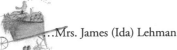

...Mrs. James (Ida) Lehman

use your favorite pizza crust
³/₄ c. Ranch dressing
2 c. shredded mozzarella
  cheese, divided
1 c. coarsely chopped broccoli
¹/₂ c. diced red or green bell
  pepper
1 med. carrot, grated
¹/₂ c. sliced black olives
¹/₄ c. Parmesan cheese

Preheat oven to 425°. Roll out your pizza dough onto pizza pan or cookie sheet. Spread Ranch dressing evenly over unbaked crust. Top with half of mozzarella cheese. Sprinkle vegetables and olives over pizza; top with remaining mozzarella cheese and Parmesan cheese. Bake 18-22 minutes or until edges are golden brown. Remove from oven; let stand 10 minutes. Cut into wedges. Yield: 16 servings.

Zesty Fried Green Tomatoes

...Mrs. John (Susan) Lehman

4 med. green tomatoes,
  sliced ¹/₄" thick
salt
¹/₂ c. cornmeal
¹/₂ c. grated Parmesan cheese
3 Tbsp. flour
¹/₂ tsp. garlic salt
¹/₂ tsp. oregano
¹/₂ tsp. ginger
dash red pepper
2 eggs

Sprinkle both sides of tomatoes with salt and let stand 10 minutes. Combine cornmeal, cheese, flour and seasonings. In another bowl place eggs and beat. Pat tomatoes dry. Dip into eggs and coat with dry mixture. Fry in butter until golden brown. Drain on paper towel.

Zucchini Fritters

...Mrs. Marvin (Mary Ann) Schrock

¹/₂ c. milk
1 egg, lightly beaten
1 c. flour
1¹/₂ tsp. baking powder
¹/₂ (1 oz.) pkg. Hidden Valley
  Ranch mix
2 c. shredded zucchini

Fill a deep fat fryer or skillet with oil to a 2" depth. Heat to 375°. Meanwhile combine milk and egg in a mixing bowl. Stir together dry ingredients and add to egg mixture; blend well. Fold in zucchini. Drop mixture by teaspoonful into hot oil. Fry until a deep golden brown, turning at least once. Drain off oil on paper towel. Enjoy with salad dressing or salsa or sour cream dip.
Note: Adding salt to the batter or salting the fritters after they are fried is delicious.

Zucchini Potato Casserole

...Mrs. Freeman (Mabel) Yoder

2-3 qt. shoestring potatoes
4 c. finely shredded zucchini
1/2 c. chopped onion
1 qt. canned sausage or 1 lb.
  bulk sausage
1 (10 1/2 oz.) can cream of
  mushroom soup
1/2-1 c. milk
16 American cheese slices
salt and pepper
1 (8 oz.) pkg. precooked
  bacon bits

Peel and fry potatoes until partially soft. Pour into a 9" x 13" cake pan or roaster; sprinkle with salt and pepper to taste. Layer on the zucchini, onion and sausage. (If using bulk sausage, fry it and drain.) Mix mushroom soup and milk; pour over all. Put cheese on top. Cover with tinfoil and bake at 350° for 35-40 minutes. Uncover and top with bacon bits and bake 5 more minutes. Ingredients may be double layered in a large roaster.

Carrot Zucchini Fritters

...Mrs. Freeman (Mabel) Yoder

3 Tbsp. chopped onion
1 Tbsp. butter
1 egg, lightly beaten
2 med. zucchini, shredded
  (about 1 1/2 c.)
1 lg. carrot, shredded
1/3 c. flour
1/3 c. Parmesan cheese
1 Tbsp. cornmeal
1/2 tsp. salt
1/4 tsp. pepper

Mix everything together in order given just until combined. In a large skillet heat 1/4 c. oil and drop by tablespoon into hot oil and fry until browned on both sides. Serve with horseradish or eat on bread. Spread with mayonnaise or salad dressing and eat with a slice of tomato on top.

Zucchini Patties

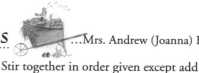

...Mrs. Andrew (Joanna) Hostetler

1/3 c. Bisquick
1/4 c. melting cheese
1/8 tsp. pepper
1/4 tsp. salt
2 eggs, slightly beaten
2 c. shredded zucchini, drained
2 Tbsp. butter
2 Tbsp. chopped onion

Stir together in order given except add zucchini last. Fry in butter like pancakes.

Zucchini Patties

...Mrs. Freeman (Mabel) Yoder

1 c. flour
³/₄ c. grated Parmesan cheese
1 tsp. dried oregano
¹/₄ tsp. pepper
³/₄ tsp. salt
3 c. shredded zucchini
2 eggs, beaten
¹/₄ c. chopped onion
¹/₄ c. mayonnaise
butter

In a bowl combine flour, cheese, oregano, pepper and salt. Beat eggs. Add zucchini, onion and mayonnaise. Add flour mixture and mix well. In a large skillet melt butter and fry pancakes until golden on both sides. Serve with sour cream, ketchup, tomatoes or mayonnaise. This is a main supper sandwich for us during the summer.

Breaded Zucchini Slices

...Mrs. Freeman (Mabel) Yoder

12-16 thin zucchini slices
3 eggs, beaten
¹/₄ c. (scant) milk
breading for zucchini (found at end of this section)
3 Tbsp. margarine
flour

Peel zucchini and slice thinly. Heat a large 12" skillet over medium heat. Add margarine and melt. Roll zucchini slices in flour. Combine eggs and milk, then dip floured slices in egg mixture, then in breading and place slices in skillet until skillet is evenly covered. Pour remaining egg and milk mixture over slices in skillet. Cover and fry until golden, then flip it over and continue frying only partially covered. This helps to get them crisp. Serve on bread with salad dressing or mayonnaise and tomatoes. Very good!

Zucchini Casserole

...Mrs. Edna Slabaugh

1 zucchini squash
1 onion
1 can cream of mushroom soup
6 slices cheese
salt to taste
1 c. buttered bread crumbs

Slice squash into buttered 1¹/₂ qt. baking dish. Add salt. Pour soup over squash. Add diced onion. Sprinkle with bread crumbs and arrange cheese slices over top. Or use crushed potato chips (barbecued) instead of bread crumbs. Bake at 350° for 30 minutes.

Eggplant Slices

...Mrs. Freeman (Mabel) Yoder

12 slices eggplant ($1/8$" thick)
3 eggs
$1/4$ c. (scant) milk
$1/4$ c. margarine
fish breading (found at the
   end of this section)

Peel and slice eggplant from narrow end (using seedy parts is fine). Beat eggs and milk. In a heavy 12" skillet heat margarine over medium heat. Dip eggplant in flour, then in egg mixture, then in breading. Place slices in pan. Use more slices if necessary to fill pan with a single layer. Pour remaining eggs over eggplant slices slowly to cover it all. Cover loosely and fry to a deep golden, then flip to brown the other side. Cut into pieces and serve with tomato slices on bread with mayonnaise or salad dressing. This is one of our favorite summer sandwiches and tastes similar to zucchini.

Broccoli Casserole

...Mrs. Freeman (Mabel) Yoder

2 lb. fresh broccoli, chopped
1 can cream of mushroom soup
$1/2$ c. mayonnaise
1 c. shredded cheddar cheese
1 Tbsp. lemon juice
1 c. crushed cheese-flavored
   snack crackers

Wash and place broccoli in a heavy saucepan. Steam 6-8 minutes until crisp-tender. Place in a casserole dish. In a bowl combine soup, mayonnaise, cheese and lemon juice. Pour over broccoli. Sprinkle with crushed cracker crumbs. Bake uncovered 20-30 minutes until heated through.

Baked Corn

...Mrs. Jonathan (Wilma) Hochstetler

2 Tbsp. lard
2 Tbsp. flour
$1 1/2$ c. milk
1 tsp. salt
$1/4$ tsp. mustard
$1/4$ tsp. paprika
2 c. cooked corn
1 egg, slightly beaten
1 Tbsp. Worcestershire sauce
buttered crumbs

Make a sauce of lard, flour, milk and seasonings. Add corn, egg and Worcestershire sauce. Pour into baking dish, cover with buttered crumbs and bake at 350° for 15-20 minutes or until heated through.

Cajun Style Beans
...Mrs. LaVern (Martha) Yoder

1 lb. ground chuck
4 c. pork and beans
¹/₂ c. ketchup
1 c. onions
1 tsp. salt
1 Tbsp. mustard
¹/₂ tsp. cayenne pepper
¹/₂ c. brown sugar
1 lb. crisply fried bacon
¹/₂ c. green pepper (optional)

Brown meat, onions, pepper and chopped green peppers. Add to beans and salt. Add ketchup, mustard and brown sugar. Stir in bacon and place in casserole dish and bake at 350° for 35 minutes.

Gravy to Put on Biscuits

...Mrs. Edward (Lizzie Ann) Schrock

1 c. shortening
flour
hot water
milk
1 Tbsp. Worcestershire sauce
4 med. potatoes, peeled, cubed
4 eggs, cooked for 12 min.
approx. 1 lb. hamburger or
    sausage, fried or canned

Melt shortening in skillet. Add enough flour to soak up all the shortening, then let it brown. Add some hot water, a little at a time; keep stirring. Then add milk and bring to a boil. Add enough milk until thin enough. Add Worcestershire sauce and salt and pepper. Cook potatoes in a little bit of water. Add potatoes and water to hot gravy plus diced eggs and crumbled meat. Ready to serve with your favorite biscuits or toasted bread.

Pan Gravy
...Mom, Elsie Yoder

1 c. lard
2 c. flour
3 qt. cold water, divided
1 can cream of mushroom soup
1 soup can milk
1 tsp. Kitchen Banquet seasoning
1 Tbsp. salt or to taste
1 tsp. black pepper

In a pan or skillet add lard and flour. Fry together until brown. Add 1 qt. cold water, mushroom soup and milk. Stir with whip and add 2 more qt. water and seasonings. Ready to serve.

Soy Sauce Marinade   ...Mrs. Danny (Vanessa) Reeves

1/2 c. soy sauce
2 Tbsp. cider vinegar
1/4 c. water
1 Tbsp. vegetable oil
1 tsp. sugar
1 tsp. ginger
garlic powder to taste

Mix all ingredients and marinate meat at least 3-4 hours. Excellent with chicken breasts.

Marinating Sauce for Meat
...Mrs. Orlie (Mary) Troyer

1 1/2 c. vegetable oil
3/4 c. soy sauce
1/3 c. lemon juice
1/2 c. vinegar
2 tsp. salt
2 tsp. pepper
2 tsp. dried parsley flakes
1/4 c. Worcestershire sauce
2 Tbsp. dry mustard

Mix all ingredients together with a wire whisk. Pour over meat to cover completely and marinate 2 hours or more. The longer you soak it the more tender your meat will be. Can be used for chicken, steak or whatever. We use it for our wild meat.

Golden Ember Barbecue Sauce
...Mrs. Willis (Mary) Bontrager

1 c. butter
1/2 c. mustard
1 c. brown sugar
2 c. ketchup
1/2 c. ReaLemon
2 Tbsp. paprika
2 tsp. black pepper
1 Tbsp. Worcestershire sauce
1 Tbsp. salt
1 tsp. Tabasco sauce

Mix together and heat to boiling. Use hot on chicken.

Barbecue Chicken Sauce...Mrs. LaVern (Martha) Yoder

2 c. vinegar
2 c. water
1/2 c. butter
5 Tbsp. Worcestershire sauce
1 Tbsp. black pepper
1/2 c. salt
1 Tbsp. garlic powder

Bring to a boil and put chicken pieces into sauce. Cook at a rolling boil for 5 minutes, then drain and put on hot grill until both sides are golden brown. Put in roaster and pour sauce over all. Finish in oven until soft and ready to eat. You can dip chicken into sauce a few times while grilling also.

Cheese Sauce

...Mom, Elsie Yoder

1 lb. butter, melted
2 1/2 c. flour
10 c. milk
1 box Velveeta cheese

Gradually add flour to butter. Add milk slowly. Use a wire whip to stir. Add cheese. Serve with haystacks or baked potatoes.

Crunchy Fish Coating   ...Mrs. Allen (Elsie) Bontrager

2 1/2 c. coarse cornmeal
1/2 c. whole wheat flour
1 tsp. onion powder
1 tsp. garlic pepper
1 1/2 tsp. Lawry's seasoning salt
2 tsp. salt
5 eggs
3/4 c. milk
3 Tbsp. canola oil

Mix cornmeal, flour, onion powder, garlic pepper, seasoning salt and salt in a bowl and set aside. In another bowl prepare eggs and milk. Beat together well. Heat oil in a skillet; make sure the bottom is well covered. Dip fish fillets in egg/milk mixture, then coat with cornmeal mixture. Fry on medium-high heat until golden brown on both sides. If you like fish, you will like this. A crisp, crunchy flavorful coating.

Zucchini, Fish and Chicken Coating
...Mrs. Freeman (Mabel) Yoder

1 1/4 lb. white crackers
1 (15 oz.) box Rice Krispies
1 (18 oz.) box cornflakes
1/4 c. salt
2 tsp. garlic powder
1 Tbsp. onion salt
1 1/2 Tbsp. paprika
1 box Frying Magic

Crush crackers, Rice Krispies and cornflakes very fine and mix well. Add salt, garlic powder, onion salt, paprika and Frying Magic. Mix thoroughly. Yield: approx. 5 1/2 qt. Store in airtight containers. Use in any recipe asking for cracker mixture.

*Provideth her meat in the summer and
gathereth her food in the harvest.*
Proverbs 6:8

Desserts

My Pantry Shelves

My mind is built like pantry shelves,
And each a purpose serves;
They do not hold mere pots and pans,
Nor cakes, pies and preserves.

The top shelf is my shelf of hope,
Of love and all that's pure;
A dish of grace to snack upon,
Freed of temptation's lure.

The next shelf holds my cluttered plans
That turned to crumbs, decayed;
It's the delight of scoffers all,
And has me sore dismayed.

The next shelf's piled with packages
Of promises unfulfilled;
These are sweetened with alibis,
To cure "digestion's ills."

The lower shelf, I'm ashamed to say,
Holds discontentment's tears,
My envies, hates, pride, jealousies,
My selfishness and fears.

My shelves are my secret domain,
And I would have those hid
That hold my peeves and meannesses
And the loveless deeds I did.

Oh, that my thoughts could ever dwell
Upon the highest shelf,
And live in Christ's celestial light,
Where I can die to self!

Fruit Cobbler

...Mrs. David (Lydia) Schwartz

1 c. flour
3/4 c. sugar
1/4 tsp. salt
2 eggs
1 1/2 tsp. baking powder
1/3 c. butter
1 tsp. vanilla
3-4 c. pie filling (your choice)

Beat eggs. Add sugar; beat until creamy. Add butter and beat again. Add rest of ingredients except pie filling. Pour pie filling into 9" x 13" pan. Then put batter on top, dropping with a spoon. Bake at 350° for 30-40 minutes or until done.

Cherry Crisp

...Mrs. John (Susan) Lehman

Pastry:
1/4 tsp. salt
1/2 c. packed brown sugar
1 c. all-purpose flour
1/2 c. butter

In mixing bowl combine salt, sugar and flour. Cut in butter. Press into 11" x 7" baking dish. Bake at 350° for 15 minutes.

Filling:
1 c. sugar
1/4 c. cornstarch
1 c. cherry juice
4 c. pitted tart red cherries
few drops red food coloring
 (optional)

Combine sugar and cornstarch in pan. Stir in juice. Cook over medium heat until thick, stirring constantly. Fold in cherries. Pour over crust and put topping on. Bake 20-25 minutes or until golden brown and bubbly around edge. Yield: 6-8 servings.

Topping:
1 1/2 c. quick-cooking oats
1/2 c. packed brown sugar
1/4 c. flour
5 Tbsp. butter, melted

Christ can do wonders with a broken heart if given all the pieces.

Berry Marble Cobbler …Mrs. Wayne (Ruth) Raber

1 c. white sugar, divided
1 c. flour
2 tsp. baking powder
¼ tsp. salt
½ c. milk
½ tsp. vanilla
1 Tbsp. butter
1 c. berries of your choice
¾ c. juice or water, boiling

Mix ½ c. sugar, flour, baking powder and salt. Stir in milk, vanilla and butter. Put batter in 10" x 6" x 2" pan. Scatter berries over batter. Put ½ c. sugar over the berries and juice or water over it all. Serve warm with milk. Bake at 375° for 25-30 minutes.

Peach Cobbler …Mrs. Dennis (Mary) Bontrager

3 eggs
¼ c. water
1 c. white sugar
1½ c. flour
1 tsp. (scant) salt
1½ tsp. baking powder
2 tsp. vanilla
1 qt. canned peaches and half of the juice*

Put peaches with the juice in a 9" x 13" cake pan. In a large bowl combine the rest of ingredients in the order given. Pour batter over the peaches and bake at 350° for 35-40 minutes or until toothpick inserted in center comes out clean. Serve with milk. *Canned blueberries can be used instead of the peaches. This is an old family favorite.

Kentucky Peach Cobbler …Mrs. Dennis (Mary) Bontrager

4 c. canned peaches
2 Tbsp. butter, melted
¾ c. sugar, divided
1 tsp. vanilla
1 c. flour
2 tsp. baking powder
dash of salt
½ c. milk
½ c. cold water

Arrange peaches in a greased 11" x 7" x 2" baking pan. In mixing bowl combine butter and ⅓ c. sugar. Beat in vanilla. Combine the flour, baking powder and salt; add to creamed mixture alternately with the milk. Pour over peaches and sprinkle with remaining sugar. Pour cold water over top. Bake at 350° for 35-40 minutes and until lightly golden. Very good served with vanilla ice cream.

Zucchini Cobbler

...Mrs. Ed (Mary) Slabaugh

8 c. chopped, seeded, peeled
  zucchini (about 3 lb.)
²/₃ c. lemon juice
1 c. sugar
1 tsp. cinnamon
¹/₂ tsp. nutmeg

In a large saucepan over medium heat cook and stir zucchini and lemon juice for 15-20 minutes or until zucchini is tender. Add sugar, cinnamon and nutmeg; simmer 1 minute longer. Remove from heat; set aside.

Crust:
4 c. all-purpose flour
2 c. sugar
1¹/₂ c. cold butter or margarine
1 tsp. cinnamon

For crust combine the flour and sugar in a bowl; cut in butter until the mixture resembles coarse crumbs. Stir ¹/₂ c. into zucchini mixture. Press half of remaining crumb mixture into a greased 15" x 10" x 1" baking pan. Spread zucchini over top; crumble remaining crust mixture over zucchini. Sprinkle with cinnamon. Bake at 375° for 35-40 minutes or until golden and bubbly. Yield: 16-20 servings. This is my surprise dessert! No one ever guesses that the "secret ingredient" is zucchini. It tastes like apples. Delicious!

Apple Crisp

...Mrs. Gerald (Rosanna) Schrock

¹/₂ c. sugar
2 Tbsp. flour
¹/₄ tsp. salt
1 tsp. cinnamon
1¹/₂ qt. sliced apples

Mix first 4 ingredients together and add to apples and mix. Put in a greased 9" x 13" pan and top with topping.

Topping:
1 c. uncooked oatmeal
1 c. brown sugar
1 c. flour
¹/₄ tsp. baking soda
¹/₂ tsp. baking powder
²/₃ c. butter

Mix until crumbly. Bake at 350° until brown and crust is formed. Serve with milk or cream. This is delicious hot or cold.
Variation: This is also very good by replacing the apple mixture with any other kind of fruit pie filling.

Apple Jack ...Mrs. David (Lydia) Schwartz

6-8 med. apples, peeled, grated
1 pkg. graham crackers
2 c. whipped cream, sweetened

Coarsely crumble the graham crackers over the apples and fold in the whipped cream. This should not be fixed long before being served or the crackers will be too soggy. Variation: Bananas, raisins and peanut butter may be added.

Baked Apples ...Mrs. John (Susan) Lehman

1 c. sugar
1/2 c. flour
1 tsp. cinnamon
1 c. brown sugar
1 c. water
2 tsp. butter
8-10 apples, peeled, halved

Boil everything except apples together until thickened. Pour mixture over apples in a 9" x 13" pan. Bake 30-45 minutes in 350° oven or until apples are soft.

Mom's Apple Dumplings ...Mrs. Eli (Martha) Mullet

2/3 c. milk
1/2 tsp. salt
2 c. flour
2 Tbsp. sugar
4 tsp. baking powder
3 Tbsp. shortening

Mix dry ingredients. Crumble in shortening. Stir in milk to make a soft dough. Roll out, then spread with butter, 4 c. chopped apples and cinnamon. Roll up and cut 1" slices. Place in 9" x 13" cake pan and bake at 350° for 3/4 hour. Remove and pour syrup over rolls. Return to oven for 15 minutes. Serve warm with milk.

Syrup:
1 1/2 c. sugar
1 Tbsp. flour
1 Tbsp. butter
1/2 tsp. salt
1 1/2 c. water

Stir all together and bring to a boil.

Peter Pumpkin

...Mrs. Jonathan (Rose) Yoder
...Mrs. John (Susan) Lehman

3 c. pumpkin
3 eggs, beaten
1 (13 oz.) can evaporated milk
  (regular milk can be used)
1 c. sugar
³/₄ tsp. salt
1¹/₂ tsp. cinnamon
³/₄ tsp. cloves
³/₄ tsp. nutmeg
1 c. brown sugar

Mix pumpkin, eggs, milk, sugars and spices together and put into 9" x 13" pan. Sprinkle with white or yellow cake mix. Drizzle ¹/₂ c. melted butter on top and sprinkle nuts over that. Good with ice cream. Bake at 350° for 40-60 minutes.

Pumpkin Torte

...Mrs. Gerald (Rosanna) Schrock

First Part:
24 graham crackers, crushed
¹/₃ c. sugar
¹/₂ c. oleo
8 oz. cream cheese
³/₄ c. sugar
2 eggs

Mix crackers, sugar and oleo and put in a 9" x 13" pan. Top with last 3 ingredients. Bake at 350° for 25-30 minutes.

Second Part:
¹/₂ c. sugar
¹/₂ tsp. salt
3 eggs, separated
¹/₂ c. milk
1 Tbsp. cinnamon
2 c. pumpkin
1 Tbsp. gelatin
¹/₄ c. cold water

Cook sugar, salt, egg yolks, milk, cinnamon and pumpkin until thickened and add gelatin soaked in water to hot mixture and set aside to cool. When cooled, beat the egg whites and add to pumpkin mixture. Pour this on top of cooled crust. Let stand in refrigerator a few hours and top with whipped topping. A family favorite!

A lot of kneeling keeps you in good standing with God.

Strawberry Tapioca

...Mrs. Steve (Martha) Yoder

9 c. water	Bring water and salt to a boil and add tapioca.
1 tsp. salt	Turn off heat and let set for 35 minutes.
1½ c. baby pearl tapioca	Bring to a boil again and add strawberry Jell-O
1 c. strawberry Jell-O	and raspberry Jell-O. Take off heat and cool.
⅓ c. raspberry Jell-O	When mixture is cold add ice cream and
½ gal. vanilla ice cream	strawberries. I prefer to not mix in ice cream
1½ pt. strawberries	and strawberries until we are ready to serve it.
	Very refreshing on a hot summer day.

Strawberry Freeze

...Mrs. Christy (Anna) Bontrager

Crust:

½ c. butter	Mix in a stainless steel bowl. Bake in a bowl
½ c. chopped nuts	for 20 minutes, stirring often. Cool. Crumble
¼ c. brown sugar	⅔ of it in a pan. Save the other ⅓ for top.
1 c. flour	

Filling:

3 egg whites	Put egg whites, strawberries, sugar and lemon
2 c. crushed fresh or frozen	juice in bowl and beat for 15 minutes or until
strawberries	mixture is thick and holds its shape. Add Cool
1 c. sugar	Whip. Spread over crumbs. Sprinkle
1 Tbsp. lemon juice	remaining crumbs on top. Freeze at least 5
1 c. Cool Whip or whipping	hours. Doubled fills a 13" x 9" pan. If using
cream	frozen strawberries, drain off some juice.

Strawberry Pizza

...Mrs. Marvin (Mary Ann) Schrock

1½ c. flour	Mix flour, butter, sugar and pecans together to
1 c. butter	form a dough. Spread onto a pizza pan and
¼ c. brown sugar	bake at 400° for 15 minutes. Mix cream
½ c. chopped pecans	cheese and powdered sugar. Fold in whipped
1 (8 oz.) pkg. cream cheese	topping. Spread on top of cooled crust. Chill
¾ c. powdered sugar	well. Top with your favorite strawberry pie
8 oz. whipped topping	filling. Chill thoroughly and serve presto!

Easy Fruit Pizza

...Mrs. Eli (Martha) Mullet

1 box yellow cake mix
1 (8 oz.) cream cheese
1 c. powdered sugar
2 c. Rich's topping

Mix cake mix as directed on box and bake on 18" x 12" baking sheet. Mix cream cheese with powdered sugar. Whip the topping and mix with cream cheese/sugar mixture. Spread over cake mix.

Sauce:
5 c. water
1½ c. sugar
1 pkg. lime Kool-Aid
¼ tsp. salt
1 tsp. vanilla
⅔ c. Perma-Flo
1 c. water

Mix first 5 ingredients and bring to a boil. Mix Perma-Flo and water and stir into mixture. Bring to a boil again until it thickens. When cool stir in apples, oranges, grapes, etc. Spoon over cake.

Pretzel Fruit Pizza

...Mrs. Freeman (Mabel) Yoder

2½ c. finely crushed pretzels
⅔ c. brown sugar
1 c. butter
1 (14 oz.) can sweetened
   condensed milk
1 tsp. ReaLemon juice
2 c. whipping cream
7 c. more or less assorted fruit—
   strawberries, grapes,
   apples, mandarin oranges, etc.

Combine pretzels and sugar. Cut in butter until coarse crumbs form. Press into a 10" x 15" pan. Bake at 350° for 10 minutes. Cool. Combine milk, ReaLemon and whipped topping. Spread over the crust. Chill well then spread with fruit. The best!

Some people have a wishbone where
their backbone ought to be.

Rhubarb Cake Dessert

...Mrs. Andrew (Joanna) Hostetler

Crumble together:
1 c. butter
1 c. brown sugar
2 c. flour

Press into a pan a little bigger than 9" x 13".

Mix together:
6 egg yolks
2 c. sugar
³/₄ c. flour
¹/₄ tsp. salt
1 c. sweet cream
5 c. rhubarb, finely chopped

Spread on top of crumb mixture. Bake at 350° for 40-45 minutes (just until custard is almost set). Take out of oven and top with meringue. Put back in oven on top shelf for approximately 20 minutes or until browned.

Meringue:
6 egg whites, stiffly beaten
1 c. sugar
pinch of salt
2 Tbsp. vanilla

Rhubarb Dumplings

...Mrs. Freeman (Mabel) Yoder

3 c. very finely chopped rhubarb

Dough:
3 c. flour
1 Tbsp. baking powder
1 tsp. salt
¹/₂ c. margarine
³/₄ c. milk

Mix all ingredients. Divide into 12 balls. Roll each one into a 4"-5" circle. In the center place approximately ¹/₄ c. rhubarb.

Crumbs:
1 c. brown sugar
¹/₈ tsp. salt
1 tsp. cinnamon
3 Tbsp. butter

Mix crumbs and sprinkle a tablespoon or so over rhubarb. Bring dough over and pinch seam shut. Place on well greased large cake pan.

Syrup:
3 c. brown sugar
3 c. water
¹/₂ c. butter
¹/₄ tsp. salt

Boil syrup. Pour over dumplings. Bake at 350°--375° for 1 hour. Serve with or without milk.

146

Rhubarb Cobbler ...Mrs. Freeman (Mabel) Yoder

4½-5 c. finely chopped rhubarb   Spread rhubarb evenly in greased cake pan.
½ c. white sugar   Combine the rest of ingredients and spread
½ c. brown sugar   over rhubarb.
½ c. butter
½ tsp. salt
2 tsp. baking powder
1 egg, slightly beaten
½ c. milk
1 c. flour

Topping:
½ c. brown sugar   Mix sugar, cornstarch and salt. Sprinkle over
1 Tbsp. cornstarch   batter. Pour water evenly over all. Bake at 375°
pinch salt   for approximately 1 hour or until golden.
1 c. water   Serve warm with milk.

Rhubarb Cream Delight
...Mrs. Reuben (Martha) Yoder

Crust:
1½ c. flour   Mix together and pat into 9" x 13" cake pan.
3 Tbsp. sugar   Bake at 350° for 20 minutes.
¾ c. butter

Filling:
2 c. sugar   Combine all filling ingredients and boil until
⅔ c. cream*   thick. Pour hot filling onto crust. Top with
4 c. chopped rhubarb   meringue.
3 Tbsp. flour   * I usually just use evaporated milk instead of
4 egg yolks, beaten   cream.
   (set aside whites)

Meringue:
4 egg whites, beaten   Return to oven and brown meringue.
¼ c. sugar
pinch of salt
¼ tsp. cream of tartar

Date Pudding

...Mrs. Edward (Lizzie Ann) Schrock

1 c. dates or raisins
1 c. hot water
1 tsp. soda
1 c. sugar
1 Tbsp. butter
1 c. flour
1 c. nuts
1 egg

Pour hot water over dates and soda. Let stand until cool. Add remaining ingredients. Pour into cookie sheet and bake. When cool, cut in squares and put in layers with butterscotch pudding mixture and bananas.

Butterscotch Pudding:
butter size of walnut
2 c. brown sugar
$^1/_2$ c. boiling water
$^1/_2$ tsp. soda
pinch of salt
2 eggs
2 c. white sugar
2 c. flour
cold water
2 qt. boiling water
1 tsp. vanilla
1 qt. whipped cream

Brown butter in a 5 qt. saucepan. Add brown sugar, $^1/_2$ c. boiling water and soda. Boil to taffy and add salt. Mix together eggs, white sugar, flour and some cold water. Then add 2 qt. boiling water. Add the mixture to taffy mixture and bring to a boil. Remove from heat and add vanilla. More water can be added. When pudding is chilled, add whipped cream. Mix whipped cream to pudding with wire whip. Ready to serve with date pudding.

Be thankful unto him, and bless his name.
For the Lord is good.
—Psalm 100:4,5

148

Date Pudding …Mrs. Samuel (Susie) Hochstetler

2 c. white sugar
2 Tbsp. butter
2 eggs
2 c. flour
2 tsp. soda
2 c. dates
2 c. nuts
2 c. boiling water

Pour boiling water over dates and soda. Let stand until cool. Combine first 4 ingredients. Then add date mixture and nuts. Bake at 350° for 30 minutes.

Butterscotch Sauce:
4 Tbsp. butter
2 c. brown sugar
3 c. water
6 Tbsp. (rounded) clear jel
   or Perma-Flo
4 tsp. vanilla
1/4 c. pancake syrup
1 Tbsp. maple flavoring
pinch salt

Boil butter, brown sugar, water and clear jel for 10 minutes. Add remaining ingredients. Cool. Layer cake, sauce and whipped topping.

Frozen Melon Mix …Mrs. Sam (Viola) Miller

Syrup:
4 c. sugar
2 qt. water
6 oz. frozen orange juice
6 oz. frozen lemonade

Bring water and sugar to a boil. Add juice, stirring until dissolved.

1 watermelon, balled or chunked
2 cantaloupes, chunked
2 honeydew melons, chunked
3 lb. seedless grapes
3 lb. peaches, peeled and sliced

Mix fruits together and put in boxes. Pour syrup over fruit leaving 1/2" headspace. Freeze. Serve partially thawed. Also delicious fresh.

149

Tropical Fruit
...Mrs. Simon (Esta) Miller

2½ c. sugar
1 c. clear jel
9 c. water
2 pkg. tropical punch Kool-Aid
3 cans pineapple tidbits, drained
3 c. seedless grapes, whole
12 bananas

Mix sugar and clear jel. Add water and Kool-Aid. Bring to a boil until thickened. Cool and add fruit. Fills a Fix-n-Mix bowl full. Very refreshing.

Banana Split Dessert
...Mrs. Freeman (Mabel) Yoder

First Layer:
2 c. crushed graham crackers
6 Tbsp. butter, melted
6 Tbsp. powdered sugar

Combine crackers, butter and powdered sugar. Press into a 9" x 13" cake pan.

Second Layer:
2 egg whites
1½ c. powdered sugar
4 Tbsp. margarine, softened

Beat egg whites until soft peaks form, then add powdered sugar and margarine. Mix well and spread carefully over first layer.

Third Layer:
3 bananas
2 c. crushed pineapple, drained
3 c. whipped topping or
   16 oz. Cool Whip
1½ c. pecans
1 c. chopped maraschino
   cherries
chocolate syrup

Slice bananas lengthwise and place over second layer. Spread drained pineapple next. Next spread whipped topping. Next spread on pecans and cherries. Chill. Just before serving drizzle liberally with chocolate syrup. This isn't as complicated as it appears and it's yummy!

Frosted Orange Salad ...Mrs. Freeman (Mabel) Yoder

3 (3 oz.) pkg. orange gelatin
3 c. boiling water
1 (20 oz.) can crushed pineapple
3 c. cold water
4 med. firm bananas, sliced
2½ c. miniature marshmallows
½ c. sugar
1 Tbsp. flour
1 egg, beaten
1 (8 oz.) pkg. cream cheese
1 c. whipping cream, whipped
¾ c. chopped pecans
½ c. coconut (optional)

In a bowl dissolve gelatin in boiling water. Drain pineapple (save juice). Stir cold water, bananas, marshmallows and pineapple into gelatin. Pour into a 9" x 13" cake pan. Refrigerate until firm. In saucepan combine sugar and flour. Stir in pineapple juice until smooth. Add beaten egg. Bring to a gentle boil until thickened, 2 minutes or so. Cool. In a bowl beat cream cheese. Add filling. Fold in whipped cream. Spread over gelatin. Sprinkle with nuts and coconut if desired.

Mandarin Pudding Tapioca
...Mrs. Harry (Edna Mae) Bontrager

1 sm. box cook-type vanilla pudding
1 sm. box cook-type vanilla tapioca pudding
1 sm. box cook-type orange pudding
2 c. whipped topping
1 can mandarin oranges or crushed pineapple

Take the juice of the mandarins or pineapple and add water until you have 3 cups. Add the puddings and cook until thick. Cool. Add whipped topping and mandarins or pineapple.

Serving the Lord is much like riding a bicycle—either you keep moving forward or you fall down.

Persimmon Pudding
...Mrs. Ed (Mary) Slabaugh & Mrs. Jonathan (Rose) Yoder

1 c. persimmon pulp
1 c. sugar
¼ c. butter
½ c. buttermilk or sour milk
½ c. cream or evaporated milk
½ tsp. soda
2 tsp. baking powder
1 tsp. cinnamon
dash of salt
2 eggs
1 c. flour

Mix all together and bake in a lightly greased 9" x 9" baking dish for 45-60 minutes at 350°. Top with whipped cream and enjoy! Delicious served with ice cream. Persimmons grow on trees and are a southern specialty. Rose uses 3 eggs, ½ c. more sugar and ¼ c. more flour.

Fruit Glaze or Sauce
...Mrs. Freeman (Mabel) Yoder

3 qt. water
1½-2 c. Perma-Flo
4 c. sugar
3 pkg. orange Kool-Aid
dash salt
1 tsp. vinegar
1 Tbsp. butter
2 tsp. vanilla
drained pineapple
drained mandarin oranges
assorted fruits of your choice
1 or 2 pkg. pineapple or
   lemonade Kool-Aid (optional)

Combine sugar and water. Include drained fruit juices and Kool-Aid. Bring to a boil. Combine Perma-Flo with cold water. Make a smooth paste and add slowly to fruit juice water. Cook until thickened. Remove from heat. Add salt, vinegar, butter and vanilla. Add more Kool-Aid if desired. Cool completely. Add fruit. Makes a big bowlful. Yield: approx. 30 c.

Lemonade Fruit Dressing
...daughter, Amy Yoder

2 eggs, beaten
¾ c. lemonade concentrate
½ c. sugar
2 c. whipped cream, whipped
assorted fruit—grapes, melons
   kiwi, strawberries, etc.

In heavy saucepan combine eggs, lemonade concentrate and sugar. Cook and stir over low heat just to boiling and slightly thickened. Cool, then add whipped cream or Cool Whip. Serve over fruit. Pictured on the front cover, left corner.

Soda Cracker Pudding ...Mrs. Edward (Lizzie Ann) Schrock

24 soda cracker squares, crushed
1/2 c. brown sugar
1/4 c. butter, melted
1/4 c. peanut butter

Mix crackers and brown sugar. Add peanut butter to the melted butter while still hot. When peanut butter is melted, add mixture to crackers. Place in pan, pressing crumbs to sides and bottom. Reserve 1/4 c. crumbs for topping.

6 c. milk, divided
4 eggs
1/4 c. cornstarch
1 1/2 c. white sugar
2 tsp. vanilla
1 c. coconut

In a saucepan heat 5 1/2 c. milk. Mix eggs, sugar, cornstarch and 1/2 c. milk. Stir into hot milk and boil over medium heat until thickened. Add vanilla and coconut. Pour slowly over crumbs and refrigerate. When cool, sprinkle remaining crumbs on top.

Tapioca Pudding ...Mrs. Samuel (Susie) Hochstetler

3/4 c. tapioca
4 1/2 c. milk, divided
1 c. white sugar, divided
pinch salt
1 egg
1 tsp. vanilla or desired flavoring
1 can crushed pineapple

Soak tapioca in 1 c. milk for 1 hour or more. Bring 3 1/2 c. milk to a boil. Stir in the soaked tapioca and simmer over low heat for 20 minutes, stirring often. Add 1/2 c. sugar and salt. Beat egg until light and fluffy. Add 1/2 c. sugar and add to hot mixture. Blend well and add vanilla or desired flavoring. Chill and add pineapple.

Hardening of the heart ages people more quickly than hardening of the arteries.

Jeweled Jell-O Dessert ...Mrs. Freeman (Mabel) Yoder

Crumbs:

1½ c. crushed graham crackers
½ c. brown sugar
½ c. butter or margarine, melted

Mix well and press into a 9" x 13" glass baking dish. Set aside.

1 (3 oz.) pkg. strawberry gelatin
1 (3 oz.) pkg. grape gelatin
1 (3 oz.) pkg. lime gelatin
1 (3 oz.) pkg. orange gelatin
1 (3 oz.) pkg. lemon gelatin
4 c. boiling water, divided
2 c. cold water, divided
1 c. pineapple juice
¼ c. sugar
1½-2 c. whipping cream or
　　nondairy such as Rich's

In a small bowl dissolve strawberry, grape, lime and orange gelatin each separately in 1 c. boiling water each. Cool, then add ½ c. cold water to each and pour into loaf pans 8" x 5" x 3" coated with nonstick spray. Let set until firm. In a saucepan bring pineapple juice to a boil and add sugar and lemon gelatin. Refrigerate until partially set. Then whip the topping and mix gently with lemon gelatin. Cut all the other gelatins into 1½" cubes and mix in gently. Pour over graham cracker crust. Refrigerate until set. This is pretty served in squares and is very colorful.

Fourth of July Jell-O ...Mrs. Freeman (Mabel) Yoder

1 (3 oz.) pkg. berry blue gelatin
2 c. boiling water, divided
½ c. cold water, divided
1 (3 oz.) pkg. strawberry gelatin
2 c. pears, cubed, drained

In a bowl dissolve blue gelatin in 1 c. boiling water. Stir in ¼ c. cold water. Repeat process with strawberry gelatin. Pour each into a 9" x 5" x 3" loaf pan. Refrigerate until firm. Cut into cubes. Just before serving mix gently with pears. This looks colorful served in a glass bowl—red, white and blue.

Any housewife, no matter how large her family, can always get some time to be alone by doing the dishes!

Crown Jewel Cake
...Mrs. Marcus (Joleen) Marner

1 box orange Jell-O
1 box cherry Jell-O
1 box lime Jell-O
3 c. boiling water, divided
1½ c. cold water, divided

Mix each box Jell-O with 1 c. boiling water and ½ c. cold water. Pour into pan and let set up.

1 box lemon Jell-O
¼ c. sugar
1 c. boiling water
½ c. pineapple juice
2 env. mixed Dream Whip or whipped topping

Dissolve lemon Jell-O and sugar in 1 c. boiling water. Stir in pineapple juice and topping. Cube colored Jell-O. Gently stir into lemon mixture. Chill until thickened.

Cheesecake
...Mrs. David (Rachel) Plank

1 sm. pkg. Jell-O (any flavor)
1 c. very hot water
1 pkg. graham crackers, crushed
¼ c. butter, melted
2 Tbsp. powdered sugar
1 (8 oz.) pkg. cream cheese
¾ c. white sugar
1 c. cream, whipped
1 med. carton Cool Whip

Dissolve Jell-O in very hot water. Set aside to cool. Crush graham crackers. Add melted butter and powdered sugar. Pat all but ¼ c. crumbs in cake pan. Cream together cream cheese and white sugar. Fold in cream and Cool Whip. To this, add the slightly set Jell-O. Mix well and pour over crust. Sprinkle leftover crackers over top. Easy and delicious!

Cheesecake Snacks
...Mrs. Willis (Mary Esther) Wagler

2 (8 oz.) pkg. cream cheese, softened
½ c. granulated sugar
2 eggs
¼ c. milk
1 Tbsp. lemon juice
2 tsp. vanilla
1 tsp. grated lemon rind
28 Triscuit wafers
canned fruit pie filling— apple, cherry, raspberry, blackberry

Beat cream cheese with sugar. Blend in eggs, milk, lemon juice, vanilla and grated lemon rind. Bake in a greased 3 qt. shallow baking dish at 350° for 20-25 minutes. Cool, then refrigerate until firm. Cut into 28 squares. Place on Triscuit wafers. Garnish with canned fruit pie filling.

155

Chocolate Cookie Cheesecake

...Mrs. Glen (Pollyanna) Hochstetler

Crumbs:

2 c. Oreo cookie crumbs
2 Tbsp. butter
¼ c. firmly packed brown sugar

Combine cookie crumbs, butter and brown sugar. After mixing, press crumbs into springform pan and bake at 350° for 12 minutes. Set aside.

Filling:

4 (8 oz.) pkg. cream cheese, softened
1¼ c. sugar
⅓ c. heavy cream
2 Tbsp. flour
2 tsp. vanilla
4 eggs
2 c. Oreo cookie crumbs

Beat cream cheese until creamy. Gradually add sugar, beating well after each addition. Add cream, flour and vanilla. Beat vigorously. Add eggs, one at a time, beating well. Pour 3½ c. batter onto cookie crust and top with cookie crumbs. Pour remaining batter on top and bake at 325° for 1 hour and 15 minutes. Turn oven off and leave cheesecake in for 30 minutes. Remove from oven and cool completely. Remove sides of pan.

Topping:

⅓ c. heavy cream
1½ c. chocolate chips
1 tsp. vanilla
Oreo cookie crumbs

Combine cream, chocolate chips and vanilla and melt over low heat. When melted, remove from heat and spread mixture over cheesecake and allow to drip over sides. Garnish with some more cookie crumbs. Store in refrigerator. So yummy! This is a family favorite!

Raspberry Swirl

...Mrs. Melvin (Mattie) Yoder

¾ c. graham cracker crumbs
3 Tbsp. margarine or butter, melted
2 Tbsp. brown sugar
3 eggs, separated
1 (8 oz.) pkg. cream cheese
1 c. sugar
⅛ tsp. salt
1 c. cream or Rich's topping
1 (10 oz.) pkg. frozen red or black raspberries

Combine crumbs, butter and sugar. Press into greased 7" x 11" pan. Bake at 375° for about 8 minutes. Cool. Beat egg yolks until thick; add cream cheese, sugar and salt. Beat until smooth and light. Beat egg whites until stiff peaks form. In a separate bowl whip topping. Fold topping and egg whites into cream cheese mixture. In blender crush raspberries to a pulp. Swirl half of fruit pulp through cheese filling and spread. Freeze.

Delicious Custard

...Mrs. Steve (Martha) Yoder

½ gal. milk
1 doz. eggs, beaten
1 Tbsp. (heaping) flour
½ tsp. salt
1 c. sugar
1 c. brown sugar
1 tsp. vanilla

Heat milk until bubbly. Beat eggs and add rest of ingredients. Add mixture to hot milk. Pour into a stainless steel cake pan. Bake at 475° for 3 minutes. Turn off oven. Leave set in oven until cool, then chill and enjoy!

Jelly Roll

...Mrs. Freeman (Mabel) Yoder

4 eggs, well beaten
¾ c. sugar
¾ c. flour
¾ tsp. baking powder
1 tsp. vanilla
½ tsp. salt

Beat eggs about 5 minutes. Gradually add sugar. Mix flour and rest of ingredients. Add to egg mixture. Pour in 10" x 15" jelly roll pan, with greased waxed paper on it. Bake 12-15 minutes or until toothpick comes out clean at 375°. Invert onto a clean towel sprinkled with powdered sugar. Roll up in towel. Remove and fill with one of the following fillings.

Filling for Jelly Roll #1:
½ tsp. salt
½ c. flour
1⅓ c. hot water
½ c. brown or white sugar
6 Tbsp. butter
1 tsp. flavoring

Combine salt, flour, hot water and sugar and heat until very thick; remove. Stir in butter and let cool. Add flavoring. Spread on cake and roll quickly.

Filling for Jelly Roll #2:
3 Tbsp. white sugar
1½ Tbsp. flour
1 egg yolk, beaten
1 c. milk
1 Tbsp. butter
vanilla

Stir together first 4 ingredients. Cook until thick. Add butter and vanilla. Let cool. Spread on cake and roll quickly.

Cottage Puffs
...Mom, Elsie Yoder

$^1/_3$ c. butter
$^1/_2$ c. sugar
1$^1/_2$ c. flour
1 tsp. vanilla
1 egg
$^1/_2$ c. milk
1$^1/_2$ tsp. baking powder
pinch of salt

Bake in well-oiled cupcake or muffin pan or may be baked in a cake pan at 350° for 20 minutes. Serve warm with cocoa sauce.

Cocoa Sauce:
1$^1/_2$ c. boiling water
1 Tbsp. cocoa
1$^1/_2$ Tbsp. flour
1 tsp. butter
$^1/_2$ c. sugar
pinch of salt
$^1/_2$ tsp. vanilla

Cook to boiling point. Pour over puffs that were put on plates separately just before serving. This was a main dish when our family was all at home yet.

Butterfinger Angel Dessert
...Mrs. Freeman (Mabel) Yoder

1 orange angel food cake
4 c. Rich's topping
1 c. caramel ice cream topping
7-8 Butterfinger candy bars, finely crushed

Whip topping until stiff peaks form; set aside. Cut cake horizontally 2 times so you have 3 layers. Place a generous layer of whipped topping on the first layer and spread $^1/_2$ c. candy bars on topping. Drizzle with caramel syrup. Place second layer on top of first layer and repeat layers. Spread remaining topping over top and sides to cover completely. Sprinkle with remaining Butterfinger bars all over and drizzle with syrup. Delicious! This is something I often make for large crowds.

158

Heath Bar Dessert   ...Mrs. Dennis (Mary) Bontrager

Crust:

2 c. crushed Ritz crackers
1 Tbsp. sugar
1/2 c. margarine

Mix and press into 9" x 13" cake pan.

Filling:

2/3 c. vanilla pudding*
2 pt. vanilla ice cream, softened
2 c. milk, heated then cooled
1 Tbsp. vanilla
12 oz. whipped topping
Heath toffee bits (garnish)

Mix everything except whipped topping and Heath bits in a medium sized bowl. Mixing it with a wire whip works great. Pour pudding mixture over crust. Top with whipped topping and garnish with a generous amount of Heath toffee bits. Refrigerate for 6 hours or overnight before serving. Can also be frozen. Absolutely delicious!
*1/3 c. vanilla and 1/3 c. butterscotch pudding may be used instead of all vanilla.

Toffee Coffee Blizzards   ...Mrs. Freeman (Mabel) Yoder

1/4 c. sugar
1 Tbsp. (rounded) cornstarch
1 Tbsp. instant coffee
1 Tbsp. butter
1 1/4 c. milk, divided
1 tsp. vanilla
1 (14 oz.) can sweetened
   condensed milk
2 c. Rich's topping
12 Oreo cookies
12 oz. English Heath toffee bits
caramel and chocolate ice
   cream syrup

In a saucepan heat 1 c. milk to boiling point. In the meantime, combine sugar, cornstarch and coffee. Mix in 1/4 c. milk and slowly add to hot milk, stirring constantly. Bring to a boil and boil 1 minute or until thickened. Remove from heat and add vanilla and butter. Cool completely and add sweetened condensed milk. Whip the topping and fold into pudding. Add Heath bits. Crush cookies into a 10" pie plate. Pour pudding mixture over cookies. Swirl with caramel and chocolate syrup. Freeze overnight or longer. A great make-ahead dessert. Our all-time favorite! Pictured on the front cover.

Easy Chocolate Dessert   …Mrs. Steve (Martha) Yoder

Bake a chocolate cake in a sheet cake pan.

3 c. milk*
1 (3 oz.) pkg. chocolate
   instant pudding
1 (3 oz.) pkg. vanilla instant
   pudding
1 c. whipped topping

Heat milk to boiling, then cool. Mix puddings with milk. Beat well and add whipped topping. Spread on top of cake. Cut the cake in squares and put a dab of whipped topping on each square.
*When using 1% or 2% milk, heating milk is unnecessary.

Maple Sponge   …Mrs. Samuel (Susie) Hochstetler

2 c. brown sugar
2 c. hot water
1/2 tsp. maple flavoring
1 Tbsp. plain gelatin
1/2 c. cold water
your favorite vanilla pudding
1 c. cream, whipped
nuts or bananas (optional)

Boil brown sugar, hot water and maple flavoring together for 10 minutes. Soak plain gelatin in cold water a few minutes. Then mix with hot syrup. Pour in pan; let set until firm. Use your favorite vanilla pudding and whipped cream. Cut maple gelatin in little squares and add to pudding. Nuts or bananas may also be added. This looks like cut glass when served.

Sherbet   …Mrs. Danny (Vanessa) Reeves

1 (3 oz.) pkg. flavored gelatin—
   lime, orange or strawberry
1 c. sugar
1 c. water
1/4 c. lemon juice
2 1/2 c. milk

Combine sugar and water. Cook together for 2 minutes. Pour hot syrup over gelatin and stir until the gelatin is dissolved. Add lemon juice and cool. When it is cool add the milk and mix well. Pour into 13" x 9" pan and freeze until firm. Put in a bowl and break into chunks. Beat with a beater until smooth and fluffy. Keep frozen until ready to serve. Very good!

Delicious Homemade Ice Cream
...Mrs. Simon (Esta) Miller

4 eggs, beaten
1 1/2 c. white sugar
1 sm. box instant pudding
1 qt. cream
1 can Eagle Brand milk
1 1/2 qt. milk
vanilla

Beat eggs. Add remaining ingredients. This is for 1 1/2 gal. freezer. For chocolate mocha ice cream add 1 Tbsp. instant coffee dissolved in 1 c. hot water and use chocolate instant pudding. Delicious.

Simple and Easy Ice Cream ...daughter, Amy Yoder

6 c. milk
1 1/2 c. instant vanilla pudding
6 eggs, well beaten
1 1/2 c. white sugar
1 1/2 c. cream or milk
1/2 tsp. salt
1 tsp. vanilla

Mix first 2 ingredients. Let set for 5 minutes. Combine beaten eggs and sugar. Add milk or cream, vanilla and salt. Stir. Add to vanilla pudding mixture. Stir until well blended. Pour into 1 1/2 gal. ice cream freezer and add enough milk to fill it 3/4 full. A very easy and delicious ice cream.

Chocolate Ice Cream Sandwiches
...Mrs. Orlie (Mary) Troyer

1/3 c. butter, softened
1/3 c. sugar
1/3 c. packed brown sugar
1 egg
1/2 tsp. vanilla extract
3/4 c. plus 2 Tbsp. all-purpose flour
1/4 c. baking cocoa
1/2 tsp. baking powder
1/4 tsp. baking soda
1/4 tsp. salt
1/2 c. semisweet chocolate chips
1 pt. vanilla ice cream

In a mixing bowl cream butter and sugars. Beat in the egg and vanilla. Combine the flour, cocoa, baking powder, soda and salt. Add to creamed mixture and mix well. Drop by rounded tablespoonsful 2" apart on greased cookie sheets, forming 16 cookies. Flatten slightly with a glass. Sprinkle with chocolate chips. Bake at 375° for 8-10 minutes or until set. Remove to wire rack to cool. To assemble sandwiches place 1/4 c. ice cream on the bottom of half the cookies. Top with remaining cookies. Wrap each in plastic wrap. Freeze until firm.

Hints for Salads

- When buying grapefruit, judge it by its weight. The heavier ones are juicer.
- Add ¼ tsp. soda to cranberries while cooking and they will not require as much sugar.
- Frosted grapes: Beat 2 egg whites and 2 Tbsp. water slightly. Dip small clusters of grapes into the mixture. Sprinkle with granulated sugar. Dry on waxed paper.
- Lemons that are heated before squeezing will give almost twice the quantity of juice.
- Lemon juice on cut bananas will keep them from darkening.
- Grease the salad mold with salad dressing, mayonnaise or salad oil and it will help the salad slip out easily.
- Save sweet pickle juice. Store it in the refrigerator and use small amounts to thin dressings for salads.
- Soak hard-cooked eggs in beet pickle juice for an interesting taste and colorful garnish.
- To make a hard-cooked egg flower: Cut white from the small end of the egg about three-fourth of the way down, petal fashion, being careful not to cut yolk. When spread apart, these white petals should show yolk as a round ball, daisy fashion. Slice green pepper for leaves. Nice for potato salad.
- Marshmallows will cut easily if the blades of the scissors are buttered.
- Try putting marshmallows in the refrigerator and they won't stick to the scissors.
- Perk up soggy lettuce by adding lemon juice to a bowl of cold water and soaking it for an hour in the refrigerator.
- The darker, outer leaves of lettuce are higher in calcium, iron and Vitamin A.
- Do not add salt to a lettuce salad until just before serving; salt makes the lettuce wilt and become tough.
- Toss salads well so you can use less dressing which is healthier.
- Prepare ingredients such as greens, chopped onions, celery, carrots and radishes ahead of time. Store in separate airtight containers for quick use in a tossed salad.
- When you will be doing extra cooking, keep shredded cheese, bread crumbs and chopped onion on hand for use in salads, casseroles and vegetables.
- Before grating cheese, brush vegetable oil on the grater and it will clean easier.
- Remove the tops of carrots before storing. Tops absorb moisture and nutrients from the carrots.
- It is easy to remove the white membrane from oranges for fancy desserts or salads by soaking them in boiling water for 5 minutes before you peel them.
- Lemon Jell-O, dissolved in 2 c. of hot apricot nectar with 1 tsp. of grated lemon added for zip, makes a perfect base for jelled fruit salad.

And the feast of harvest, the firstfruits of thy labours,
which thou hast sown in the field: and the feast of
ingathering, which is in the end of the year, when thou
hast gathered in thy labours out of the field.
Exodus 23:16

Soups & Salads

How to Be Thankful

Count your blessings, instead of your crosses;
Count your gains, instead of your losses.
Count your joys, instead of your woes;
Count your friends, instead of your foes.
Count your smiles, instead of your tears;
Count your courage, instead of your fears.
Count your full years, instead of your lean;
Count your kind deeds, instead of the mean.
Count your health, instead of your wealth;
Count more on God, instead of yourself.

Virginia Potato Soup

...Mrs. David (Fannie) Miller ...Mrs. Andrew (Joanna) Hostetler

9 c. water
7 c. diced potatoes
1 c. carrots
1 c. celery
1 c. (scant) onion
5 chicken bouillon cubes or
   chicken seasoning
2 cans cream of chicken soup
   (or thick chicken gravy)
¹/₂ lb. Velveeta cheese
salt and pepper to taste

Cook vegetables until soft. Add soups and seasonings. Bring to a boil. Simmer a little. Remove from heat. Add cheese. Cover and let set until cheese is melted.

Ham and Potato Soup for Church

...Mrs. Daniel (Fannie) Hershberger

1 lb. butter
3 c. flour
1 lg. onion
6 qt. shredded potatoes
6 qt. milk
5-7 lb. ham, chopped
1 box Velveeta cheese
salt

Brown butter, flour and onion together. Boil shredded potatoes in enough water to cover; add this and milk to first mixture, including the potato water. Also add 5-7 lb. chopped ham. Last add Velveeta. Don't let it boil after it is all together. Doesn't need much salt because of the meat and cheese. Yield: 1 canner full. Takes 5 lb. crackers.

Hearty Ham Soup

...Mrs. Sam (Mary) Hershberger

1 c. diced potatoes
1 c. diced carrots
¹/₄ c. chopped onions
¹/₂ c. diced celery
1¹/₂ c. chopped ham
1¹/₂ tsp. chicken soup base
¹/₄ c. butter
1 qt. milk
Velveeta cheese

In a saucepan cook potatoes, celery, carrots, onions, butter and chicken base in enough water to cover vegetables. Cook until tender. Add ham and milk. Bring to a boil, then thicken with cornstarch and water as desired. Add cheese.

165

Bean-n-Bacon Soup

...Mrs. Orva (Marietta) Yoder

4 lb. dried navy beans, soaked
   overnight, then cooked
   until soft
2 lb. ham
1 c. onions
6 qt. tomato juice
4 c. carrots
8 c. potatoes
3 c. celery
1 pkg. bacon, fried, then
   crumbled into pieces

Mix cooked beans, vegetables and ham together. To each quart add 1 tsp. salt. Yield: about 16 qt. Pressure cook at 10 lb. pressure for 1 hour.

Chili Soup

...Mrs. Melvin (Mary) Stutzman

2 lb. ground meat
1-2 tsp. chili powder, as desired
salt
2 c. ketchup
2 c. salsa
1 qt. water
1 qt. tomato juice
1 c. brown sugar
2 Tbsp. mustard
2 (16 oz.) cans chili beans

Fry meat with chili powder and salt. Add everything except juice and water. Mix thoroughly. Add juice and water. Simmer for 30 minutes or more.

Chili Soup

...Mrs. Edna Slabaugh

5 lb. hamburger
1/2 tsp. red pepper
1 Tbsp. salt
2 Tbsp. ground chili powder
1/2 c. chopped onion
6 qt. water
2 c. flour
2 qt. ketchup
1 c. brown sugar
2 qt. Busch pork and beans

Combine first 5 ingredients and fry until hamburger is brown. In a large kettle heat water to boiling. Combine sugar, flour and ketchup. Mix slowly into boiling water. Add hamburger mixture and pork and beans. Heat through. Very tasty and unusual since it takes no tomato juice. Children love it!

166

Chicken Chowder Soup

...Mrs. Andrew (Joanna) Hostetler

2 c. chicken
2 c. chicken broth
2 c. diced celery
2 c. diced potatoes
2 c. diced carrots
2 Tbsp. butter
salt and pepper to taste
2 c. milk
2 Tbsp. flour
1 c. Velveeta cheese

Cook first 7 ingredients together until tender. Slowly add flour mixed with milk and bring to a boil. Add cheese. I use less vegetables or more broth.

Turkey Chowder Soup

...Mrs. Marvin (Mary Ann) Schrock

4 c. turkey broth
1 c. shredded potatoes
1 c. chopped celery
1 c. shredded carrots
$^{1}/_{4}$ c. butter
2 c. milk
6 Tbsp. flour
1 c. shredded cheddar cheese

Boil broth, potatoes, celery and carrots together until tender, approximately 20 minutes. Then add butter. In a blender combine milk and flour. Stir into soup mixture to thicken. It will become like a thin gravy. When this has boiled thoroughly add cheddar cheese. Stir until melted.

Cheeseburger Chowder

...Mrs. Gerald (Rosanna) Schrock

1 lb. hamburger
2 med. potatoes, chopped
$^{1}/_{2}$ c. chopped celery
1 onion, chopped
$^{1}/_{2}$ tsp. salt
$2^{1}/_{2}$ c. milk
3 Tbsp. flour
1 c. cheddar or Velveeta cheese

Cook potatoes, celery, onion and salt in 1½ c. water until tender. Add browned and drained hamburger and 2 c. milk. Use the remaining ½ c. milk to blend with flour to thicken soup. Add cheese.

167

Vegetable Cheeseburger Soup

...Mrs. Melvin (Mary) Stutzman

1 lb. browned meat or chicken
2 med. potatoes
1 (16 oz.) pkg. mixed vegetables
¼ c. chopped onion
¼ c. uncooked rice
¼ c. flour
4 c. water
2 c. milk
12 or more slices Velveeta cheese

Brown meat unless using chicken. Cook vegetables and rice. Add flour to meat, then add cooked vegetables and water. Season with chicken seasoning, salt, pepper and parsley flakes. Add milk and cheese.

Chunky Veggie Chowder

...daughter, Amy Yoder

2 med. onions, finely chopped
2 garlic cloves, minced
2 Tbsp. butter or margarine
3 med. carrots, chopped
2 celery ribs, sliced
2 med. potatoes, cubed
1 sm. zucchini, cubed
2 (10½ oz.) cans chicken broth
¼ c. minced fresh parsley
¾ tsp. dried thyme
1 c. frozen peas
1 c. frozen corn
¼ c. all-purpose flour
3 c. milk
salt and pepper to taste

In a large saucepan or soup kettle sauté onions and garlic in butter until tender. Add carrots, celery, potatoes, zucchini, broth, parsley and thyme. Bring to a boil. Reduce heat. Cover and simmer until vegetables are tender, about 20 minutes. Stir in peas and corn. In a bowl combine flour, milk, pepper and salt if desired until smooth; gradually add to soup. Bring to a boil. Cook and stir until thickened. Yield: 2 qt.

It isn't our position but our disposition that makes us happy.

Zucchini Hamburger Stew

...Mrs. Freeman (Mabel) Yoder

1 lb. ground hamburger
1 lb. bulk pork sausage
2 (14 oz.) cans diced tomatoes
2 med. green peppers, chopped
2 c. celery, finely chopped
³/₄ c. chopped onion
peeled zucchini, cut into chunks
1 pt. tomato juice
1 tsp. salt
1 tsp. Italian seasoning
1 tsp. oregano
Parmesan cheese (optional)

Brown hamburger and sausage, then drain and set aside. Drain diced tomatoes. Place reserved tomato juice in a large saucepan. Add peppers, celery and onion. Cover and cook 10 minutes. Add meat, tomatoes, zucchini, tomato juice and seasonings. Cook approximately 15 minutes or until zucchini is tender. Garnish with cheese if desired. Pictured on the back cover.

Pumpkin Soup

...Mrs. David (Lydia) Schwartz

¹/₄ c. green pepper, chopped
1 bay leaf (optional)
2 Tbsp. butter or oleo
2 c. water
2 chicken bouillon cubes
1 Tbsp. flour
1 tsp. butter
2 Tbsp. chopped onion
1 tsp. parsley flakes
1 diced tomato
2 c. mashed cooked pumpkin
   or squash
2 c. milk
¹/₈ tsp. pepper

Sauté pepper, onion, parsley and bay leaf in butter until tender. Do not brown. Add tomatoes, pumpkin or squash, water and bouillon. Bring to a boil. Reduce heat. Simmer for 30 minutes, stirring occasionally. In small bowl combine flour and milk; blend well. Stir into soup mixture. Add salt and pepper. Cook over medium heat, stirring frequently, until mixture boils.

Salad

...Mrs. John (Mary) Hochstetler

1 lg. head lettuce, chopped
1 sm. head cauliflower, chopped
1 sm. onion, chopped
1 lb. fried bacon, crumbled
1 1/2 c. shredded cheese

Layer ingredients in order given except cheese. Put dressing on top. Spread evenly. Sprinkle shredded cheese on top. Put in Tupperware and seal to use the next day. Before serving, toss salad. Do not wash vegetables as it makes salad wilt.

Dressing:
1 1/2 c. salad dressing
1/3 c. Parmesan cheese
1/4 c. sugar

Mix together.

Zucchini Garden Salad

...Mrs. Freeman (Mabel) Yoder

5-6 c. garden lettuce or
   1 head, chopped
2 lg. carrots, shredded
1 c. chopped celery or
   2 Tbsp. celery flakes
4 med. tomatoes
2 c. cooked spiral macaroni
6 hard-boiled eggs, chopped
1 med. zucchini, seeded, peeled, chopped
1 c. red, green and yellow peppers, chopped
1 med. onion, chopped
1 (8 oz.) pkg. shredded cheddar cheese

Toss all salad ingredients in a large bowl.

Dressing:
2 c. mayonnaise
1 c. sour cream
1 c. brown sugar
1/4 c. milk
1/4 tsp. liquid hickory smoke
1 tsp. salt
1 1/2 Tbsp. prepared mustard
1/4 tsp. pepper
2 Tbsp. red wine vinegar

Mix well with a wire whisk and pour over salad just before serving and mix just until greens are coated. Do not overmix.

Cucumber Salad

...Mrs. Freeman (Mabel) Yoder

4 c. peeled, sliced med.
    cucumbers
$^1/_2$ c. sliced onion
$^1/_2$-1 tsp. salt
$^1/_4$ tsp. pepper
1 tsp. red wine vinegar or
    regular vinegar
1$^1/_4$ c. sweet cream or half and half

Place sliced cucumbers and onions in a bowl.
Sprinkle salt and pepper over them. Let soak
15-20 minutes, then add vinegar and cream.
Serve with potatoes.

Hot Taco Salad

...Mrs. Steve (Linda) Kauffman
...Mrs. John (Mary) Hochstetler

1 head lettuce
1 onion
4 tomatoes
4 oz. cheddar cheese
8 oz. Thousand Island dressing
2 lb. hamburger (ground beef)
1 can kidney beans
    (or pork and beans)
$^1/_4$ tsp. salt
2 Tbsp. hot sauce
1 pkg. taco-flavored corn chips

Cook hamburger and onion. Then drain. Add
cheese, dressing, hot sauce and kidney beans.
Simmer a little. Chop lettuce and tomatoes.
Topped with sour cream is good. A delicious
summer meal. Mary adds 1 c. salad dressing
and 1 c. salsa instead of Thousand Island
dressing.

Thousand Island Dressing:
2 c. salad dressing
$^1/_4$ c. relish
2 Tbsp. catsup
onion, finely chopped

You can use this for your dressing in taco salad.

Thou openest thine hand, and satisfiest
the desire of every living thing.
—Psalm 145:16

171

Chili/Taco Salad
...Mrs. Freeman (Mabel) Yoder

3 c. shredded lettuce
3 c. thick chili soup, warmed
1 c. refried beans
1 c. salsa
2 c. shredded cheddar cheese
sour cream
tortilla chips

Divide lettuce into 4 soup plates. Heat chili and refried beans in a saucepan, then divide evenly onto lettuce in plates. Add $1/4$ c. salsa to each plate, sprinkle with cheese and spread with sour cream and tortilla chips as desired. This salad is filling enough to be a main course meal. It is good to eat with garlic bread on the side. Yummy!

Corn Bread Salad
...Mrs. Steve (Martha) Yoder

1 (8 oz.) pkg. Jiffy corn
  bread mix
1 can green chilies
$1/8$ tsp. cumin
$1/8$ tsp. oregano
$1/8$ tsp. sage
1 c. mayonnaise
1 c. sour cream
1 env. Ranch dressing mix
1 (15 oz.) can pinto or kidney
  beans
1 (15 oz.) can whole kernel corn,
  drained
1 c. green onions
1 c. green peppers
10 slices bacon, fried and crumbled
2 c. shredded cheese
3 med. tomatoes

Mix and bake corn bread according to directions and add green chilies, cumin, oregano and sage. Bake at 400° for 20-25 minutes. Cool. In small pan mix dressings together and set aside. Crumble half of corn bread in 9" x 13" pan. Layer with half of the rest of the ingredients in order, beans, dressing mix, corn, tomatoes, peppers, onion, cheese, bacon, then repeat the layers. Refrigerate at least 2 hours.

A dog is a man's best friend, because he
wags his tail, not his tongue!

Bean Salad

...Mrs. John (Mary) Hochstetler

1 pt. yellow beans, drained
1 pt. green beans, drained
1 pt. kidney beans, drained
1 pt. lima beans
1 pt. carrots
1 c. celery
1 c. chopped onions
1 c. chopped peppers

Partly cook lima beans, carrots and celery (not soft). Put everything in 4 qt. Tupperware bowl.

Sauce:
4 tsp. salt
3 c. white sugar
2 c. vinegar
1¹/₂ c. oil

Mix and pour over bean mixture. Cool in refrigerator overnight. Serve.

Potato Salad

...Mrs. Jonathan (Naomi) Wagler
...Mrs. Daniel (Fannie) Hershberger

12 c. (3 qt. kettle full) cooked and shredded potatoes
12 hard-boiled eggs, diced
1¹/₂ c. (2¹/₂-3 lg. stalks) chopped celery
¹/₂ c. chopped onion

Dressing:
3 c. salad dressing
2 c. sugar
3 Tbsp. mustard
¹/₄ c. vinegar
4 tsp. salt
¹/₂ c. milk

Mix dressing ingredients and pour over potatoes, eggs, celery and onions. Let stand overnight to blend. Yield: 1 gal.
Variation: Fannie uses only 1 c. sugar.

Pasta Salad

...Mrs. Simon (Esta) Miller

1¹/₂ lb. spiral macaroni (don't overcook)
8 oz. ham, cubed
¹/₂ c. chopped celery
2 med. tomatoes
1 med. onion, chopped
1 green pepper, chopped
2 c. shredded cheddar cheese

Dressing:
3 c. Miracle Whip
¹/₄ c. brown and spicy mustard
³/₄ c. oil
¹/₂ tsp. salt
¹/₄ c. vinegar
1¹/₂ c. white sugar
1 Tbsp. salt
¹/₂ Tbsp. celery

Mix and pour over pasta mixture.
Refrigerate and serve. Yield: 1 gal.

Macaroni Salad

...Mrs. Sam (Mary) Hershberger

2 c. spaghetti macaroni
1 c. sour cream
1 c. salad dressing
³/₄ c. sugar
1 tsp. garlic salt
2 tsp. celery seed
¹/₂ c. diced celery
1 tsp. mustard

Cook macaroni with 2 tsp. salt until soft, then
rinse in cold water. When cooled, add rest of
ingredients. Does not get watery.

Thankfulness is the beginning of gratitude.
Gratitude is the completion of thankfulness.
Thankfulness may consist merely of words.
Gratitude is shown in acts.
—Henri Frederic Amiel

174

Coleslaw

...Mrs. Willis (Mary Esther) Wagler

14 c. (5 lb. 2 oz.) shredded cabbage, put in water a few seconds, then drain
1 lg. green pepper
1 lg. onion
salt to taste

Dressing:
$^7/_8$ c. vinegar
$^7/_8$ c. salad oil
$1^1/_2$ c. sugar

Mix and heat to boiling point. Set aside for 30 seconds. Pour over cabbage mixture. Cover and put aside for 30 minutes. Toss and refrigerate for a day before eating. You can freeze this, then to use thaw and drain. Add mayonnaise to serve.

Creamy Chicken Salad

...Mrs. John (Susan) Lehman

2 c. cubed, cooked chicken breast
1 c. cooked small pasta
1 c. halved seedless red grapes
1 c. mandarin oranges, drained
3 celery ribs, chopped
$^1/_2$ c. sliced almonds (optional)
1 Tbsp. grated onion
1 c. mayonnaise
1 c. whipped topping
$^1/_2$ tsp. salt

Mix all ingredients except mayonnaise, whipped topping and salt. In another bowl mix rest of ingredients and pour over chicken mixture. Stir to coat.

Too Busy Mother

Are you too busy to help them play?
Too busy to hear them what they say?
Are you too busy to watch them swing?
Too busy to hear the songs they sing?
If you're too busy except to scold,
They may be too busy when you grow old.

Crunchy Veggie Sandwiches
...Mrs. Freeman (Mabel) Yoder

1 c. chopped green peppers
1 c. chopped cucumber
1 c. chopped celery
1 c. chopped tomatoes
1 sm. onion, sliced
2 Tbsp. minced fresh parsley
1/4 c. chopped dill pickles
1/2 c. fat-free sour cream
1/4 c. reduced-fat mayonnaise
1/2 tsp. salt
1/4 tsp. pepper
lettuce
6 sandwich buns

In a bowl combine all ingredients except lettuce. Line 6 sandwich halves with lettuce. Spoon veggie mixture on top and top with the other half of sandwich. Yummy and nutritious!

Deluxe Salad Eggs
...Mrs. Freeman (Mabel) Yoder

12 eggs
1/2 c. mayonnaise
2 Tbsp. flour
1/3 c. brown sugar
1/4 tsp. salt
1/4 tsp. (scant) minced garlic
3 Tbsp. finely chopped onion
2 Tbsp. real bacon bits (optional)
1 tsp. vinegar
1 Tbsp. prepared mustard
1/8 tsp. liquid hickory smoke
parsley flakes

In saucepan cook eggs with water until hard-boiled, approximately 10 minutes, then let sit in the hot water for 5 minutes, covered. The eggs will peel easier this way. Peel and cool completely. Cut eggs lengthwise and remove yolks. Mash yolks until fine. Mix mayonnaise, mustard, vinegar and liquid smoke. Set aside. Mix sugar, flour, salt, garlic, onions and bacon bits. Add to yolks and mix well. Spoon into the egg white cavities until rounded. Sprinkle parsley flakes over all.

The greatest remedy for anger is "delay."
When one will not, two cannot quarrel.

Marinated Tomatoes

...Mrs. David (Fannie) Miller

1 c. oil
⅓ c. vinegar
½ Tbsp. sweet basil
½ tsp. dry mustard
1 Tbsp. sugar
½ tsp. garlic (optional)
¼ c. chopped parsley
½ tsp. salt

Mix well, then add sliced tomatoes and onions. Marinate and refrigerate for 2 hours before serving.

Refreshing Fruit Salad ...Mrs. Glen (Pollyanna) Hochstetler

1 fresh pineapple
2 c. crisp grapes
2 small kiwis, diced
1 apple, diced

Cut fresh pineapple; core and dice into bite-size chunks. Add grapes, kiwis and apple. Mix well and chill until very cold. Very tasty and refreshing!

Harvest Mold

...Mrs. Freeman (Mabel) Yoder

First Layer:
1 (3 oz.) pkg. orange Jell-O
¾ c. hot water
1 c. cold water
1 c. shredded carrots

Dissolve Jell-O in hot water, then add cold water. Chill until slightly thickened and add carrots. Pour into mold or glass bowl.

Second Layer:
1 (3 oz.) pkg. lime or
 lemon Jell-O
1 c. hot water
1 (8 oz.) pkg. cream cheese
1 c. drained crushed pineapple
2 c. whipped topping

Dissolve Jell-O in hot water. Chill slightly. Beat in cream cheese until smooth. Add pineapple. Fold in whipped topping. Spoon carefully on first layer. Let set until firm.

Third Layer:
1 (3 oz.) pkg. raspberry Jell-O
¾ c. hot water
1 c. cold water
1 c. shredded apples

Dissolve Jell-O in hot water, then add cold water. Chill until slightly set. Add apples and spoon carefully over second layer. Refrigerate 6 hours or overnight. Unmold on a glass plate. Pictured on the front cover.

Spring Jell-O Salad   ...Mrs. Gerald (Rosanna) Schrock

2 pkg. lemon Jell-O
3 c. boiling water
1 can crushed pineapple
2 bananas, cubed
1 c. pineapple juice
2 Tbsp. flour
1²⁄₃ c. miniature marshmallows
  or 12 large, cut up
¹⁄₂ c. sugar
2 eggs, beaten
8 oz. Cool Whip
shredded cheddar cheese

Dissolve lemon Jell-O in boiling water. Cool until it starts to thicken, then add drained pineapple, bananas and marshmallows. Pour into a 9" x 13" pan and let set until firm. Beat eggs and add sugar, flour and pineapple juice. Cook until thickened, stirring constantly. Remove from heat and let set until cool, then add Cool Whip and spread on top of Jell-O mixture. Top with shredded cheese.

Pistachio Mallow Salad   ...Mrs. Freeman (Mabel) Yoder

16 oz. whipped topping
1 (3.4 oz.) sm. box instant
  pistachio pudding
6 drops green food coloring
3 c. miniature marshmallows
1 (20 oz.) can pineapple
  tidbits or crushed
¹⁄₂ c. chopped pistachios or walnuts

In a large bowl combine topping, pudding mix and food coloring. Fold in marshmallows and pineapple. Mix in nuts. Refrigerate at least 2 hours and garnish with additional nuts.

Punch-Apple Jell-O Salad

...Mrs. Edna Slabaugh

3 c. strawberry Jell-O
¹⁄₂ c. cherry Jell-O
1¹⁄₂ c. orange Jell-O
10 c. boiling water
10 c. cold water
16-18 apples, shredded

Place all flavors gelatin in large bowl. Dissolve with boiling water. Stir well. Add cold water. Refrigerate until syrupy, then stir in apples. Refrigerate until set. Fills a fix and mix bowl.

178

Waldorf Salad
...Mrs. Steve (Linda) Kauffman

1 c. pineapple juice
²/₃ c. sugar
1 Tbsp. cornstarch
¼ tsp. salt
1 egg
3-4 Tbsp. water
6 apples, diced
2 c. chunk pineapple
½ c. chopped celery
2 c. seeded grapes
½ c. nuts

Bring pineapple juice to a boil. Stir together sugar, cornstarch and salt. Add egg and blend. Stir in water. Add to the hot pineapple juice. Cook over low heat. Cool and add to the remaining ingredients.

Bright Christmas Salad
...Mrs. Freeman (Mabel) Yoder

²/₃ c. or 1 (6 oz.) box lime gelatin
4 c. boiling water, divided
1 (20 oz.) can crushed pineapple
4 c. marshmallows, large or miniature (I prefer miniature)
²/₃ c. raspberry or cherry gelatin or 1 (6 oz.) box
1½ c. cherry pie filling

In a bowl dissolve lime gelatin in 2 c. boiling water. Let set a few minutes. Stir in pineapple. Pour into a 9" x 13" x 2" pan. Cover with marshmallows and chill until set. Dissolve raspberry or cherry Jell-O with remaining 2 c. boiling water. Cool slightly. Add pie filling gently. Pour over marshmallows. Cover and refrigerate until set.

Cranberry Salad
...Mrs. Ed (Mary) Slabaugh

2 sm. boxes cherry Jell-O or ⅔ c.
3 c. hot water
2 c. ground cranberries
2 c. ground apples
2 c. Rich's topping, beat until stiff
2 Tbsp. lemon juice
¼ c. orange juice concentrate
1 c. sugar
pinch salt
4 eggs, well beaten

Mix Jell-O and hot water. Let set until cool. Add the cranberries and let stand 4 hours. Cook lemon and orange juice, sugar and beaten eggs over low/medium heat until it thickens. Takes only a few minutes. Let it cool. Mix topping and sauce together, then add to Jell-O mixture and apples. Pour into bowl. Let set. Yield: 16-20 servings.

Creamy Grape Salad
...Mrs. David (Rachel) Plank
...Mrs. Melvin (Mattie) Yoder

1 (8 oz.) pkg. cream cheese, softened
1 1/2 c. powdered sugar
1 c. sour cream
1 tsp. lemon juice
8 oz. Cool Whip
4 lb. whole seedless grapes

Beat together the first 4 ingredients. Fold in Cool Whip and grapes. Chill and serve. Mattie uses only 1 c. powdered sugar.

Coated Grapes
...Mrs. Sam (Mary) Hershberger

1 (8 oz.) pkg. cream cheese
1 c. powdered sugar
1 c. sour cream
2 tsp. vanilla
2 lb. grapes (red or green)

Mix cream cheese and powdered sugar. Mix with sour cream and vanilla. Pour over grapes. This is very refreshing.

Mexican Salad Dressing
...Mrs. Andrew (Joanna) Hostetler

1 c. sugar
1/4 tsp. pepper
1 tsp. salt
1/2 tsp. celery seed
2 tsp. prepared mustard
1/3 c. vinegar
1 c. salad oil
1 med. onion, finely chopped (optional)

Mix in order given. Gradually add oil and keep beating so oil won't separate. Serve with assorted vegetables and salad greens. Andrew's favorite.

Life is like an onion—you peel off one layer
at a time and sometimes you weep.

God Bless

This Nest

Canning & Freezing

...*I give unto you, and shall reap the harvest thereof, then ye shall bring a sheaf of the firstfruits of your harvest.*
Leviticus 23:10

The Harvest Time

While gazing out the window on a somber autumn day,
I ponder on the season, colors bright, then skies of gray—
Indian summer with its beauty, then the autumn rains at last
All are just a step ahead of the winter's icy blast.
But there's something extra special in this bounteous time of year—
As we survey the harvest, hunger pains we need not fear.
We've carrots in our garden, Chinese cabbage, turnips, beets
And the cellar nigh o'erflowing, freshly cleaned and full of treats.
Bags of apples in the corner, and potatoes in their sacks,
Spaghetti squash and butternuts, each one in separate racks.
With jars of peaches on the shelf, a hundred quarts or more,
We needn't shop for cans of fruit when we go to the store.
With blueberries, applesauce and pears, and cherries for our pies,
We're really blessed, the shelves are stocked with plenty of supplies.
There are peas and beans and golden corn and pickles sweet and sour;
We're feeling well rewarded for each busy summer hour.
Baked beans are in the corner, for a change from usual fare,
And if you look for beef or pork, you'll find it over there.
Tomato soup and vegetables, another kind or two,
There are jams and jellies of all kinds, and pasta sauces, too.
Fruit juice to serve at breakfast time, or else when we are sick.
There is so much variety, sometimes it's hard to pick.
The harvest has been bountiful, and occupied our days,
For God has blessed us richly—we owe Him hearty praise.
Though we can plow and we can hoe and we can scatter seed,
And we can cultivate with care, each thistle and each weed,
Yet only God can send the rain, the sunshine from on high,
And God alone can give us strength, and health to us supply.
So we will thank and praise the Lord, for blessings He bestows.
For life, for health, for sun and rain—each living thing that grows.

—B. Zimmerman

Beef Chunks to Can ...Mrs. Jonathan (Rose) Yoder

1½ c. Tenderquick
2 c. brown sugar
1 Tbsp. black pepper
½ c. liquid smoke
6 c. water (or more)

Mix with beef or ham chunks, approx. 20 lb. meat. Soak 6 days in cool place. Rinse pieces in cold water, or do not rinse for more spicy meat. If meat chunks are coarse-ground, only soak 3 days. Pressure can quarts 1 hour at 10 lb. We like this very well with ham pieces approximately 2" square. Heat up only; a very handy meal.

Meat Loaf to Can ...Mrs. Vern (Irene) Schlabach

15 lb. hamburger
36 white crackers, crushed
7 slices bread, crumbled
1 c. oatmeal
½ c. (scant) salt
4 eggs
2 c. onion
pepper to taste

Mix hamburger and other ingredients. Form into balls. Bake a little. Put in jars and fill up cans with gravy. A very handy meat to have on hand. Pressure can 1 hour at 10 lb. pressure. Making a pan gravy with water instead of milk is best.

Corned Beef ...Mrs. Ed (Mary) Slabaugh

approx. 10 lb. choice cut—
    beef, steak, roast, etc.
2 gal. water
3 lb. salt
1 oz. (2 Tbsp.) salt petre
1 lb. brown sugar
2 tsp. (heaping) soda

Place meat in a crock or other suitable container. Heat dry ingredients and water until dissolved. Let cool, then pour over meat to cover. You may want to put a weight on top so meat is completely covered. Will be cured and ready to cut up to can or freeze in 2 weeks. Or you can drain off brine, reheat to boil, let cool and pour over meat for several more weeks and will not spoil if kept in cold place. When cured is good to cook until tender and use for sandwiches when cold.

183

Sausage to Can or Freeze ...Mrs. LaVern (Martha) Yoder

50 lb. ground pork
1½ c. salt
¾ c. pepper
4 tsp. mace
4 tsp. sage
4 tsp. dry mustard

Mix salt, pepper, mace, sage and dry mustard to ground pork. Shape into balls the size of a walnut and drop into jars. Can at 10 lb. pressure for 1 hour or put in containers and freeze.

Pork Sausage
...Mrs. Leland (Orpha) Yoder
...Mrs. Harry (Edna Mae) Bontrager

To every 50 lb. pork add:
10-12 oz. (1¼-1½ c.) salt
2 oz. (¼ c.) black pepper
¼ c. sage
1 Tbsp. red pepper
1 c. brown sugar

Sprinkle these seasonings over meat and mix well before grinding. Very good to make into patties and bake awhile before putting into jars and canning, but can also be canned as is for slicing later or can be frozen. Very good! 10 lb. pressure for 1½ hours if raw in jars.

Polish Sausage
...Mom, Rosa Bontrager

10 lb. ground chicken
2 lb. water
2 c. nonfat dry milk
6 Tbsp. salt
1 Tbsp. sugar
½ tsp. cure
1 Tbsp. black pepper
1 tsp. garlic
1 tsp. (heaping) marjoram

Mix all ingredients and stuff into jars and pressure can at 10 lb. pressure for 1½ hours or place in freezer bags and freeze.

If my problems or workload overwhelms me,
my focus is on my problems instead of on God.

184

Homemade Bologna to Can
...Mrs. Jonathan (Rose) Yoder ...Mrs. Samuel (Susie) Hochstetler

25 lb. beef (We like it better
  with sausage.)
³/₄ lb. (1¹/₂ c. heaping) Tenderquick
1 qt. warm water

Mix and let set overnight.

1 Tbsp. pepper
¹/₄ c. seasoning salt
¹/₂ c. brown sugar
1 tsp. garlic salt
1 Tbsp. liquid smoke
1 qt. warm water

Add. Mix together and stuff into jars. 1¹/₂ pt.
jars are great as you can just slide the meat out
and slice. Warm up and use for sandwiches.
Pressure can at 10 lb. for 90 minutes.

Turkey Bologna
...Mrs. Christy (Anna) Bontrager

25 lb. fresh turkey, cut off
  bones
¹/₂ lb. Tenderquick
1 oz. black pepper
¹/₂ c. sugar
2 tsp. salt petre
¹/₄ tsp. garlic powder
3 Tbsp. liquid smoke
¹/₂ gal. water

Grind turkey once. Mix other ingredients and
mix into the meat well. Grind 2 more times.
Put into jars for canning or packaging for
freezing. Let set 24 hours before canning or
freezing. Pressure can at 10 lb. for 1¹/₂ hours.

Venison Bologna
...Mrs. Samuel (Susie) Hochstetler

38 lb. deer meat
12 lb. pork
1¹/₂ lb. Tenderquick
¹/₃ c. salt
¹/₃ c. black pepper
1¹/₈ c. brown sugar
¹/₄ c. Worcestershire sauce
¹/₂ c. Lawry's seasoning salt
1 oz. (2 Tbsp.) Accent
1 Tbsp. cayenne pepper
¹/₄ c. liquid smoke

Grind 2 times. Mix all dry ingredients and
sprinkle over meat. Add liquids and mix well
and grind third time. Let set in cool place 3-4
days. Grind and stuff in 2¹/₂"-3" casing. Put
bologna in large cooker. Cover with cold
water. Heat to 155°-160°. Simmer for 45
minutes or until done. When bologna
floats, it's done. Put in cold water to cool. Is
good to eat cold with cheese and crackers.

Pork and Beans to Can

...Mrs. Melvin (Katie) Miller

8½ lb. navy beans
⅓ c. salt
3½ lb. pork of any kind

Tomato Sauce:
3 qt. tomato juice
2 lb. brown sugar
1 lb. white sugar
2 tsp. dry mustard
1 tsp. cinnamon
1 qt. ketchup
2 qt. water
1 tsp. pepper
½ c. flour or cornstarch

Soak beans overnight. Boil until soft with
pork and salt, adding as little water as possible.

Mix all together and add to bean mixture.
Put in jars and cold pack for 2 hours or
pressure cook for 40 minutes at 10 lb.
pressure. This was my mother's recipe and is
very good!

Favorite Soup to Can

...Mrs. Sam (Mary) Hershberger ...Mrs. Daniel (Fannie) Hershberger

5 lb. hamburger
4 onions, chopped
salt and pepper to taste
6 qt. chopped potatoes
3 qt. chopped carrots
4 lb. mixed vegetables
1 lb. ABC macaroni
2 qt. chicken broth
5 qt. tomato juice
4 c. brown sugar
2 Tbsp. chili powder
2 Tbsp. chicken soup base

Fry hamburger, onions, salt and pepper.
Cook potatoes. You may add potato water.
Cook and salt vegetables. Combine chicken
broth and tomato juice, chicken base, sugar
and 1 stick butter. Thicken this slightly with
Perma-Flo or clear jel. Add meat and vegetables.
You may add more seasoning to your taste.
Pressure cook at 10 lb. pressure for 30 minutes.
Fannie uses more hamburger and tomato juice
and no chicken base. Yield: 20 qt.

When the children are rowdy and we are tired, remember
strength comes from the One who blessed us with these angels.

Vegetable Soup
...Mrs. Roy (Lovina) Yoder

10 lb. mixed vegetables
12 lb. hamburger
1-2 c. ABC macaronis
2 stalks celery, chopped
5 qt. carrots, chopped
5 qt. potatoes, chopped
8 onions, finely chopped
6 qt. tomato juice
1 c. butter
4 qt. hot water
3/4 lb. beef soup base
1 c. salt
3 c. white sugar
1 c. clear jel or Perma-Flo

Cook mixed vegetables 5 minutes. Add salt. Save water in which vegetables were cooked. Fry hamburger. Cook and drain macaronis. Cook celery, carrots and potatoes for 5-10 minutes. Save water. Mix mixed vegetables, hamburger, macaronis, celery, carrots, potatoes and onions together. Add tomato juice. Brown butter in 6 qt. kettle. Add hot water, beef soup base, salt and sugar. Bring to boiling. Add clear jel mixed with water to make a thin paste. Stir into boiling mixture and stir until boiling again. Add other vegetables. Put in jars. Bathe or cold pack 2-3 hours. Yield: 40 qt.

Cream of Tomato Soup
...Mrs. Sam (Viola) Miller

2 c. butter
1/4 c. finely chopped onion
2 1/4 c. flour
3/4 c. sugar
1/4 c. salt
2 tsp. pepper
7 1/2 qt. tomato juice

Melt butter. Add onions and fry a little. Stir in flour, sugar, salt and pepper. Cook until smooth and bubbly, stirring constantly. Remove from heat and add tomato juice. Stir. Cold pack for 15-20 minutes.

Tomato Juice Cocktail
...Mrs. Dennis (Mary) Bontrager

12 qt. tomato juice
1 1/3 c. sugar
1/4 c. garlic salt
4 tsp. celery salt
4 tsp. onion salt
1/4 c. plain salt

In a large saucepan combine all ingredients. Heat, put in jars and cold pack for 15 minutes. This is a healthy drink/snack for little children.

Canning Apple Snitz   ...Mrs. Edna Slabaugh

Peel and core apples. I peel mine with peeler, then chop to size. Put in layers in 5 gal. bucket or in big stockpot. Put layer of apples, then sugar, apples, sugar...about 2 lb. sugar for 5 gal. bucket. Let stand overnight. Next day put apples in jars along with the syrup that has formed. Hot water bath: 1 qt. = 10 minutes, ½ gal. = 15 minutes. Take out immediately.

Strawberries to Can with Glaze
...Mrs. Freeman (Mabel) Yoder

10 c. sugar
12 c. water
2 c. (or more) Perma-Flo
⅔ c. strawberry or raspberry Jell-O
6-8 qt. sliced strawberries
¼ c. lemon juice
dash salt

First slice strawberries and place in a bowl with holes to drain. Use some of drained juice for the water. Combine sugar, water and Jell-O in a large kettle. Bring to a boil. In a small bowl combine Perma-Flo and 1-2 c. cold water to make a paste and add gradually to boiling sugar water. Bring to a boil again until thickened, about 2 minutes. If it's not thick enough, add a bit more Perma-Flo mixed with a little water. Add lemon juice and salt. In a large bowl gently fold berries and sauce together. Ladle into jars and water bath. Bring water to a rolling boil, then turn burner off and let set 10 more minutes. Remove jars from water. Good to use in cobblers or as a fruit with cake.

Tip: Always use Perma-Flo when canning thickened fruits. Stays nice for years. Clear jel is better to use for immediate use.

You can tell more about a person by what he says about others than what others say about him.

Canning Strawberries

...Mrs. David (Lydia) Schwartz

Fill jars with clean, capped whole strawberries. Make a heavy syrup of 1 part sugar and 1 part water. Use less sugar if desired. Screw on lids and water bath, filling the water so it almost covers the jars. Bring to a boil and boil 3-5 minutes. Turn off heat and let jars sit 15 minutes, then take out of water.

Another way to can them is after they are washed, pour sugar over them, approx $^1/_3$-$^1/_2$ c. per qt. of berries. Toss to coat. Put in fridge or cool place a few hours or overnight. This will form its juice. Put berries in jars and pour juice over berries dividing evenly. More sugar syrup may be added or just plain water for a less sweet berry. These are now ready to seal. Same as above. Do not boil more than 5 minutes. Strawberries are best the first year. Strawberries this way are good used with fruit cobblers.

To Can Ground Cherries for Pie Filling

...Mrs. Mervin (Emma) Yoder

$3^1/_2$ qt. ground cherries
3 c. sugar
1 tsp. almond extract
3 qt. water
$^1/_3$ tsp. salt
2 c. (heaping) Perma-Flo
1 c. water
1 (20 oz.) can crushed pineapple
$^3/_4$ c. lemon Jell-O

Mix Perma-Flo with 1 c. water. Add to boiling cherries, sugar, almond extract, 3 qt. water and salt. Add pineapple and Jell-O. Bring to a boil again. Put in jars and cold pack for 20 minutes.

To Can Peaches

...Mrs. Sam (Mary) Hershberger

20 c. water
8 c. sugar
3 c. Therma-Flo
$^3/_4$ c. orange Jell-O
$^3/_4$ c. peach Jell-O
$^1/_2$ c. pineapple Jell-O
3 Tbsp. lemon juice
1 tsp. salt

Cook water, sugar and Therma-Flo together, then add Jell-O, lemon juice and salt. Add peaches and pineapple. Cold pack for 15 minutes. When you open a jar, add grapes. This is very refreshing.

Pineapple-Orange Fruit to Can

...Mrs. Mervin (Emma) Yoder

1 gal. crushed pineapple
1 gal. mandarin oranges
1 gal. peaches
2 gal. water
4 lb. sugar or less
2¹/₂-3 lb. Perma-Flo
24 oz. orange or apricot Jell-O

Heat pineapple, water and sugar to boiling. Add Perma-Flo mixed with 1 qt. water. Bring to boil again and add other fruit and Jell-O. Put in jars and cold pack for 10 minutes. Adds a nice variety to your canning shelves. Is good on cheesecakes.

Glaze for Fruit Cocktail to Can

...Mrs. Jonathan (Rose) Yoder

1 lg. can pineapple juice
2 c. crushed pineapple
7 c. water
4 c. sugar
3 c. mashed peaches
2 c. Perma-Flo
1 c. water
1 c. sugar
3 tsp. vanilla
1 c. peach Jell-O
1¹/₂ tsp. salt

Heat pineapple juice, crushed pineapple, water, 4 c. sugar and mashed peaches to boiling. Add Perma-Flo, water and 1 c. sugar. When thickened, add vanilla, peach Jell-O and salt. One and a half batches is enough for ¹/₂ bushel peaches, 2 gal. pears, 2 bags grapes and 3 cans chunk pineapple. Yield: approx. 22 qt.

Canning Muskmelons

...Mrs. Jonathan (Rose) Yoder

Syrup:
3¹/₂ c. sugar
2 c. water
1 tsp. salt
¹/₂ c. vinegar

Soak chopped melons in salt water a couple hours or overnight. Put melons in jars. Hot water bath. Boil for 10 minutes. Yield: 4 qt.

Freezer Corn

...Mrs. Leland (Orpha) Yoder ...Mom, Rosa Bontrager

16 c. raw corn
1/2 c. sugar
5 tsp. salt
4 c. ice water

Measure corn into a large bowl. Add sugar and salt, then put 3 c. water in a pitcher with 1 tray of ice cubes (approximately) and pour over corn. Mix well; let set for a little while, stirring occasionally. When ice has melted put in containers or freezer bags and freeze immediately. Tastes very fresh. Since corn is still raw, it must be cooked for 5-10 minutes before serving.

Dilled Beans

...Mrs. Leland (Orpha) Yoder

1 clove garlic, do not cut
1 head of dill
¹/₈ tsp. red cayenne pepper

Snip and wash beans. Leave beans whole. Using pint jars, place 1 clove garlic, 1 head dill and ¹/₈ tsp. red cayenne pepper in bottom of each jar. Stand beans in jar (make full). Then add brine.

Brine:
5 c. white vinegar
5 c. water
¹/₂ c. (scant) canning salt

Boil brine. Pour into jars. Put on lids. Hot water bath for 5 minutes. Yield: 10 pt. Wait 3 weeks before enjoying.

Kosher Dill Pickles

...Mrs. Nathan (Barbara) Lehman

To each quart pickles add:
1 tsp. dry mustard
¹/₂ tsp. turmeric
1 tsp. (rounded) minced garlic
2 tsp. dill seed or dill weed
¹/₂ tsp. black pepper
1 grape leaf or
    ¹/₈ tsp. powdered alum

Slice cucumbers lengthwise or use small whole ones. Stuff jars with cukes, and measure spices into each jar, then pour boiling brine over it. Put grape leaf on top before closing with lids. Preheat oven to 250°. Set jars into cake pans, fill pans with boiling water and bake for 20 minutes. Set jars upside down on towel and cover with towel for 12 hours. The crispest pickles with no chance of turning mushy.

Brine:
1 qt. vinegar
3 qt. water
³/₄ c. salt

Cook brine.

Crisp Lunch Pickles

...Mrs. Sam (Rachel) Kauffman

approx. 2 gal. cucumbers
3 onions
1/2 c. salt
5 c. white sugar
3 c. vinegar
2 c. water
1 tsp. celery seed
1 tsp. mustard seed
1/2 tsp. turmeric

Slice cucumbers and 3 onions in a large bowl. Add salt and cover with cold water. Let stand overnight. Drain and pack in jars. Bring sugar, vinegar, water and spices to a boil and pour over the pickles in jars. Seal and cold pack for 5 minutes. When fixing these in the summer time to have fresh for church lunch; just put the drained pickles in a big container and pour boiling syrup over them and let set a day. Very good and crisp.

Pickle Relish to Can

...Mrs. Marcus (Joleen) Marner

2 gal. ground pickles
4 c. onion, chopped
4 red peppers, chopped
3 stalks celery, chopped

Put these ingredients in a colander to drain.

1/4 c. salt
6 c. sugar
2 tsp. mustard seed
2 tsp. turmeric
1 Tbsp. celery seed
2 c. vinegar

Mix these ingredients well. Add pickles, onion, peppers and celery to vinegar mixture. Mix well. Let set for 2 hours. Bring to a boil for about 5 minutes. Pack in jars and set upside down to seal. Yield: about 10-12 pt.

Hamburger Relish

...Mrs. Lonnie (Norma) Bontrager

12 extra lg. cucumbers (peel, remove seeds and grind)
4 lg. onions, ground
4 green peppers, ground
2 red peppers, ground

Add:
1 Tbsp. salt
1/4 c. mustard seed
3 Tbsp. turmeric
1 qt. vinegar
1/2 tsp. cloves
2 1/2 c. sugar

Bring to a boil for 5 minutes and hot water bath for 30 minutes.

192

Canned Peppers ...Mrs. Marvin (Mary Ann) Schrock

Cut peppers into small pieces and pack into pint or quart jars. It is very colorful if you have some red peppers to mix in with your green peppers. Add 1 Tbsp. corn oil to each quart of peppers. If you use pint jars add ½ Tbsp. corn oil.

Boil together:

2 qt. white vinegar
1 qt. water
2 c. sugar

Pour hot mixture into each jar to the neck of the jar. Seal immediately. Note: It is important to use corn oil and not vegetable oil. The peppers are almost like pimentos.

Pickled Onions ...Mrs. Freeman (Mabel) Yoder

1 c. sugar
1 c. canning salt
2 qt. water
1 qt. vinegar
garlic buds
dill seed
onions
green peppers (optional)
red peppers (optional)

Combine first 4 ingredients in a large kettle. Bring to a boil and simmer. Slice desired amount of onions into pint jars and (pepper slices if desired, looks pretty this way) place a garlic bud and ½ tsp. dill seed in each jar or a medium head of homegrown dill. Pour brine over onions to the neck of the jars. Screw on lids and place jars in a cake pan of hot water. Water bath in oven at 250°-300° for 25 minutes. Very crisp; a family favorite! May use ½ tsp. minced garlic instead of buds. Wait 3 weeks before opening a jar. Serve with any meat or hot dish.

Barbecued Onions ...Mrs. Freeman (Mabel) Yoder

1 qt. spaghetti sauce
¾ c. ketchup
2 c. brown sugar
1 tsp. salt
½ c. barbecue sauce
¾ c. vinegar
1 c. vegetable oil

Mix together and heat. Add 1 gal. sliced onions or chopped. Simmer 30 minutes. Put in jars and seal. This is a good way to use up those extra onions and delicious with any meat and/or tomatoes.

Red Beets to Can

...Mrs. Vern (Irene) Schlabach ...Mom, Elsie Yoder

3 c. brown sugar
1½ c. vinegar
1½ c. hot water
1 c. beet water (that was used
   to cook beets in)
1 Tbsp. salt

Dissolve sugar in hot water, then add rest of ingredients and pour over beets packed in jars. This is enough brine for 5-7 qt. Cook the red beets soft, then the peelings just slip off. I usually pressure cook mine for 5-10 minutes at 10 lb. pressure. To can I just cold pack for 10 minutes in hot water bath.

Sauerkraut

...Mrs. Willis (Mary Esther) Wagler

Put 1 tsp. salt in bottom of quart canning jar. Fill with shredded cabbage and add to each jar 1 tsp. salt, on top, 1 tsp. sugar, 1 tsp. white or apple cider vinegar. Then cover with boiling water and seal tight. Fill each jar to 1" from top and seal. No need to cold pack. Ready to use in a few weeks. When opened for use, kraut will be white and crisp.

Cabbage Slaw to Freeze or Can

...Mom, Rosa Bontrager

4½ qt. shredded cabbage
6 med. carrots, finely chopped
3 onions, finely chopped
3 green or red peppers, finely chopped
1 Tbsp. salt
2¼ c. oil
1 Tbsp. mustard seed

Mix and let set 1 hour.

1 c. vinegar
1 c. water
3 c. sugar
1 lg. box lemon Jell-O

Boil vinegar, water and sugar. Add Jell-O. Cool and add to cabbage. If you can it, just bring to a boil, then turn off burner and let cool in canner before taking jars out.

Salsa Sauce

...Mrs. Melvin (Mary) Stutzman

10-12 c. chopped, peeled
    tomatoes
2 c. chopped green peppers
1¼-1½ c. chopped hot pepper
4½ c. chopped onions
3 c. chopped celery
2 Tbsp. garlic powder
2 Tbsp. parsley flakes
2 Tbsp. salt
2 tsp. oregano
1 c. vinegar

Cook everything for 30 minutes. Add ⅓ c. Perma-Flo mixed with a small amount of water. Ladle into jars and hot water bath pints for 15 minutes. Yield: 17 c.

Charlene's Salsa

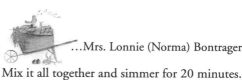

...Mrs. Lonnie (Norma) Bontrager

2 lg. bunches celery, chopped
6 lg. onions, chopped
6 cloves garlic, chopped, or
    garlic powder
6 green peppers
16 c. tomatoes, chopped
4 jalapeño peppers (optional)
1 qt. vinegar
1 c. brown sugar or enough to suit your taste
4 tsp. salt
4 (8 oz.) cans tomato paste
2 Tbsp. oregano
2 pkg. taco seasoning mix
2 tsp. Tabasco sauce

Mix it all together and simmer for 20 minutes. Hot water bath for 30 minutes.

The eyes of all wait upon thee; and thou
givest them their meat in due season.
—Psalm 145:15

195

Super Sauce

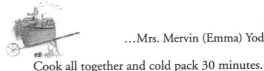

...Mrs. Mervin (Emma) Yoder

3 gal. tomato juice
1½ c. onions
½ tsp. red pepper
1½ tsp. garlic powder
1½ tsp. oregano
1 Tbsp. Vega-salt
1½ c. vinegar
1 Tbsp. cumin
2 Tbsp. paprika
5 c. (scant) sugar
¼ c. salt
¼ c. Lawry's seasoning salt
3 Tbsp. parsley
1 c. Perma-Flo, or more for desired thickness

Cook all together and cold pack 30 minutes. A good sauce that works well for spaghetti and pizza both.

Sandwich Spread

...Mrs. Wayne (Ruth) Raber

6 lg. onions
6 lg. cucumbers
6 green peppers
6 red peppers
6 green tomatoes
¼ c. salt
1 qt. vinegar
1 pt. water
5 c. white sugar
1¼ c. flour
1 pt. mustard
2 Tbsp. turmeric
1 pt. vinegar

Grind or chop the vegetables and add salt. Stir together, then let stand 1 hour. Put in colander and drain 1 hour. Put in kettle and add 1 qt. vinegar, water and white sugar. Boil together for 15 minutes. While this boils mix flour, mustard, turmeric and 1 pt. vinegar. Mix into boiled mixture.

For he satisfieth the longing soul, and filleth
the hungry soul with goodness.
—Psalm 107:9

Tips for Canning and Freezing

... Syrup for canning fruit:
   heavy syrup – 1 c. sugar to 1 c. water
   medium syrup – 1 c. sugar to 2 c. water
   light syrup – 1 c. sugar to 3 c. water.

... When filling jars for canning, leave approximately 1" headspace. If jars are too full, food may cook out through lids and jars may not seal.

... Check jars carefully. If there are any chips or cracks, they will not seal.

... To process foods with the boiling water bath method: Place jars on a rack in a cooker and fill with water, covering jars. Start timing when water comes to a full rolling boil. Lower heat slightly, making sure water continues to boil.

... Boiling water bath method

Time Table for Fruit	
Peaches	15 minutes
Pears	15 minutes
Cherries	10 minutes
Applesauce	10 minutes
Tomato Juice	15 minutes

Turn off heat and let set for 5 minutes before removing jars from hot water.

Home Canning Methods

Water-Bath Method

Water-bath method is a way of processing foods at a temperature of 212°F. This method is recommended for processing fruits, tomatoes, pickles, relishes and other acid foods. Enough heat is supplied by the boiling water to destroy the bacteria, enzymes, molds and yeasts which cause spoilage in acid foods. Butters, conserves, jams and preserves should be processed at simmering (180°-185°F) for 10-20 minutes in a water-bath canner.

A water-bath canner is a large kettle with a cover and rack or metal basket to keep the jars from resting directly on the bottom of the kettle. The canner needs to be deep enough for water to cover the tops of the jars one or two inches without boiling over. The steam-pressure canner may be used as a water-bath canner. In this case, place the cover on the canner but do not fasten it down; leave vent wide open.

Water-bath canners are available on the market. Any big metal container may be used as a boiling-water-bath canner if it is deep enough so that the water is well over tops of jars and has space to boil freely. Allow two to four inches above jar tops for brisk boiling. The canner must have a tight-fitting cover and a wire or wooden rack. If the rack has dividers, jars will not touch each other or fall against the sides of the canner during processing.

If a steam-pressure canner is deep enough, you can use it for a water bath. Cover, but do not fasten. Leave petcock wide open, so that steam escapes and pressure does not build up inside the canner.

Steam-Pressure Method

Steam-pressure method is a way of processing foods under pressure at a temperature of 240°F. This method is recommended for processing beans, beets, corn, meats and all other low-acid foods. A steam-pressure canner, or cooker, is the kitchen utensil which supplies enough heat to destroy the spores of bacteria which cause flat-sour botulism and some other types of spoilage.

A steam-pressure canner is a heavy kettle with a cover which can be clamped or locked down to make the kettle steamtight. The cover is fitted with a safety valve, a petcock (vent) and a pressure gauge. All parts of the canner must be clean and in good working order. The pressure gauge should be checked at least once a year.

Open-Kettle Method

Open kettle canning, putting hot food into hot jars and putting a prepared lid on it with no further processing is no longer a recommended practice. It previously was used for sealing pickled products and jams and jellies. The correct procedure for these products today is to process in a boiling water bath (jams and jellies) or in a simmering water bath (pickling products).

While the earth remaineth, seedtime and harvest, and cold and heat, and summer and winter, and day and night shall not cease.
Genesis 8:22

Candy, Snacks, Jellies, Jams & Misc.

The Legend of the Snowflake

Long ago, a glittering star led the way to a Holy Child, and today it is said that snowflakes are tiny pieces of that very star, sent to lead our hearts anew to Jesus, the Light of the World.

For as the rain cometh down, and the snow from heaven, and returneth not thither, but watereth the earth, and maketh it bring forth and bud, that it may give seed to the sower and bread to the eater.
Isaiah 55:10

Caramel Candy
...Mrs. Willis (Mary) Bontrager

1 lb. brown sugar
1 c. light corn syrup
1 tsp. cream of tartar
14 oz. sweetened condensed milk
dash salt
½ lb. butter
1 tsp. vanilla

Mix together all ingredients except vanilla; bring to a boil. Cook to 234°-240° on candy thermometer, stirring all the time. Add vanilla and pour in a greased pan. When cool, cut in squares. Coat with chocolate or wrap with kiss wrap or waxed paper squares. Yield: approx. 3 lb. This is the caramel recipe to use for turtles. Could also sprinkle pecans over the top and then dip squares in chocolate. 240° is almost too hard, though thermometers do vary slightly.
Hint: Always add solid shortening to this chocolate candy coating. Never add milk, water, butter, oil or margarine. Approx. 1 Tbsp. to 1 lb. of coating.

Never-Fail Fudge
...Mrs. David (Lydia) Schwartz

3 c. sugar
⅔ c. evaporated milk
1 (7 oz.) jar marshmallow creme
¼ lb. butter or margarine
1 (12 oz.) pkg. semisweet
    chocolate chips
1 c. chopped nuts (optional)

Melt butter in heavy 2-qt. saucepan; stir in milk and sugar. Bring to a full rolling boil, stirring constantly. Continue boiling over medium heat, stirring constantly, until mixture reaches the medium soft ball stage (238° on a candy thermometer). Maintain 238° boiling for a minimum of 5 minutes, stirring constantly. Remove from heat and stir in chocolate chips until melted. Add marshmallow creme and nuts, stirring until well blended. Pour into greased 13" x 9" pan. Cool at room temperature. Cut into squares.

God has promised...strength for each new day,
rest from our labor and light for our path.

Peppermint Fudge   ...Mrs. Freeman (Mabel) Yoder

2 tsp. butter
2 oz. cream cheese, softened
2 c. powdered sugar
3 Tbsp. cocoa
1/2 tsp. milk
1 tsp. vanilla
1/4 c. chopped nuts

Line a loaf pan with foil 8" x 4" x 2". Grease foil with butter. In a bowl beat cream cheese, powdered sugar, cocoa, milk and vanilla. Stir in nuts. Spread into prepared pan. Chill until firm.

Peppermint Layer:
2 oz. cream cheese
2 c. powdered sugar
1/2 tsp. milk
1/2 tsp. peppermint extract
1/4 c. crushed peppermint candy

Mix cream cheese, milk and powdered sugar, then add everything else. Spread gently over chocolate layer. Chill for 1 hour. Using foil, lift fudge from pan, peel off foil and cut in squares.

Butter Pecan Fudge   ...Mrs. Freeman (Mabel) Yoder

1/2 c. butter
1/2 c. sugar
1/2 c. brown sugar
1/2 c. heavy whipping cream
1/8 tsp. salt
1 tsp. vanilla
2 c. powdered sugar
1 c. pecan halves, coarsely chopped

In a large kettle combine the butter, sugars, cream and salt. Bring to a boil over medium heat, stirring occasionally. Boil for 5 minutes, stirring constantly. Remove from heat; stir in vanilla and powdered sugar until smooth. Fold in pecans. Spread into 8" buttered pan. Cool, then cut in squares. Store in refrigerator.

Cheese Fudge   ...Mrs. Monroe (Mary) Hochstetler

1 lb. butter
4 lb. powdered sugar
2 Tbsp. vanilla
1 lb. softened cheese
1 c. cocoa
2 c. chopped nuts

Melt butter and cheese together in large pan. Add other ingredients. Pour into 9" x 13" buttered pan. Let cool. Yield: 7 lb. fudge.

Candy Cereal Treats   ...Mrs. Freeman (Mabel) Yoder

$^1/_2$ c. butter or margarine,
   softened
$^2/_3$ c. brown sugar
2 egg yolks
1 tsp. vanilla extract
$1^1/_2$ c. flour
$^1/_2$ tsp. baking powder
$^1/_2$ tsp. salt
$^1/_4$ tsp. baking soda
3 c. miniature marshmallows

In a mixing bowl cream butter and brown sugar. Beat in egg yolks and vanilla. Combine flour, baking powder, salt and soda; add to creamed mixture until it resembles coarse crumbs. Do not overmix. Press into a 9" x 13" pan. Bake at 350° for 12-14 minutes or until golden brown. Sprinkle with marshmallows and bake 3 minutes longer. Cool.

Topping:
$^2/_3$ c. corn syrup
$^1/_4$ c. butter or margarine
1 (10 oz.) pkg. peanut butter
   chips
2 tsp. vanilla
2 c. Rice Krispies
1 c. salted peanuts
1 c. plain M&Ms

Combine syrup, butter and peanut butter. Cook over medium heat until chips are melted. Remove from heat and add vanilla, cereal, peanuts and M&Ms. Spread over marshmallow layer.

Sweet Jumble Treats   ...Mrs. Freeman (Mabel) Yoder

$^1/_2$ c. peanut butter
$^1/_2$ c. margarine or butter
$^3/_4$ tsp. salt
$^1/_2$ tsp. (scant) garlic powder
$4^1/_2$ tsp. Worcestershire sauce
8 c. Rice or Corn Chex
8 c. Cheerios
$1^1/_2$ c. salted peanuts
2 c. corn candy or M&Ms

Melt margarine and peanut butter until it's shiny, about 5-8 minutes. Stir in seasonings. Add cereals and peanuts. Stir until well coated. Bake at 250° for 1 hour, stirring every 10-15 minutes. Bake on 15" x 10" x 1" pans. Remove from oven and cool slightly. Stir in candy. Red and green M&Ms are good to use at Christmas time. Spread on paper to cool.

God meant it unto good. No second cause I see,
For my God appoints each day, and plans my life for me.

Chex Muddy Buddies ...Mrs. David (Lydia) Schwartz

9 c. Chex cereal
1 (8 oz.) bag semisweet
  chocolate chips
1/2 c. peanut butter
1/4 c. butter
1 tsp. vanilla
1 1/2 c. powdered sugar

Measure cereal into large bowl; set aside. Heat butter, chips and peanut butter in 1-qt. saucepan over low heat, stirring frequently until melted. Remove from heat. Stir in vanilla. Pour chocolate mixture over cereal. Stir until evenly coated. Pour into a clean brown grocery bag and add powdered sugar. Fold top shut and shake until well coated. Yield: 9 c.

Favorite Snack Mix ...Mrs. Simon (Esta) Miller
...Mrs. Orlie (Mary) Troyer

6 c. Crispix cereal
1 (10 oz.) can mixed nuts
1 (10 oz.) bag pretzel sticks
3/4 c. butter
3/4 c. brown sugar

In a large bowl combine cereal, nuts and pretzels. In small saucepan melt butter over low heat. Add brown sugar. Stir until dissolved. Pour over cereal mixture. Stir to coat. Toast on a large cookie sheet in 325° oven for 8 minutes. Stir and return to oven for another 8 minutes. Spread on wax paper to cool. Yield: 14 c. yummy crunchies. Variations: Mary uses only 1/3 c. butter and 4 c. Honeycomb cereal as optional.

Happy Trails Snack Mix ...Mrs. Freeman (Mabel) Yoder

3 c. miniature pretzels
2 c. mixed nuts
1 c. Kix cereal
1 c. chopped dried apple
1 c. raisins
3/4 c. chopped dried pineapple
1/2 c. Skittles, bite-size candies
1/2 c. milk chocolate M&Ms

Combine all ingredients in a large bowl. Store in an airtight container. Yield: 2 qt.

Seasoned Pretzels ...Mrs. David (Rachel) Plank

1 c. oil
3 Tbsp. cheddar cheese powder
3 Tbsp. sour cream and onion powder
1 lb. pretzels

Mix together oil and seasonings. Pour over pretzels; mix thoroughly. Bake at 250° for 30 minutes, keeping stirred often. Let cool and enjoy.

Seasoned Crackers ...Mrs. Marvin (Mary Ann) Schrock

1 lb. saltine crackers
1 c. vegetable oil
3 Tbsp. cheddar cheese powder
¼ c. sour cream and onion powder
2 Tbsp. chicken soup base

Pour crackers into a large mixing bowl. Mix remaining ingredients together. Pour mixture over crackers and stir well. Bake 20 minutes at 250°, stirring several times. A very good snack! Note: For a different flavor substitute taco seasoning for the chicken soup base. Plain saltines turn into a delicious snack!

Nutty Toffee Popcorn ...Mrs. Freeman (Mabel) Yoder

10 c. popped popcorn
1 c. pecan halves, toasted
1 c. whole unblanched almonds, toasted
1⅓ c. packed brown sugar
1 c. butter, no substitutes
½ c. light corn syrup
½ tsp. cream of tartar
½ tsp. baking soda
½ tsp. rum extract (optional)

In a large bowl combine the popcorn and nuts. In a heavy saucepan combine the brown sugar, butter, corn syrup and cream of tartar; stir until sugar is dissolved. Cook without stirring over medium heat until a candy thermometer reads 300°-310° (hard crack stage). Remove from heat; stir in baking soda and extract. Immediately pour over popcorn mixture; toss gently. Spread into 2 greased 15" x 10" baking pans. Press gently to flatten. Cool completely. Break into pieces. Yield: about 2 qt.

God is...
the arm that protects,
the help that assures,
the wisdom that guides
the love that endures.

Popcorn Candy Cake ...Mrs. Freeman (Mabel) Yoder

1 (16 oz.) pkg. miniature
  marshmallows
³/₄ c. vegetable oil
¹/₂ c. butter or margarine
5 qt. popped popcorn
1 (24 oz.) pkg. spiced gumdrops
  or 1 c. M&Ms
1 c. salted peanuts

In a large saucepan melt marshmallows, oil and butter until smooth. In a large bowl combine popcorn, gumdrops and peanuts. Add marshmallow mixture and mix well. Press into a greased 10" tube pan. (A one piece tube pan is recommended, but I have used an angel food cake pan.) Cover and refrigerate for 5 hours or overnight. Dip pan in hot water for 5-10 seconds to unmold. Slice cake with an electric or serrated knife.

Peanut Butter Popcorn Bars
...Mrs. Freeman (Mabel) Yoder

10 c. popped popcorn
¹/₂ c. sugar
¹/₂ c. light corn syrup
¹/₂ c. creamy peanut butter
1 tsp. vanilla extract

Place popcorn in a large bowl. Set aside. In a saucepan over medium heat bring sugar and corn syrup to a boil, stirring constantly. Boil for 1 minute. Cool slightly. Stir in peanut butter and vanilla; mix well. Pour over popcorn and mix until coated. Press into a buttered 13" x 9" x 5" pan. Cool before cutting. Children love this!

Ice Cream Finger Jell-O ...Mrs. Simon (Esta) Miller

1¹/₂ c. Jell-O of your choice
¹/₄ c. unflavored gelatin
¹/₂ c. cold water
4 c. boiling water
2 c. vanilla ice cream

Soak gelatin in cold water. Mix Jell-O and gelatin. Add boiling water. Mix thoroughly. Add ice cream. Pour into Tupperware Jell-O mold. Let it set. Slice and enjoy.

Zucchini Marmalade

...Mrs. Wayne (Ruth) Raber ...Mrs. John (Susan) Lehman

6 c. peeled, seeded, finely
   shredded zucchini
6 c. white sugar
1 lg. box orange Jell-O
1 (20 oz.) can crushed
   pineapple, not drained

Boil zucchini and sugar together for 6 minutes. Add Jell-O and pineapple. Stir and heat. Pour into hot jars and seal. Yield: 9 c.

Zucchini Butter

...Mrs. Wayne (Ruth) Raber
...Mrs. Samuel (Susie) Hochstetler

4 c. cooked and mashed zucchini
$1/4$ c. vinegar
1 tsp. lemon juice
2 c. sugar
1 tsp. cinnamon
$1/8$ tsp. allspice

Stir everything together and cook until thick over medium heat. Ladle into jars while hot and seal.

Honey Butter

...Mrs. Orlie (Mary) Troyer

1 c. butter
$1/2$ c. honey
1 c. powdered sugar
2 tsp. cinnamon

Heat butter and honey until melted. Remove from heat and add powdered sugar and cinnamon. Mix thoroughly and cool completely, stirring occasionally as it cools. This is delicious on hot rolls or toast.

Pumpkin Honey

...Mrs. Freeman (Mabel) Yoder

6 c. pumpkin
2 Tbsp. ginger
2 Tbsp. cinnamon
1 tsp. allspice
2 lemons
2 c. water
5 lb. brown sugar

Peel pumpkin; chop fine or put through a food chopper. Add spices and sugar. Add chopped lemons, rind and all. Mix well and let set overnight. In a large kettle boil water and pumpkin mixture. Boil gently until mixture is thick. Pour into sterilized jars and seal.

Pear Honey

...Mrs. Freeman (Mabel) Yoder

5 lb. pears
10 c. sugar
2 (8¼ oz.) cans crushed
   pineapple

Peel pears; remove hard cores and discard. Put pears through food chopper, using coarse blade. Combine pears, sugar and pineapple. Cook until the mixture is thick and pears are clear. Pour into hot jars. Adjust lids at once and process in boiling water bath (212°) 5 minutes. Yield: 7 pt. Very good.

Peanut Butter for Church

...Mom, Rosa Bontrager

6 lb. peanut butter
3 lb. marshmallow creme
½ gal. white Karo
pancake syrup, enough to make
   it as thin as you like

We like creamy peanut butter best; it stays fresh longer if you have some left. Yield: 13 qt. mixing bowl not quite full.

Caramel Spread

...Mrs. David (Barbara) Wagler

3 c. brown sugar
2 c. cream
½ gal. white syrup
½ tsp. maple flavoring

Boil brown sugar and cream to 260°. Add white syrup and maple flavoring. Boil this to 230°. Yield: 3 qt. It is very good to spread on bread or use to put over ice cream. Will keep for a long time.

Red Beet Spread

...Mrs. Leland (Orpha) Yoder
...Mrs. Ed (Mary) Slabaugh

3 c. red beet juice
3 c. water
2 pkg. Sure-Jell
½ c. lemon juice
8 c. sugar
6 oz. raspberry Jell-O

Heat beet juice, water, Sure-Jell and lemon juice to a full rolling boil. Add the sugar and Jell-O all at once. Boil for 6-10 minutes. Seal hot in jars or freeze.
Variation: Orpha uses 6 c. beet juice and no water.

Corncob Jelly

...Mrs. Freeman (Mabel) Yoder

12 clean freshly shelled corncobs
3 pt. water
1 pkg. Sure-Jell pectin
3 c. sugar
red food coloring

In a large kettle heat 3 pt. water. Break cobs into small pieces and add to water in kettle. Bring to a boil and boil 35 minutes. Strain 3 c. of this juice. Add water to make 3 c. if necessary and add the pectin. Add sugar. Bring to a full rolling boil for 3-5 minutes. Remove from heat and add a few drops of red coloring. Pour into jars and seal. For variation, add mint flavor and green coloring.

Corncob Molasses

...Mrs. Freeman (Mabel) Yoder

15 clean fresh corncobs,
  broken up
1 gal. water
sugar
½ gal. light corn syrup*
¼ tsp. baking soda (optional),
  this keeps it from sugaring

In a large kettle bring cobs and water to a boil. Boil 2 hours or until water is a nice pink or amber color. Strain and measure water. Add as much sugar as the measured water (I use a few cups less). Bring to a boil and boil until thickened. Add corn syrup, vanilla and red food coloring if desired.
*I add corn syrup right away, then it only needs to be boiled approximately 2-2½ hours. Check periodically by taking ½ c. out and cooling it to see the thickened consistency. Very good on bread or ice cream.

Instant Strawberry Jam

...Mrs. Wayne (Ruth) Raber

16 c. strawberries
16 c. white sugar, divided
2½ c. instant clear jel

Mix strawberries and 10 c. sugar and let set 10 minutes. Mix clear jel and 6 c. sugar. Stir into strawberry mixture. Let set a few minutes. When thickened, put in containers. Let set ½ day before freezing.

No-Cook Strawberry Jam

...Mrs. Melvin (Katie) Miller

4 c. crushed strawberries
⅓ c. (1 pkg.) pectin
1 c. white Karo syrup
5½ c. white sugar

Mix strawberries and pectin. Stir and blend well. Let stand 20 minutes but stir occasionally. Add Karo and gradually add sugar. When all is dissolved, fill freezer containers and freeze. This is a family favorite.

Freezer Jam

...Mrs. David (Lydia) Schwartz

2 c. crushed strawberries
4 c. sugar
1 c. water
½ c. fruit pectin

Mix strawberries and sugar; set aside. In a saucepan bring water to a boil. Boil for 1 minute. Add fruit pectin and boil 3 more minutes. Take off stove and immediately stir into strawberry mixture. Mix well and put in jars. Cold pack for 15 minutes.

Chocolate Syrup

...Mrs. Reuben (Martha) Yoder

1½ c. water
½ c. cocoa
1¼ c. sugar
½ tsp. salt
1½ Tbsp. (rounded) Perma-Flo
1 tsp. vanilla

Bring water to a boil water; stir in mixed dry ingredients and boil 5 minutes. Remove from heat and add vanilla. Add 1-2 Tbsp. syrup to 8 oz. milk. More or less to suit taste. Also good to use as a topping on ice cream. Store in refrigerator.

Peanut Butter Fudge Sauce

...Mrs. Allen (Elsie) Bontrager

1 c. Nésquik
¼ c. creamy peanut butter
⅓ c. milk
3 Tbsp. light corn syrup
2 Tbsp. butter

In 1-qt. saucepan combine Nésquik, peanut butter, milk and corn syrup. Bring to a full boil over low heat, stirring constantly. Remove from heat; stir in butter. Serve warm or cold over ice cream. Yield: approx. 1 c.

Hard Shell Ice Cream Sauce …daughter, LuAnn Yoder

1 c. semisweet chocolate chips	In heavy saucepan on low heat melt
1/4 c. butter	chips, butter and milk slowly. Stir until
3 Tbsp. evaporated milk	mixture is smooth and thin. Serve
	immediately over ice cream; reheat if
	necessary. Is almost like the store-bought hard
	shell syrup and is delicious!

Homemade Sour Cream …Mrs. Jonathan (Wilma) Hochstetler

Pasteurize cream in double boiler to 185°, stirring constantly. Cool quickly on ice. Pour into sterile jar. Add 1 Tbsp. cultured buttermilk per 1 c. cream; shake it. Set out at room temperature for 24-48 hours. If it separates, shake it.

Homemade Sweetened Condensed Milk
…Mrs. Freeman (Mabel) Yoder

1 c. instant dry milk powder	Combine in blender or with wire whip until
2/3 c. sugar	totally smooth. Yield: Equal to a 14 oz. can
1/2 c. boiling water	store bought sweetened condensed milk. Will
3 1/2 Tbsp. butter or margarine	keep in refrigerator for 3 weeks.

Miracle Whip …Mrs. Melvin (Katie) Miller

Part 1:

2 1/2 c. water	Heat water and vinegar to boiling. Make paste
1 c. vinegar	of clear jel and cold water. Add to boiling water
1/2 c. clear jel	and cook until thick. Remove from heat and
2/3 c. cold water	add sugar. Cool.
1/2 c. sugar	

Part 2:

3 egg yolks	Beat egg yolks, sugar, dry mustard, salt and
1/2 c. sugar	vinegar. Beat until light and lemon colored.
1 tsp. dry mustard	Measure out 1 c. salad oil and water and add
2 tsp. salt	slowly to egg mixture until thoroughly blended
1 Tbsp. vinegar	and thickened. Add to cooked mixture and
1 c. salad oil	beat only enough to blend. Store in refrigerator.
1 Tbsp. water	Yield: 1 1/2 qt. This is very tasty but takes a lot
	of beating.

211

Yogurt
...Mrs. Vern (Irene) Schlabach

2 qt. milk
1 Tbsp. gelatin
¹/₄ c. plain yogurt

Put milk in saucepan. Add gelatin. Let set for 10 minutes. Heat to scalding (180°). Let cool to 115°, then add yogurt. Mix well. Put in jars and keep warm (117°). Keep warm with towels or set in gas oven with pilot light on for 4-8 hours.

Gak
...Mrs. Daniel (Fannie) Hershberger

First Bowl:
4 (4 oz.) bottles Elmer's glue
¹/₂ c. water
food coloring

Mix.

Second Bowl:
1 c. water
2 tsp. (level) borax

Dissolve borax in water. Slowly stir this mixture into glue mixture. Use hands to finish mixture. Pour off excess water. Have fun playing!

Liquid Homemade Soap
...Mrs. Mervin (Emma) Yoder

4 gal. water, divided
1 can lye
2 c. 20 Mule Team borax
3 c. liquid Wisk
1 c. ammonia

Use 5 gal. pail. Pour in 2 gal. water and add lye, then rest of ingredients. Stir well and add 2 more gal. of water. Put in containers.

Bird Cake
...Mrs. David (Emma) Hershberger

2 c. peanut butter
2¹/₂ c. cornmeal
1 c. mixed bird seed
¹/₂ c. beef suet

Mix together and melt over low heat. Pour into a bread pan. Let cool. When set, put into mesh bag (like oranges come in). Hang out and let the birds enjoy it.

Today is ours, God has given it to me.
He has taken back all our yesterdays,
And all our tomorrows are in His care.
For gentle guidance, for constant love,
We owe our thanks to God above.

When the billows toss your vessel,
When you sail uncharted seas,
May you hear the captain saying,
"Fear not, I will pilot thee."

Pancakes &
Cereals

Because Jesus Came, We Can...

be a child of God

be rooted and grounded in love.

be under grace.

be filled with all joy.

be alive toward God.

be more than conquerors.

be justified freely.

be conformed to His image.

have peace with God.

be to the praise of His glory.

be renewed day by day.

have a hope laid up in Heaven.

Lonnie Y.

Breakfast Roll-Ups
...Mrs. Orlie (Mary) Troyer

1 (8 oz.) pkg. cream cheese
1 egg yolk
¹/₄ c. sugar
1 loaf white or wheat bread
¹/₂ c. butter, melted
¹/₂ c. sugar, mixed with
    2 tsp. cinnamon

Cream cream cheese, egg yolk and sugar together. Remove crusts from bread (this is optional). Roll each slice out flat with a rolling pin. Spread cream cheese mixture on bread slices. Roll up each slice and cut in half crosswise. Dip each roll in butter, then cinnamon sugar mixture. Place on greased cookie sheet and bake at 400° for 15 minutes.

Waffles
...Mrs. Christy (Anna) Bontrager

2 c. flour (I use Prairie Gold
    whole wheat flour)
4 tsp. baking powder
¹/₄ tsp. salt
2 eggs, separated
1¹/₂ c. milk*
6 Tbsp. butter, melted

Mix everything except egg whites together until smooth. Beat egg whites until stiff; fold into batter. Fry on hot waffle iron. Serve with maple syrup. A family favorite!
*If using whole wheat flour, use 2 c. milk.

Whole Wheat Pancake Mix
...Mrs. Lonnie (Norma) Bontrager

4 c. whole wheat flour
4 c. unbleached flour
¹/₂ c. sugar
¹/₂ c. wheat germ
¹/₄ c. baking powder
1 Tbsp. salt
1¹/₂ c. butter or margarine

Mix dry ingredients and cut in butter. Place in covered container and store in refrigerator for up to 6 weeks. Yield: 3¹/₂ qt. mix.

For pancakes mix:
2¹/₄ c. mix
1 egg
1¹/₄ c. milk

Golden Pancakes
...Mrs. Allen (Elsie) Bontrager

2½ c. flour (1 c. buckwheat
and 1½ c. white)
2 Tbsp. baking powder
½ c. sugar
4 eggs, beaten
2 c. milk
¾ c. vegetable oil
½ tsp. soda

Mix dry ingredients. I like to experiment with using different kinds of flour for a nutritious change. Add eggs, milk and vegetable oil. Beat well and fry on hot griddle. Serve with maple syrup.

Oatmeal Wheat Cakes
...sister, Elvesta Bontrager

1 c. flour
1 c. whole wheat flour
2 c. quick oats
6 Tbsp. brown sugar
1 tsp. salt
4 tsp. baking powder
2 tsp. baking soda
4 eggs, separated
6 Tbsp. vegetable oil
2 c. buttermilk (more or less)

In bowl mix buttermilk, egg yolks, sugar, oats and oil until well blended. Add dry ingredients and mix well, then fold in beaten egg whites. Fry for pancakes. Enjoy! These are good as leftover with butter and jam or jelly.

Country Potato Pancakes

...Mrs. Ed (Mary) Slabaugh

3 lg. (approx. 2 lb.) potatoes,
peeled
2 eggs, slightly beaten
1 Tbsp. grated onion
2 Tbsp. all-purpose flour
1 tsp. salt
½ tsp. baking powder
vegetable oil

Finely grate potatoes. Drain any liquid. Add eggs, onion, flour, salt and baking powder. In frying pan add oil to the depth of ⅛"; heat over medium high (375°). Drop batter by heaping tablespoons in hot oil. Flatten to form patties. Fry until golden brown, then turn and cook other side. Serve immediately. Yield: about 24 pancakes.

Apple Pancakes ...Mrs. Allen (Elsie) Bontrager

2 c. flour
4 tsp. baking powder
2 Tbsp. sugar
1 tsp. salt
2 c. milk
2 Tbsp. butter, melted
2 eggs, separated
1 c. grated, peeled apples

Combine flour, sugar, baking powder and salt in mixing bowl. Combine milk, well beaten egg yolks and butter in small bowl; mix well. Add to flour mixture and beat until smooth. Stir in apples; fold in beaten egg whites. Grease hot griddle for first pancakes only. Pour batter by 1/2 cupfuls onto griddle; cook until puffy and bubbly. Turn; brown other side. Serve with syrup.

Chocolate Chip Pancakes ...Mrs. Freeman (Mabel) Yoder

2 c. flour
1/4 c. sugar
2 Tbsp. baking powder
1 tsp. salt
2 eggs
1 1/2 c. milk
1/4 c. vegetable oil
1/2 c. mini milk chocolate chips

Combine flour, baking powder, sugar and salt. In another bowl combine eggs and milk. Beat well. Add oil and add to dry ingredients. Last add chocolate chips. Bake on a hot griddle. Serve with your favorite syrup. Our children love these chocolate chip pancakes as a change of pace.

Stuffed Apricot French Toast
...Mrs. Orlie (Mary) Troyer

1 (8 oz.) pkg. cream cheese, softened
1 1/2 tsp. vanilla
1 loaf French bread (we use homemade)
4 eggs
1/2 tsp. nutmeg
1/2 c. orange juice
1 c. heavy cream
1 (12 oz.) jar apricot jam

In mixing bowl beat cream cheese and 1 tsp. vanilla until fluffy. Set aside. Cut bread in thin slices. Spread one piece with cream cheese mixture and add another one on top to form a sandwich. In another bowl beat eggs, cream, nutmeg and remaining vanilla. Dip both sides of bread into egg mixture. Fry on lightly greased griddle until golden brown on both sides. Place on ungreased baking sheet. Bake at 300° for 20 minutes. Meanwhile combine jam and orange juice in a saucepan and heat until bubbly. Drizzle over hot French toast and serve immediately. This is delicious with smoked ham and hash browns for brunch.

217

Crunchy Pancake Pizza ...Mrs. Freeman (Mabel) Yoder

2 c. pancake mix*
2 eggs, beaten
1³/₄ c. milk
2 Tbsp. vegetable oil
1 tsp. vanilla or maple flavoring
³/₄ c. granola (without raisins)
1 c. chopped pecans

Combine pancake mix, eggs, oil and milk; mix well. Pour into a greased 14" pizza pan; sprinkle with granola and pecans. Bake at 400° for 12-15 minutes or until a toothpick comes out clean. Serve with your favorite syrup. *I use my own pancake recipe instead of mix. Use a recipe using 1¹/₂-2 c. flour. It's wonderful served with maple syrup.

Granola ...Mrs. Jonathan (Naomi) Wagler

21 c. quick oats
7 c. Cheerios
2 c. wheat germ
2 c. coconut
2¹/₂ c. brown sugar
2 c. oleo or butter, melted
2 Tbsp. vanilla
1 pkg. graham crackers, broken up
2 Tbsp. cinnamon
¹/₂ c. flour

Mix everything together until crumbly. Toast at 300° in shallow pans for 30 minutes, stirring every 15 minutes.

Granola Cereal ...Mrs. Melvin (Mary) Stutzman

5 c. uncooked quick oats
1 c. wheat germ
1 c. coconut
¹/₄ c. (not packed) brown sugar
¹/₂ c. honey
1 c. cooking oil
raisins (optional)
dry powdered milk

Mix first 4 ingredients together. Mix honey and oil and pour over first mixture. Mix until moist. Pour into baking pans and bake 30 minutes at 250°, stirring occasionally. Cool 10-15 minutes. Sprinkle with powdered milk and mix in. Add raisins when cooled completely.

Blessed be the God and Father of our Lord Jesus Christ who hath blessed us with all spiritual blessings in heavenly places in Christ.
—Ephesians 1:3

Graham Granola

...Mrs. Willis (Mary) Bontrager
...sister, Elvesta Bontrager

10 c. oatmeal
2 pkg. graham crackers, crushed
2 c. coconut
1½ c. brown sugar
2 tsp. soda
½ lb. oleo
1½ c. mini chocolate chips

Mix everything except chocolate chips and toast in oven at 200° for 2 hours. Stir every half hour. Cool and add chocolate chips.

Chocolate Chip Granola Cereal

...Mrs. Nathan (Barbara) Lehman

6 c. quick oatmeal
1½ c. brown sugar
4 c. whole wheat flour
2 tsp. salt
1½ c. butter, melted with
   ½ c. peanut butter
1 c. coconut
1½ tsp. soda
1 c. chocolate chips or raisins

Mix all dry ingredients except chocolate chips or raisins. Add melted butter. Mix well with hands. Place in 2 cake pans and bake at 300° for 1 hour, stirring every 15 minutes. Add chips after cereal is cooled or raisins as soon as it comes out of oven. Very delicious and nutritious! The children enjoy eating it dry as an after-school snack.

Butterscotch Granola

...Mrs. Aaron (Mary Ada) Yoder

10 c. oatmeal
2 pkg. graham crackers, crushed
2 c. coconut
1 c. chopped pecans (optional)
4 sticks oleo
¾ c. brown sugar
2 tsp. soda
1 tsp. salt
1 c. mini butterscotch chips

Melt oleo and mix everything except butterscotch chips. Spread evenly on 2 large cookie sheets. Bake at 300° for 40 minutes. Stir every 10 minutes for the first 30 minutes, then every 5 minutes until done. Add butterscotch chips last minute of baking.

Grapenuts
...Mrs. Jonathan (Naomi) Wagler

13 c. wheat flour
4½ c. brown sugar
2 Tbsp. salt
1 c. oleo or butter, melted
1½ Tbsp. vanilla
1 tsp. maple flavoring
6½-7 c. buttermilk
1½ Tbsp. soda

Mix dry ingredients together. Dissolve soda in milk and add to dry ingredients. Add butter and flavorings; mix well. Spread in 2 greased 11½" x 16½" pans. Bake at 350° for 45 minutes. Cut in large pieces. When cooled, put through Salad Master (shoestring cone). Toast at 375°-300° in shallow pans until dry, stirring every 15 minutes.

Oat Bran Grapenuts
...Mrs. Edward (Lizzie Ann) Schrock

10 c. oat bran
1 Tbsp. soda
2 c. brown sugar
2 tsp. salt
2 tsp. vanilla
3-4 c. milk or water

Mix dry ingredients, then add the rest. Put in 3 cake pans and bake at 350° for almost an hour. When done baking, wrap each cake in a towel while still warm and also in plastic. Keep wrapped in towel and plastic overnight, then crumble, dry and eat like any other grapenuts. Soaking in milk a good 15 minutes or more before eating makes them better.

Oatmeal Grapenuts
...Mrs. Nathan (Barbara) Lehman

6 c. graham flour
3 c. brown sugar
2 c. oatmeal
1 c. butter, melted
2 eggs, beaten
4 tsp. soda
2 c. milk

Bake as a cake. Crumble fine; dry in oven at 275° until browned, stirring every 15 minutes. Put into jars immediately and seal. It will stay fresh for months.

Crunchy Puffed Cereal
...Mrs. Mervin (Emma) Yoder

6 c. puffed wheat
6 c. Cheerios
6 c. puffed rice
6 c. oatmeal
3 c. wheat germ
3 c. coconut
3 c. sunflower seeds (optional)
1 c. oil
1 c. honey
2 tsp. vanilla

Heat oil and honey for 3 minutes. Add vanilla and pour over dry cereal. Toast in 300°-325° oven until light brown. Add raisins if desired.

Humble yourselves therefore under the mighty hand of
God, that he may exalt you in due time: Casting all
your care upon him, for he careth for you.
I Peter 5:6-7

Lunch Box Ideas

Autumn Scenes

Some people say that summertime
   Just suits their senses best,
While others think the earth in
   spring
   Is at its loveliest;
But as for me, I like the days
   The autumn brings around,
When skies are blue and air is crisp
   And leaves are on the ground.

When days begin to shorten and
   A chill comes to the air,
When people's steps are brisker as
   They hurry here and there.
When the harvest now is gathered
   From garden and from field,
When overflowing plenty crowns
   The autumn's generous yield.

Then are the days of slower pace
   When evenings seem to call
For crunchy popcorn in a bowl
   And mugs of cider tall.
A wood fire blazing in the stove,
   Dispelling warmth and cheer,
And all the family gathered 'round—
   A special time of year.

It is the year's fulfillment of
   The promise of the spring.
The summer months have brought
   at last
   A bounteous harvesting.
Now as we view the fruits for which
   Our days of toil were spent,
How could the heart be any less
   Than thankful and content?

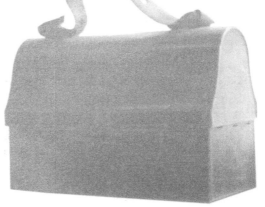

Lunch Box Rules

Lunch packing as we all know can be a big task, but it can also be a satisfying experience if we do a little planning ahead. Here are a few rules we have found helpful in lunch packing. These are only suggestions and people have different preferences.

If you are not a morning person, pack lunches the evening before and store containers in your refrigerator.

• • • • •

Always pack a sandwich, some kind of fruit and a glass of milk or juice.

• • • • •

Plan ahead and bake a big batch of cookies or bars for a week of lunches. Some for lunches and some for meals at home.

• • • • •

Cut up a big bowl of celery sticks, carrot sticks, cauliflower and broccoli. Store in an airtight container or a salad bowl with breathing holes and store in fridge and use for lunches only. Prepare a simple dip with a quart of mayonnaise and salad dressing and mix 4-5 Tbsp. sour cream and onion powder. Mix well and place in small containers for each child.

• • • • •

Do not use food prepared for lunches for your other meals. Keep separate containers somewhere of food for lunches even if it's the top pantry shelf!

• • • • •

We have found it helps to have only 1 or 2 kinds of variety of lunches for one week and then have something else the next week.

• • • • •

When planning lunches shop accordingly.

• • • • •

Set rules for your children, such as if they don't eat the fruit in their lunches, they may not have a snack when the rest of the children do. Of course, there are exceptions to every rule.

• • • • •

We have found it helpful to have snacks such as potato chips, pretzels, corn chips, popcorn, etc. on Monday, Wednesday and Friday. On alternating days for an extra filler, we put in an extra cookie, s'mores or veggies and dip. Snacks are used for lunches and are considered enough of a luxury to use them carefully.

223

Never start fixing each child's lunch to order, such as one sandwich gets mayo, another salad dressing and yet another butter; one wants peaches, another pears and another grapes. Let's teach our children that we try to pack a meal that's healthy and the same for everyone. It's not a meal made to order. This can avoid a lot of stress.

. . . . .

Line your children's lunch boxes with a paper towel to catch spills, etc. They can then use this towel to wipe their hands and mouth when finished eating. Can't afford paper towels or napkins? A thin washcloth works just as well!

. . . . .

Short messages written on your child's napkin (with a black marker) will take only seconds of your time, but will do wonders for his/her day. For example: *Have a good day! Praying for you* or just simply *I love you—Mom.*

. . . . .

Hopefully with some of these tips in mind you won't stand at your counter in the morning wondering what goes in the lunches today! Trying to stay 3 days to a week ahead in planning reduces a lot of hassles. And last but not least, as we pack these lunches for our dear little souls, let's remember to pray for them and their teachers and that the food we prepare for them may nourish their bodies and help them to grow. Keep their well-being in mind.

Here are a few things our grandparents had in their lunches as children. It is good to sometimes remind our children of lunches that our grandparents had.

lard sandwiches	cold beef gravy over bread
cracklings	apple butter with bread
liverwurst and mustard	cold egg sandwiches

They didn't have nice plastic baggies to put food in and used newspaper or wax paper to wrap food in and the food was often dry by noon. They used tin pails or tin buckets that often got rusty. We truly live in a land of plenty. Let us be thankful.

Lunch Box Menus

Complete lunches for school children. Any of these suggestions may be switched to suit individuals.

Ham and cheese sandwich, cake, fruit, a glass of milk and popcorn.

· · · · ·

Bologna and cheese salad dressing sandwich, cookies, chocolate milk, apple and Ritz Cracker S'mores.

· · · · ·

Pizza burger on toast (can be eaten warm or cold), a glass of lemonade, granola bar, fruit and Dorito chips.

· · · · ·

Fried egg and cheese sandwich (heated), Lemon Long Johns, an orange and popcorn.

· · · · ·

Pizza cups (heated), peaches, cake, milk and potato chips.

· · · · ·

Tuna egg salad sandwich, Butter Brickle Bars, apple with peanut butter in the middle or canned fruit, a glass of frozen juice which will be slushy by noon and a small bag of Trail Mix.

· · · · ·

Tuna Snack Spread (for sandwich), No-Bake Oatmeal Cookies, apple or cherry pie filling, chocolate milk, Seasoned Crackers and a piece of candy (optional).

· · · · ·

Lettuce and turkey ham sandwich, fruit, yogurt, cookies of your choice and Chex Muddy Buddies or chips.

· · · · ·

Peanut butter and jelly sandwich, carrots and dip, drink of your choice, chocolate chip cookies and favorite snack mix.

· · · · ·

Summer sausage slices with round crackers, a glass of milk or juice, pumpkin bars and caramel or plain popcorn.

· · · · ·

Spinach or lettuce with home-canned bologna or store-bought for a sandwich, Tri-Level Brownies, orange juice, small jar of raisins and mixed nuts and celery ribs.

. . . . .

Mix 4 oz. cream cheese with $\frac{1}{2}$ c. chopped dried beef or bologna; spread on bread for a sandwich, peanut butter in celery sticks, zucchini cookies or molasses cookies, fruit, potato chips and juice or milk.

. . . . .

Bacon, lettuce and tomato on bread as a sandwich, Pumpkin Whoopie Pies, glazed fruit mix, lemonade and popcorn. (Using real dried bacon bits sprinkled on bread saves time.)

. . . . .

Turkey ham, onions and lettuce sandwich, Sour Cream Raisin Bars, chocolate milk, carrot sticks and finger Jell-O.

. . . . .

Lettuce and summer sausage sandwich, sweet rolls, Simple Fruit Slush or fruit of your choice, juice of choice and popcorn or pretzels.

. . . . .

Toasted cheese sandwiches (warmed), a glass of frozen chocolate milk, Twinkies (homemade), popcorn balls and apples, grapes or oranges.

. . . . .

Hot dog wrapped in tinfoil and warmed up, Maple Butterscotch Brownies or coffee bars, broccoli and cauliflower with dip, fruit, snack and juice.

. . . . .

All recipes found in this cookbook.

Lunch Box Ideas

Cut an apple in half. Cut out the core and fill with crunchy peanut butter. Wrap in Saran wrap for the lunch box. Children love it! Peel and chop 1 apple until coarsely chopped. Add $\frac{1}{2}$ tsp. vanilla, pinch salt, 5-6 Tbsp. milk and 2 tsp. sugar. Stir all together. A delicious different fruit.

. . . . .

Make a glass of your favorite beverage—Kool-Aid, lemonade or chocolate milk—and put in freezer overnight. Put in lunches and by lunchtime, they'll have a cool, slushy drink. Refreshing!

. . . . .

Spread peanut butter and jelly between 2 graham crackers for a delicious alternative to bread.

. . . . .

Carrot sticks dipped in peanut butter make a great snack.

. . . . .

Soda crackers spread or dunked in apple butter is a treat our children love. Fill a small container with apple butter and crackers in a bag for a lunch box treat.

. . . . .

Cut $\frac{1}{2}$ c. fresh cucumbers fine. Add 1 c. cottage cheese, 2 Tbsp. chopped green onions and $\frac{1}{4}$ c. grated carrots. Add salt and pepper to taste. Spread on bread.

. . . . .

Melt 1 c. chocolate chips. Spread on 2 sides of graham cracker halves, as many as desired, then let them dry. Next spread with marshmallow creme and put 2 crackers together. A great school lunch snack.

. . . . .

2 pkg. refrigerated biscuit dough. 16 oz. package hot dogs. Wrap biscuit dough all around each hot dog and bake until light brown. These are handy to wrap in tinfoil and warm up at school. All they need to do is cut a small slit along the top of the bun and put ketchup in. Children think this is a novelty!

. . . . .

Bacon and Onion Bread—Press dinner rolls into a 9" x 13" pan to $\frac{1}{4}$" thickness (or use store-bought biscuit dough). Spread with 1 lb. cooked crumbled bacon and chopped onions as desired. Let rise and bake at 375° until light brown. Cut in squares for lunches and serve with a piece of cheese.

. . . . .

Mix honey and peanut butter (equal amounts). Spreading on bread for a sandwich is a nice change from meats.

. . . . .

Mix 3 oz. pkg. cream cheese, softened, with 1 pkg. drained beef, chopped, 4 oz. shredded marble cheese, ¼ c. mayonnaise and ¼ tsp. minced garlic. A great sandwich spread. Recipe may be doubled.

. . . . .

Mix ¾ c. cottage cheese with ½ c. chopped homemade bologna or lunch meat of your choice (ham or bologna), 2 hard-boiled eggs, chopped, and ¼ c. chopped garlic dill pickles. Spread on bread.

. . . . .

Cream cheese spread on crackers (Ritz or graham) make a good snack and is good when traveling and have problems with car sickness. Also is very soothing to eat when you are sick with flu, etc. But do not put on crackers too long before you eat them or crackers will get soggy.

. . . . .

Pizza Cups

¾ lb. ground beef
1 (6 oz.) can tomato paste
1 Tbsp. minced onion, or raw
1 tsp. Italian seasoning
½ tsp. salt
1 (10 oz.) can refrigerated biscuits or use your own
½-¾ c. shredded cheese

Brown and drain beef. Stir in tomato paste, onion and seasonings (mixture will be thick). Cook over low heat for 5 minutes, stirring frequently. Place biscuits in a greased muffin tin. Spoon about ¼ c. of meat mixture into biscuit-lined cups and sprinkle with cheese. Bake at 400° for 12 minutes or until golden brown. Yield: 12 pizza cups. These are handy to put in lunches!

Ham Roll-Ups

12 oz. cream cheese, softened
1 c. shredded carrots
4 tsp. dill weed
2 tsp. celery flakes
1 lb. fully cooked thin sliced ham

Combine first 4 ingredients and mix well. Place 2 Tbsp. on 1 or 2 pieces of ham and spread evenly. Roll up tightly and place side by side, seam down, in an oblong pan. Cover and refrigerate overnight. Cut in 1" slices. A yummy finger food! May also wrap each one in plastic wrap to refrigerate.

Indiana Style Corn Dogs

$1/2$ c. yellow cornmeal
1 c. all-purpose flour
1 Tbsp. baking powder
1 Tbsp. sugar
1 tsp. salt
$1/4$ tsp. paprika
$1/2$ tsp. dry mustard
1 c. evaporated milk or
   1 c. sweet cream
1 egg, beaten

Mix all together in a bowl, then pour mixture into a tall glass. Dip the precooked hot dogs into mixture and deep fat fry at 375° until golden brown. Drain on paper towels.
Yield: 10-16 corn dogs.
Note: These corn dogs don't get so soggy when reheated, so we like to make several recipes. Freeze the leftovers, then wrap them in foil when you need something quick for children's lunches. They are just delighted to have a hot corn dog on a cold winter day! For easier handling, put wooden skewers into your hot dog before dipping into cornmeal mixture.

Open-Faced Tortillas

3 (10") flour tortillas
1 c. refried beans
1 c. salsa
1 c. shredded mozzarella
1 c. shredded cheddar cheese
$1/3$ c. real bacon bits
$1/4$ c. chopped green onions
chopped tomatoes (optional)

Spread ingredients over tortillas, dividing evenly. Broil in oven until cheese melts. Cut into fourths. Wrap in tinfoil for lunch sandwich. Delicious! Can also use bread.

Tuna Snack Spread

1 (6 oz.) can tuna, drained
   and flaked
1 (8 oz.) pkg. cream cheese,
   softened
2-3 tsp. lemon juice
1 tsp. onion salt
3-4 drops hot pepper sauce
$1/2$ c. salad dressing
shredded cheese (optional)

Serve with crackers. Our children like this in school lunches instead of sandwiches for a change.

229

Tuna Egg Salad

10-12 hard-boiled eggs, chopped
2 (6 oz.) cans tuna, drained
1 c. finely chopped celery
³/₄ c. salad dressing
1 tsp. onion powder
1¹/₂ tsp. Lawry's seasoning salt

Mix all together and refrigerate. Serve on slices of buttered bread or buns.

Tortilla Pinwheels

2 c. sour cream
1 (8 oz.) pkg. cream cheese, softened
1 pkg. Hidden Valley Ranch dip mix
10 flour tortillas
1 c. broccoli
1 c. cauliflower
1 c. grated cheese
1 c. crumbled bacon or diced ham

Mix sour cream, cream cheese and Ranch mix. Spread on tortillas. Top with remaining ingredients. Roll up and chill overnight or 5-6 hours. Slice ¹/₂" thick and serve.

Chocolate Dessert Wraps

1 c. creamy peanut butter
8 (8") flour tortillas
2 c. mini marshmallows
1 c. mini milk chocolate chips
vanilla ice cream
chocolate syrup or shavings

Spread peanut butter evenly over tortillas. Sprinkle with marshmallows and chocolate chips. Roll up, then wrap in heavy tinfoil. Place on a cookie sheet and place in oven at 250°-300° for 8-10 minutes or until heated through. Serve with ice cream and syrup.

Whole Wheat Coffee Bars

2 eggs	Mix coffee with water. Beat sugar, eggs and oil.
2 c. brown sugar	Add dry ingredients. Gradually add coffee
1 c. vegetable oil	water. Pour onto a greased 10" x 15" x 1"
1 c. water	cookie sheet. Bake at 350° for 25-30 minutes.
2 tsp. instant coffee	Drizzle with coffee glaze while warm.
2 tsp. vanilla	
1 tsp. salt	
1 tsp. baking soda	
1 c. chocolate chips	
1 c. whole wheat flour	
2 c. white flour	
1 c. chopped peanuts (optional)	

Glaze:

¹/₂ tsp. instant coffee	Mix coffee and water. Add margarine and
4 tsp. water	powdered sugar. Mix and drizzle over bars.
1 Tbsp. margarine	
1 c. powdered sugar	

Crispy Pretzel Bars

1 c. sugar	In a large saucepan combine the sugar and
1 c. light corn syrup	corn syrup. Cook for 3 minutes or until sugar
¹/₂ c. peanut butter	is dissolved. Stir in peanut butter until blended.
5 c. Rice Krispies	Add the cereal, pretzels and M&Ms; stir until
2 c. pretzel sticks	coated. Press into a greased 15" x 10" x 1"
1 c. plain M&Ms	pan. Cut into bars.

3-Step Peanut Butter Cookies

1 c. peanut butter	Mix all together. Shape into balls and roll in
1 c. sugar	sugar. Flatten onto cookie sheet with a fork.
1 egg	Bake at 350° for 10 minutes. This makes a
	delicious, melt-in-your mouth cookie.

Warm Day No-Bakes

1/2 c. corn syrup or honey 1/2 c. butter 1/2 c. sugar (raw or brown)	Boil for 7-8 minutes on top of stove over medium heat. Let cool. Add peanut butter, oatmeal, coconut and Rice Krispies. Also add powdered sugar if you wish until balls the size of golf balls can be formed. Press a few M&Ms on top and flatten slightly. Enjoy!

No-Bake Oatmeal Cookies

First Ingredients:

2 c. sugar 1/2 c. cocoa 1/2 c. rich milk or cream 1 stick margarine pinch of salt	Mix and boil 1 minute. Remove from heat.

Second Ingredients:

1/2 c. peanut butter 3 c. quick oats 1 tsp. vanilla	Add to first set of ingredients. Mix well and drop by teaspoons on waxed paper.

Monster Squares

3 eggs 1 c. brown sugar 1 tsp. vanilla 2 tsp. corn syrup 2 tsp. baking soda 1/2 c. margarine 3/4 c. peanut butter 4 1/2 c. quick oats 1/2 c. flour 1 c. chocolate chips 1 c. M&Ms	Mix in order given. Press into a greased jelly roll pan and bake at 350° just until set. Do not overbake. Makes soft, chewy bars. Bake approximately 20-25 minutes.

Butter Brickle Bars

saltine crackers
1 c. butter
1 c. brown sugar
1½ c. chocolate chips

Line a cookie sheet with tinfoil. Place a single layer of saltine crackers on sheet. Cook butter and brown sugar for 3 minutes. Pour on crackers and bake for 5 minutes at 400°. Remove from oven and sprinkle with chocolate chips. Wait for 2 minutes, then spread chocolate chips evenly over butter and sugar layer. Cool and cut into pieces. Easy for school children to make and a great snack.

Lemon Long Johns

3 Tbsp. clear jel or Perma-Flo
1½ c. white sugar
3 egg yolks, beaten
1¼ c. boiling water
2 Tbsp. lemon juice
dash salt
wiener buns

Mix sugar, lemon juice and clear jel. Add egg yolks, then hot water. Cook in double boiler until thick and clear. Let cool. Open wiener buns and spoon filling carefully into buns. Frost tops of buns lightly with your favorite frosting. A simple and easy specialty for lunches.

Cake Cones

Mix a cake mix or the cake of your choice and fill ice cream cones ⅔ full. Set in a cake pan or muffin pans. Bake at 350° for 15 minutes or until done. You can frost them if you like or sprinkle chocolate chips on top. A quick and easy lunch box treat!

Cake Mix Rolls

2½ c. warm water
1 box yellow cake mix
2 Tbsp. yeast
4½ c. flour or enough to
make a soft dough

Mix like bread dough and let rise until double in size. Roll out and spread with butter, brown sugar and cinnamon. Roll up and cut. Lay on a greased cake pan and let rise again. Bake at 350° until nicely browned. Frost with your favorite frosting while they are warm.

233

Kiddy's Apple Mix

2 c. chopped apples 1 c. mini marshmallows 1 c. mini chocolate chips nuts and raisins (optional)	Mix all together, then add dressing. More apples may be added. This is a great quick and nutritious mix for lunches.

Dressing:
1/2 c. crunchy peanut butter
1/2 c. brown sugar
1/4 c. half and half or cream
1/2 c. mayonnaise

Popcorn Snack Mix

3 qt. popped corn 1 (15 oz.) pkg. puffed corn 1 (15 oz.) pkg. corn chips 22 oz. white melting chocolate	In a large bowl combine first 3 ingredients. In a saucepan on low heat melt chocolate and pour over corn mixture. Toss to coat. Spread in pans and cool. Store in airtight containers.

Chocolate Popcorn Balls

1 1/2 c. sugar 1 c. light corn syrup 3 Tbsp. vinegar 2 Tbsp. oleo 1/2 tsp. salt 1/2 tsp. baking soda 6 qt. popped corn 1 1/2 c. milk chocolate chips	Cook first 4 ingredients until it forms a soft ball in cold water. Remove from heat and stir in chocolate chips. Stir until melted. Add salt and soda, stirring quickly. Pour over 6 qt. lightly salted popcorn. Butter hands and form balls. Store in airtight container in layers between wax paper. Omit chocolate chips for plain balls and add 1 tsp. vanilla and food coloring if desired or Jell-O of your choice.

Golden Cornflake Balls

$^1/_2$ c. sugar
$^1/_2$ c. light corn syrup
1 c. peanut butter
3 c. cornflakes
$^1/_2$ c. Rice Krispies
dash of salt

In a saucepan over low heat melt sugar and corn syrup. Add peanut butter and stir well. Remove from heat. Pour over cereal. Stir gently until coated. Butter hands. Take a rounded tablespoonful at a time and form into balls. Cool syrup mixture slightly before pouring over cereal and working with it. Easy for children to do and simple for lunches.

Fruity Colored Cheerios

$^3/_4$ c. raspberry or orange Jell-O
1 c. light corn syrup or
   molasses
$4^1/_2$ Tbsp. butter, softened
8 c. plain Cheerios

Melt Jell-O, butter and syrup in heavy saucepan. Heat and stir until melted. Pour over Cheerios. Press into a greased 9" x 13" pan.

Ritz Cracker S'mores

10 Ritz crackers
peanut butter
marshmallow creme

Spread 5 Ritz crackers with peanut butter and another 5 with marshmallow creme. Put together for an unusual treat. Using a Tupperware to place them in is not so messy as a baggie.

Granola Bars

5 c. quick oats
$4^1/_2$ c. Rice Krispies
1 c. coconut
1 c. chocolate chips
1 c. graham cracker crumbs
$^1/_2$-$^3/_4$ c. butter
$^1/_4$ c. oil
$1^1/_2$ lb. marshmallows
$^1/_4$ c. honey
$^1/_4$ c. peanut butter

Mix first 5 ingredients. Melt butter in saucepan. Add oil and marshmallows and melt. Remove from heat and add honey and peanut butter. Mix to dry ingredients. Press into 2 large cookie sheets and cut in pieces. This is a no-bake snack that is easy for school lunches.

Finger Jell-O

2 c. boiling water
1 lg. box Jell-O of your choice

Dissolve Jell-O in boiling water and pour into a lightly oiled pan. Chill until firm. Cut into squares or desired shapes. Put in lunches.

Applesauce and Jell-O

1 c. applesauce
2/3 c. raspberry or strawberry Jell-O
1 (12 oz.) can lemon/lime soda
1 c. crushed pineapple, undrained

Bring applesauce to a boil. Stir in Jell-O until dissolved. Slowly add soda and pineapple. Pour into a small cake pan. Refrigerate until firm. Cut into squares for lunches.

Simple Fruit Slush

1 qt. peaches, mashed
1 (20 oz.) crushed pineapple
1 c. sugar
1 can lemonade concentrate
1 can orange juice
1 qt. water

Mix peaches with pineapple. Mix sugar with lemonade, orange juice and water. Bring to a boil. When cool add fruit. Place in small containers and freeze. Put in lunches for a slushy fruit at noon. May add pears, grapes or bananas.

Frozen Pops

3 c. vanilla ice cream
1 c. orange juice concentrate

Mix together and spoon into dessert cups. Freeze overnight and then put into lunches for a frosty treat. Put buckets in a cool or cold place.

Take a cup of kindness; mix it well with love.
Add a lot of patience and faith in God above.
Sprinkle very generously with joy and thanks and cheer.
And you'll have lots of angel food to feast on all the year.

Basic Oil Mixture for Bugs on Houseplants

1 c. vegetable oil
1 Tbsp. Murphy's oil soap

Pour the oil and oil soap into a plastic bottle and store at room temperature. Mix 1 Tbsp. of the mixture in 2 c. water in a hand-held sprayer bottle. Spray pest-ridden plants from top to bottom and it's bye-bye bugs.

Solution for Washing Coverings

1 oz. Clorox 2 (liquid)
1 oz. Cascade (liquid)
1 oz. Whisk or some kind of
   bluing

Use $1\frac{1}{2}$ gal. pail. Place soaps in pail and add water. Place 1 covering into water and soak for a few hours. Rinse with clear water. This makes them nice and white.

String Cheerios on strong thread and tie ends together. Give to your baby 6 months to $1\frac{1}{2}$ years old. This keeps them quiet and occupied for long periods of time in church or when quiet time is needed.

• • • • •

Use up greeting cards by cutting off the front and using them as gift tags or write a note on the back for a friend or shut-in. Use as a recipe card or book marker.

• • • • •

Make your hands wet to press any cookie dough into pans that has a thick sticky dough.

• • • • •

God has for you...
a light for every shadow
a plan for every tomorrow
a key for every problem
and a balm for every sorrow.

Notes

Index

Cookies & Bars

Cakes & Frostings

Pies

Meats & Main Dishes

Desserts

Soups & Salads

Canning & Freezing

Candy, Snacks, Jellies, Jams & Misc.

Pancakes & Cereals

Lunch Box Ideas

Helpful Hints

Notes

Harvest of Blessings

Please send _____ copies of *Harvest of Blessings* cookbook
at $9.99 + $1.50 shipping and handling per book.

Ship to:

Name _____

Address _____

City _____ State _____ Zip_____

Make checks payable and send to:
Mabel Yoder
7850 Dutch Bethel Rd., Freedom, IN 47431

....

More Cookbooks by Mabel Yoder!

Please send

_____ copies of *Family Treasures I*

_____ copies of *Family Treasures II*

_____ copies of *Harvest of Blessings*

SPECIAL PRICE
Order all 3 for $30
postpaid

at $9.99 + $1.50 shipping and handling per cookbook.

Ship to:

Name _____

Address _____

City _____ State _____ Zip_____

Make checks payable and send to:
Mabel Yoder
7850 Dutch Bethel Rd., Freedom, IN 47431